Marlborough's Duchess

Also by Louis Kronenberger

Kings and Desperate Men (1942)
The Pleasure of Their Company (1946)
The Thread of Laughter (1952)
The Republic of Letters (1955)

MARLBOROUGH'S DUCHESS

A Study in Worldliness

by

LOUIS KRONENBERGER

WEIDENFELD AND NICOLSON
7 CORK STREET, LONDON, W.1.

To
EMMY, JOHN AND LIZA
KRONENBERGER

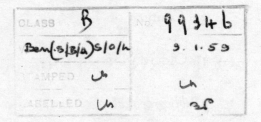

MADE AND PRINTED BY OFFSET IN GREAT BRITAIN
BY WILLIAM CLOWES AND SONS, LIMITED, LONDON AND BECCLES
N. 6120

CONTENTS

Note

IN BIOGRAPHICAL TERMS, there is this peculiarity to the Duchess of Marlborough's life: it is inseparable from the Duke's, as the Duke's, again, is a part of the history of Europe. There is the further peculiarity that, with most of Sarah's letters to her husband destroyed, she often—in terms of posterity—is cut out of scenes and situations in which, while alive, she vitally figured. Hence there are stretches in this book where she hardly appears; but they seem for all that not just contributory to the main narrative, but an actual part of it. For the decisive thing about Sarah's career was her not wishing to be, indeed her refusing to be, a mere Court lady, however grand. She insisted on becoming a figure of politics, a contestant for power, an active promoter of her husband's interests. Hence, to grasp at trivial scenes and pointless small talk just because they permit Sarah a speaking part, while omitting scenes where she does not appear but yet greatly figures, would in the end misrepresent her story.

The unity of that story rests, for me, in the worldly nature of everything that attracted and affected the Marlboroughs. Sarah, to be sure, had a worldling's interests and ambitions while quite lacking the manner and methods. But, however obstreperous a woman of the world, she was not really a dissenting one; and both the comedy of her story and the drama of it lie in how little she differed from those she opposed in what she wanted, and how enormously she differed in her efforts to get it.

This book represents much reading, but nothing by way of original research: for all its *facts* I am indebted to my predecessors in the field. In certain places involving secondary characters and background material, I have drawn on my own *Kings and Desperate Men.*

For his editorial suggestions I am deeply indebted to Herbert Weinstock. James L. Clifford has given generously of his time and expert knowledge to read the book in galleys and make several valuable comments, and my wife has been of very special help both in reading the manuscript and in supervising the illustrations.

L. K.

Illustrations

Titles and Connections

Children and grandchildren of JOHN and SARAH:

1. HENRIETTA
B. 1681
Married Francis, later 2nd Earl of Godolphin; at John's death, became Duchess of Marlborough in her own right

HER CHILDREN:
1. William ("Willigo"), D. 1731—Marquis of Blandford on his mother's becoming Duchess
2. Harriet, M. the Duke of Newcastle
3. Mary, M. the Duke of Leeds

2. ANNE
B. 1682
Married Charles Spencer, later 3rd Earl of Sunderland

HER CHILDREN:
1. Robert, D. 1729, later 4th Earl of Sunderland
2. Charles, 5th Earl of Sunderland and (at Henrietta's death) 3rd Duke of Marlborough
3. John (Jack) Spencer
4. Anne, M. William, 1st Viscount Bateman
5. Diana, M. John, 4th Duke of Bedford

3. ELIZABETH
B. 1685
Married Scroop, 4th Earl (and later Duke) of Bridgewater

HER CHILDREN:
Two sons who died young and Anne, M. (1) 3rd Duke of Bedford; (2) 3rd Earl of Jersey

4. JOHN
B. 1686
Marquis of Blandford, D. 1703

5. MARY
B. 1687
Married John, Lord Monthermer, later 2nd Duke of Montagu

HER CHILDREN:
1. Isabella, M. (1) William, Duke of Manchester; (2) Earl Beaulieu
2. Mary, M. 4th Earl of Cardigan (later Duke of Montagu)
3. and two sons and a daughter

GEORGE I: son of the Electress Sophia of Hanover; father of George II; grandfather of Frederick Prince of Wales; great-grandfather of George III
HALIFAX: Charles Montagu (1661-1715), Earl of Halifax, member of the Junto
HALIFAX: Sir George Savile (1633-1695), Marquis of Halifax ("The Trimmer")
HARLEY: Robert, created (1711) Earl of Oxford
HILL: Abigail, successively Mrs. Samuel Masham and Lady Masham
JAMES II: until 1685, Duke of York MARRIED:
    (1) Anne Hyde, daughter of Lord Clarendon and mother of the future Mary of Orange and the future Queen Anne
    (2) Mary of Modena, mother of "James III" (The Old Pretender)
ST. JOHN: Henry, created (1712) Viscount Bolingbroke
VILLIERS: Barbara, successively Barbara Palmer; Lady Castlemaine; Duchess of Cleveland

PART ONE

THE WINDING STAIR

I

ON THE 29th of May 1660, just one week before Sarah's birth, Charles II, after long years of troubled exile, returned to London in triumph. It was accordingly into a world of old attachments and new luster, the kind of world that she herself would be resplendently a part of, that the future Duchess was born. About her birth itself there is no sense of lights or music, ceremony or celebrity: Sarah's father was a Royalist country squire named Richard Jennings; her background was sound and solid but not illustrious; her prospects were genial and dignified but far from opulent. Indeed, it is not known even now precisely where Sarah was born, any more than where or when she was married or where, long after, she died. But very likely she was born—the youngest of five or, as some say, seven children—at Holywell House, the family place near St. Albans in Hertfordshire, where quite certainly she lived as a child.

Not much is recorded of Sarah's childhood; doubtless not much requires to be. The Jennings family had once been exceedingly well off: her father "had in Somersetshire, Kent and St. Albans," Sarah wrote later in life, "four thousand pounds a year"; [1] while one of the family properties, as no

---

[1] Because money plays so leading a role in the story, it seems well to remind the reader right off that, to be given their present-day value, all sums mentioned must be multiplied some ten times.

one can resist pointing out, was a manor called Churchill. But Richard Jennings, who in 1643 had married the daughter of a Kentish baronet, became impoverished during the Civil Wars. During Sarah's babyhood his stanch Royalism bore fruit—he became a member of Charles II's Parliament, as he had once been of Charles I's. But he never greatly mended his fortunes; nor did he live long under the Restoration, dying in 1668 when Sarah was a little girl. There is a tradition that he and Sarah were particularly close to each other, but as one biographer asserts it on no higher grounds than that "a special intimacy often binds father and daughter," some license exists to doubt it.

What, in any case, first opened the great world to Sarah was her older sister Frances's place in it. Frances was the great beauty of the family; by way of Gramont, indeed, she survives as one of the great beauties of English history. While Sarah was still a little girl, Frances became a maid of honor to the first Duchess of York, to that daughter of Clarendon's who died young and was the mother of Queen Mary and Queen Anne. Setting Frances about the Court was "a cheap way of repaying the Jennings" for their Royalist service. As maid of honor to the Duchess, Frances understandably caught the eye of the Duke, the future James II; what is much more noteworthy, she eluded his grasp, ostentatiously scattering, "like hailstones," his unopened billets-doux for all to see. With him, and indeed with everyone else, Frances remained charmingly virtuous. She was accompanied to Court, and chaperoned on arriving there, by her mother, so that Sarah was left at St. Albans with the servants—and perhaps a governess—to pick up what education, to indulge in what amusements she could. All but the barest facts of her early life is hearsay and conjecture, but she is not too recklessly supposed to have been "saucy" and

—left as she was among servants—rather spoiled. Her education was not extensive. "Prithee," she herself once remarked, "do not talk to me of books. I know only men and cards." So much, to be sure, might have been pleasantry; but that, when a grown woman, she knew no French and that "her methods in arithmetic, though infallible, were unique" are established facts.

Meanwhile, at Court, Gramont's "la belle Jennyns" went her way, achieving popularity without provoking scandal; and when Sarah was twelve or thirteen, she also was brought from St. Albans to St. James's to become a member of the second Duchess of York's household. Here for the first time the light falls directly upon her; and at her first entrance she assumes a characteristic stance. Mrs. Jennings and Sarah, a letter of the time reports,

> have had so great a falling out that they fought; the young one complained to the Duchess that if her mother was not put out of St James's where she had lodgings to sanctuary her from debt, she would run away; so Sir Alleyn Apsley was sent to bid the mother remove, who answered "with all my heart; she should never dispute the Duke and Duchess's commands, but with the Grace of God she would take her daughter away with her." . . . So rather than part with her, the mother must stay, and all breaches are made up again.

But the breaches were not made up for very long: a month later, Mrs. Jennings—denounced by Sarah as a madwoman—was sent packing, while her daughter remained behind. Once the two ceased to be near-neighbors, they presumably managed to be friends; plainly they were too much of the same kidney to get along under the same roof. What Mrs.

Jennings was like generally is harder to say. We are not much enlightened when one of Sarah's contemporaries refers to her as "your noble mother"; nor much convinced when, many years later, the vilifying Mrs. Manley calls her a sorceress who used black magic to establish Frances at Court. What *is* known about her is her unbridled temper and her unpaid debts; because of the debts, the alternative to St. James's might well have been prison. With her dismissal from Court, Mrs. Jennings passes out of the story; but we know that she died at an advanced age in comfortable circumstances; and Sarah, by then, was on good enough terms with her to inherit her estate.

Already in childhood, during visits to Frances at Court, Sarah had met the little Princess Anne. Anne, it would appear, was a very sad little princess—her mother was dead, her father neglectful, her older sister Mary always with a bosom friend; and Anne herself, colorless by nature, was made unconfident by circumstance. To the hesitant, awkward child, the prancing and positive Sarah—four years older and decidedly freer and prettier—was someone to envy, to look up to and want for a friend. After Sarah joined the household of Anne's kindly young stepmother, Mary of Modena, the two girls were very naturally thrown together; they both, for example, took part in Court theatricals the Christmas when Sarah was fourteen. By the following Christmas, 1675, Sarah was an acknowledged young lady who attended Court balls. She was never so dazzling a beauty nor so courted a belle as Frances had been; but along with "a fury temper" she had "a fairy face"; she, like Frances before her, was fruitlessly ogled by the Duke of York; she enjoyed "advantageous offers of marriage" and no breath whatever of scandal.

In terms of courtship her fate, however she might tempt

and trifle with it, was really sealed from the outset. Sarah was fifteen when she first began dancing, at Court balls, with John Churchill, who at twenty-five was a lieutenant colonel and whose "every step" as he danced ". . . carried death with it." But one night, when the dancing was over, Churchill in his turn found himself passionately in love—as it happened, for life. Few men in history have had a more realistic temper or cooler brain than the future Duke; few, either, so undivided a heart. There was a certain similarity—though hers was rather better—about Sarah's and John's positions. John, like Sarah, was the child of an impoverished Royalist, a country gentleman named Winston Churchill who, soon after the Restoration, was made a knight. Sir Winston, like Richard Jennings, sat in Charles II's Parliament; indeed the historian of the Tory party calls him one of the period's leading Tories. He, however, was also of a somewhat scholarly turn, writing a book called *Divi Britannici* which chronicled every king of Britain "from 2855 B.C. to 1660 A.D." If an often ponderous historian, Sir Winston was a not altogether despicable phrasemaker: when Charles II, characteristically seeking money from the House of Commons, refused in turn what the Commons sought of the King, Sir Winston rose and declared: "No song, no supper"; and "No song, no supper" became the cry. Drunk with success, Sir Winston later evolved, less effectively, "No penny, no paternoster." Most important, as A. L. Rowse points out, Sir Winston was given a minor position in the royal household, whence ensued that "intimate contact with the Court" which in the next generation made one after another of the Churchill fortunes. John, the oldest boy in a large family of children, was born and grew up at Ashe House, the Churchill manor in Devonshire. When, shortly after the Restoration, Sir Winston was made Commissioner of the Court of Claims at Dublin, John went for a while to school there; later, in London, he went to school at St. Paul's. But the Great Fire of 1665, when John was fifteen, finished St. Paul's off for a season, and John's book learning for all time. Chesterfield, in after years, called him "eminently illiterate."

From St. Paul's John went, as a page to the Duke of York, to St. James's; and he too had a sister at Court, and she too was in the household of the Duchess. John's sister Arabella was no such tearing beauty as Sarah's sister Frances: indeed, she seemed all skin and bones until a hunting accident made clear, to those who stood around, her unforeseeably exquisite "limbs." Among those standing around, or soon coming up, was the Duke of York: he was moved to admiration, and Arabella, no long time after, to assent. She became the mistress of the future King and the mother of the future Duke of Berwick. She also became of some use to the future Duke of Marlborough. Doubtless the extent of her assistance has been as much magnified by scandalmongers as it has been minimized by apologists. Arabella would seem to have had nothing to do with her young brother's coming to Court; nor with his being asked by the Duke of York what profession he would like to follow and his pleading for a "pair of colors" in one of the Duke's regiments. She may have had something to do with John's receiving those colors not long after—which is to say that she may have seconded her brother's entreaties, or that the Duke may have favored John the more from her being his sister. But none of this can be turned to any particular account: even if Arabella did get John his first commission, it bore little on his subsequent career. In an age pre-eminent for soldiering, a handsome wellborn youth with such a turn for it could hardly have mislaid his talents:

the right young men then forged ahead at making war as they advance themselves today in corporations.

By the time he met Sarah—during an interval of peace when he was the Duke of York's Master of the Robes— John had presumably served at Tangier; had helped the French fight the Dutch, winning praise from Louis XIV and Turenne; and had been successively ensign, captain, and lieutenant colonel. He had also become the lover of the King's established mistress, Barbara Palmer, Countess of Castlemaine and Duchess of Cleveland, a connection not without its perils or prestige, nor without its rewards. By birth a Villiers, of that gifted erratic line,[2] Barbara was by blood John's second cousin once removed. She is said to have been beautiful and charming; she is known to have been violent and unprincipled. Becoming Charles's mistress shortly before he was proclaimed King, she was for years "the reigning beauty" and the raging whirlwind of the palace. John seems to have attracted her notice, and have won her affection, while still a page: he was about twenty when he became her lover. By then, no doubt, Barbara— who had borne the King a number of children and ac- quired various other lovers—was of diminished luster about the Court. All the same, she was still the King's mistress; and whatever, now, his pleasure in her company, he must re- sent a young officer's outrivaling him and, as Gramont maintains, boasting of it into the bargain. So pretty as to seem apocryphal is the tale of how John Churchill, being in Barbara's bedroom when the King came calling, leaped from her window into the courtyard—a leap for which she

---

[2] In addition to John Churchill, what Maynard Keynes called "the great Villiers connexion" includes Lord Rochester, Lady Mary Montagu, Fielding, the two Pitts, Charles James Fox, Lord Shelburne, Lady Hester Stanhope, and Castlereagh.

rewarded him with five thousand pounds. In a companion story, John does not leap from a window but hides in a cupboard, where the King spies him out. Whereupon, after the culprits fall on their knees, Charles orders him away, saying: "Go: you are a rascal, but I forgive you because you do it to get your bread." One may wonder about either story: the window feat suits any dashing gallant; the bread remark suits almost too well the King. On the other hand, the five thousand pounds was very definitely not stage money: it is *known* that at twenty-three or twenty-four John Churchill purchased for forty-five hundred pounds—"of my grandfather Halifax," wrote Lord Chesterfield—an annuity of five hundred pounds for life. What is not known is where he got the money; but even his descendant Sir Winston Churchill is forced to concede that there is no plausible "other source than Barbara." [3] Both John's way of earning this money and his way of disposing of it have drawn obloquy upon him; comparison has even been made to Tom Jones being kept by Lady Bellaston. Yet, considering the backdrop against which the liaison was carried on—never was there a court financially more corrupt or less sexually restrained—it would be absurd to moralize about John's conduct. Posterity, to be sure, has found his conduct reprehensible, but rather because he violated its notions of romance than of virtue. He did the sensible instead of the stylish thing; he refused to act like a storybook hero; he *invested* what were ill-gotten gains to begin with, and thus fell foul of cynics and romantics alike. But John Churchill, notwithstanding, was much too fond of money.

[3] John is thought to have been the father of Barbara's last child, a girl also named Barbara, who was brought up by nuns in Paris to become a nun and—at length—the prioress of a convent.

And yet there can be no slightest doubt that he married
for love. And married for love a girl who for the longest
time—out of pride, out of prudence, out of an ungracious
need to have the last word—refused him. His was a thorny
courtship indeed, for his family, who felt he ought to marry
money, opposed the match almost as fiercely as the girl herself appeared to oppose it. His family even had in reserve
the right sort of bride: Catharine Sedley, whose father Sir
Charles is remembered even now for his poetry and his wit,[4]
and was known then for a rich and famous rake. The
thought of Catharine vexed Sarah, but also emboldened
her.

That Sarah became what in such a relationship is called
coy, though in any other it would be deemed cantankerous;
that Sarah meant to become in every respect John's consort
and not simply his wife; that Sarah was determined to play
out the whole thing for drama while even we, three centuries later, cannot merely rig it up for comedy: all this
emerges in the many letters from John which she preserved,
and in the few from her which he failed to destroy.[5] For all
the set phrases he sometimes used, John's infatuation seems
plain, his ardor almost monotonous:

> My head did ache yesterday to that degree . . . that
> nothing should have persuaded me to have gone abroad
> but the meeting of you who is much dearer than all the
> world beside to me.

> I did no sooner know that you were not well, but upon
> my faith without affectation I was also sick.

[4] Which his daughter inherited. She later became the mistress of
James II; and when Mary of Orange, after the Revolution, snubbed her
at Court, Catharine said: "If I broke one of the commandments, ma'am,
with your father, you have broken another against him."

[5] Because of her insistence, most of Sarah's letters to John, at all
periods, were destroyed.

There is no pain so great to me as that when I fear you do not love me.

Pray write two words before you go. You ought to do it, for I love you with all my heart and soul.

John's difficulties seem even plainer. Though Sarah, after the fashion of the age, might let him fasten her garter or come chastely visiting her in her bedroom, his place in her affections was extremely unclear. "You say I pretend a passion to you when I have other things in my head," he writes, adding a few lines later: "I do despair of your love" and "How unjust you are." "I cannot remember what it was I said to you that you took so ill . . ." and then he bursts out: "Ah my soul, did you love so well as I, you could never have refused my letter so barbarously as you did, for if reason had bade you do it, love would never have permitted it."

All this was in reply to, or in the face of, such of Sarah's outbursts as: "As for seeing you I am resolved I never will in private nor in public if I could help it" or "I find all you say is only to amuse me and make me think you have a passion for me." But the cat is out of the bag when she runs on:

I protested that I would never write nor speak to you more; but as you know how much kindness I had for you, you can't wonder or blame me if I try once more to hear what you can say for your justification.

Then back again to raillery and sarcasm: "At four o'clock," Sarah writes,

I would see you, but that would hinder you from seeing the play, which I fear would be a great affliction to you, and increase the pain in your head. . . .

At this point in the correspondence—or the courtship—John's passion was curbed or his patience exhausted: his answer has been lost, but accompanying it was a note of protest to Sarah's waiting woman:

> Your mistress's usage to me is so barbarous that sure she must be the worst woman in the world, or else she would not be thus ill-natured

and concluding:

> Let her read my letter and answer it, and not use me thus like a footman.

This marks the turn. Sarah answered, as Sarahs always will, that she had "done nothing to deserve such a . . . letter," that she was grieved to find he had so ill an opinion of her; that "you shall have it in your power to see me or not—and if you are contented without it, I shall be extremely pleased." She now reproached rather than rebuffed him; and far from slamming the door in his face, opened it appreciably wider. Her answer brought him round quickly enough, but his quick defiance had in some sense brought her round also.

Though Sarah was exploiting his devotion to the hilt, her own position was by no means so assured as his remonstrances might indicate. There is at least the possibility that John at the outset sought to make her his mistress rather than his wife; there is the known fact that, at a later stage, Catharine Sedley was still being pressed upon John—which could be more for Sarah than a private grief, could be indeed a very public humiliation. In November 1676 the French ambassador wrote to Versailles of a "small ball" given by the Duchess of York at which the "uncommonly good-looking" Sarah "had far more wish to cry than to dance":

> Churchill who is her suitor says that he is attacked by consumption and must take the air in France. I only wish I were as well as he. The truth is that he wishes to free himself from intrigues. His father urges him to marry one of his relations who is very rich and very ugly, and will not consent to his marriage with Miss Jennings.

Thus it is clear that however certain Sarah might be of John's heart, she could by no means be so sure of his hand; and that while all was doubt on her part over what might presently happen, all was knowledge on everyone else's as to what was currently going on. She must have known—or have heard—too, how much John Churchill loved money. She might have supposed that nothing favored their marriage except love: each had his fortune to make, and each the means of making it, but neither could make the other's. In addition, she was only sixteen years old, which, even in those days, was not the most propitious age for conducting adroit campaigns or arriving at sound decisions.

Clearly her fears were not unfounded, nor her calculations—if such they can be called, for pride played as great a role as prudence—unnecessary; and if she behaved throughout as imperiously as Sarah always did, she behaved as shrewdly as Sarah almost never did again. We are a little prone to judge the contest by the outcome; would it have been so easy, three hundred years ago, to guess the outcome by the contestants? John Churchill, fired by ambition and flawed by avarice, had every incentive to essay a brilliant marriage. Moreover, John Churchill—at all other times a model of coolness, patience, and self-discipline—could not have been supposed on this occasion to sweep the board clean for love. On any basis of realistic fiction, John's behavior does not ring true. He could only have married Sarah in a very bad novel, in a very brilliant novel, or in real life. Sarah, again, reveals all the wiles and stratagems of hackneyed romances. At a crucial moment she informs John that she is going to France with her sister. "My heart," he writes back, "is ready to break . . . Since you are grown so indifferent, death is the only thing that can ease me." And he tells of his efforts with their confidante, the Duchess of York, to add to his income. This being the very music Sarah's ears had sought, she first confides that "you need not fear my sister's coming can make any change in me," then instructs him just how to proceed with the Duchess.

John having asserted himself, and Sarah having so far as was expedient relented, he made his suit and was accepted. They were not to be married quite yet, however, nor was Sarah to melt once for all into tenderness and compliance. John would continue to sue: "If you do not think me impertinent for asking, I should be glad to know what made you go away"; or he might complain of her "unkind, indifferent letter." But the last phrase turns up in a communication having to do with their marriage plans—the marriage itself being performed so secretly that to this day the time and place remain hidden. The date was presumably late in 1677 or early in 1678; the scene very possibly the apartments of the Duchess of York, who now served as their benefactress. John's finances were shaky; further, just when he planned to marry he was asked—and agreed—to surrender the entail on his father's estate to help pay his father's debts. His only income, accordingly, was his army pay and the annuity of five hundred pounds; all Sarah had was her "expectations." For the life they desired, and would be compelled, to live, there was need of a substantial amount of money. It was almost certainly the Duchess who somehow made it available: having for a long while smiled on the match, Mary of Modena at length eased the path to marriage. At the time it was performed, John's parents presumably still opposed it; but they must afterwards have accepted it with a good grace, for it was to their house in Dorset that summer, when such honeymoon as there may have been was over, that John led home his bride.

II

Love had triumphed, and not just in a breast where self-interest seemed to reign, but also during an age when men could be as mocking of love as they were lyrical. The Restoration—and by that, to be sure, one means the highborn, for it was their place in life that had been restored—has become a byword for cynicism, profligacy, duplicity: we find it too much damned by lack of heart to be saved by its show of style. So dissolute was its King that he was called the Merry Monarch out of euphemism rather than compliment. Who, furthermore, knows the name of his Queen; who does not know the name of Nell Gwynne? So indecent were the Restoration's plays that for two centuries after, the theater was outlawed by the God-fearing; and the Restoration's plays, it is assumed, not unfairly reflected its attitudes. Certainly the period's most famous diarist, Pepys, does nothing to gainsay its most notorious dramatist, Wycherley; and Gramont's scandalous Court memoirs are born of fact, however adulterated by fiction.

Yet Restoration morality has probably been too much stressed and set apart. There is almost no high life that does not also mean high living; and the Restoration's worst folly may simply have been its frankness. All the same, there was a most conspicuous amount of high living. It was an era bound to lack discipline, predestined to lack ideals. Under Cromwell, Puritanism had starved men's emotions and submerged their instincts: to be gay had been almost as reprehensible as to be godless; the amenities had been everywhere distrusted, as gilding and embossing vice; and as wide a gulf had been set between love and sex as commonly divides love from loathing. The age, remarked Macaulay, that follows a period of severe repression is always far more lax than the age that preceded it. Moreover the aristocracy, having beggared and martyred and exiled itself for the Stuarts, resumed the old life with voracious new appetites; was in the patrician mood that corresponds to the plebeian sacking of cities; and had lived so long in the shadow of an improbable Puritan God as to be all too eager to sup—with no care for the length of its spoon—with the Devil. Accordingly, there was no dissembling one's vices; there was, if anything, a desire to parade them, a positive wish, a strenuous rush, to inhabit glass houses. The prevailing mood perhaps finds its nearest modern parallel in the mood of the 1920's, the key to which was less how wicked people were than how pleased they were to be thought wicked.

Naturally, just by making so brave an ideal of iniquity, such a world has trouble being as bad as it pretends to be; also, where there is no such thing as forbidden fruit, there is not much fun to robbing orchards. We know that the

first Lord Nottingham enjoined his son "never to become
that thing of horror, a man about town"—which the son,
whom we shall meet again, sufficiently heeded as to be
nicknamed "Dismal." We know that at the Court of
Charles II in his prime there were such good girls as Frances
and Sarah Jennings and Margaret Blagge (John Evelyn's
Margaret Godolphin); we know that Evelyn himself,
Pepy's nearest rival as a diarist, was at the farthest remove
from him as a man; we know that the Elias Ashmole who
founded the Ashmolean, or the Robert Boyle who established Boyle's Law, or the Clarendons, father and son, were
all God-fearing men. It was an age of martyrdom for Catholic and Protestant, peasant and peer, alike; and we may
wonder whether its chroniclers, as perhaps those of the
1920's, did not disseminate an attitude whereby men became cynical lest they be thought naïve, and were forced
to be frank however little there was to be frank about.
Certainly, on any basis of *events*, not cynicism but fanaticism is the master trait of the age.

Yet, in strong contrast to the 1920's, the world the
Churchills were to live in, the only world that mattered,
made genuine frankness impossible. How fare well at
Court, how conceivably thrive as a courtier but by being
a hypocrite? How hope to rise unless one strove to please?
Theirs was an age when no world of mere wealth could
rival or even ape the Court, and the arbiter, indeed the auto-
crat, of fashion was the King. The great Lord Halifax—
who, though called "The Trimmer," was not meant to be
castigated by the term—had it that "a place at Court, like
a place in Heaven, is to be got by being upon one's knees";
and painfully valid was Bacon's famous dictum that "all
rising to great place is by a winding stair." Such assump-
tions were part of one's ingrained view of life, were part,

in a way, of one's upbringing. If John Churchill's parents went by the book, it was doubtless by Francis Osborne's *Advice to a Son*, first published in John's childhood: its being banned for instilling "principles of atheism" merely made it sell the better. The core of Osborne's teaching was an undisguised and perfect worldliness, which made no attempt to yoke morality and expediency in the same injunction. Thus Osborne warns against hawking and hunting: it is so easy to be "accidentally" shot by an enemy. He counts it nothing sinful "to serve one who has come to power by crime"; he judges free schools better than tutors for ambitious boys: a gang of boys robbing an orchard uses all the stratagems required for taking a town. Feeing servants he considers useful on arrival, but foolish on taking leave; and he holds it very foolish in a man to marry, as marriage only compounds sin by making fornication adultery. Here indeed is all the prudence of Poor Richard with none of the cant.[1]

But if the way of the world seldom really alters, how much do its outward look and shape: England under Charles II consisted largely of people who lived on the land: it had not a city except London with more than 30,000 people. Thus the great landowners constituted the voice, and the squirearchy—"half nobles and half boors"— the backbone of the country. A squire's great rambling house might be densely tenanted—sometimes "the family," with its cousinships and connections, ran to sixty people. It would be lavishly staffed—John Evelyn's father kept 116 servants in livery—and might be royally maintained, with five or six tables always laid in readiness for visitors and

[1] More engagingly downright was that "versatile pathfinder" Sir William Petty. As nearsighted as he was enlightened, he proposed— when challenged to a duel—a dark cellar and hatchets.

their retinues. (A country house like Audley End, with its 750 rooms, was compared to a walled town.) It seems a spacious and baronial existence, but its pleasures ran largely to hunting by day and reminiscences of the hunting by night.

A courtier's life, to be sure, was a good deal livelier, as when, for example, "the King and Queen and all the court went about masked, and came into houses unknown, and danced there with wild frolic." But Court life too—in a sense, even the life of the King—shows an appalling sameness. Day after day Charles elected to share the fate of a drama critic and attend the theater; night after night, with Sundays no exception, his Queen and his mistresses sat over cards. At Newmarket the royal routine scarcely varied for years: the morning walk, the midday dinner (served the King by peers on bended knee), the races, a cockfight, a play, supper, Lady Castlemaine.[2] The working day—and not only for the workingman—began, after a bolted breakfast of, say, bread, butter, radishes, and ale not later than seven, and quite possibly at five; and a "debauch" of guzzling and gorging might—as at the Marquess of Winchester's —last "from one at noon till one in the morning." Though by no means everyone got drunk—Charles II, for example, almost never did—practically no one, even children, drank water. The mass of people drank beer, and even three-year-olds were veteran pipe-smokers. People of quality took coffee and chocolate, but not yet tea—tea, in the year of Sarah's marriage, was called "a base unworthy Indian practice." Spices, those flavorers and disflavorers during so many generations, were going out; sugar was coming in.

[2] Who, Pepys declared, had more jewels than the Queen and the Duchess of York together, and thought nothing of wearing £40,000 worth to the play.

Despite Charles II's feeling for the amenities, few people used forks, most men dined with their hats on, it was still common to clean one's teeth at table, still not uncommon to spit. At the very same table the well-trained housekeeper must yet carve to perfection, so as to display a crane, disfigure a peacock, or lift a swan.

It seems, as it was, a distant age when many people still believed in witchcraft, thousands rotted away in prison, and great numbers went to the block and even the stake; and when His Majesty's warships sailed down the river filled with women swilling punch and brandy and singing "Loath to Depart." As well as how strange, we shall presently see how black with treachery the age could be, how rife with bigotry and crime. Yet one encounters some curiously modern touches, like the use of fountain pens and—among model employers—sickness and old-age benefits for workers. And indeed the last forty years of the seventeenth century constitute one of the most astonishing periods in the annals of British genius—boasting England's greatest scientist, Newton; her lustiest satirist, Dryden; her supreme classical scholar, Bentley; the heyday of Wren in architecture and of Purcell in music; the years of England's foremost diarist, Pepys; most polished playwright, Congreve; most influential philosopher, Locke; though of England's only second-greatest poet, Milton.

It was not the period of England's greatest King—though had it been, John Churchill might have had less chance to emerge as her greatest soldier. John Churchill, in due time, had to break the power of France because Charles let France dismember that of England. Charles was by no means the mere fribble, rake, and witty cynic of tradition; the things he did, despite Rochester's tattered epigram,

could be quite as shrewd as the things he said. It will sufficiently indicate how brilliant a king he was among his own
subjects—and all the more by contrast with his father, who
was beheaded, and his brother, who was deposed—that he
achieved immense popularity while never forfeiting an iota
of power; died a communicant with Rome while remaining King of England; completely dominated his ministers
and dispensed, where he chose, with Parliament. He not
only weathered costly and sanguinary wars, and explosions
first against Catholics and then against Protestants, but in a
country that had but lately got rid of monarchy, actually
strengthened monarchical sentiment. He made a good king
because, in a sense, he made a good courtier, and what he
courted was popular regard. Dashing by nature, he was
affable by design; he had wit; and his greatest extravagance,
women, being pardoned in most men, is if anything admired in a monarch. He had, to be sure, a great and unpar-
donable fault: he was in the pay of France. By the secret
Treaty of Dover he had agreed—and it meant exercising his
"supreme power in ecclesiastical matters"—to suspend all
penal laws affecting Catholics and to do all he could for
Roman Catholicism generally, in return for which Louis
XIV would pay most of Charles's bills. After the gray
drizzle years under Cromwell, sunlight now seemed to
stream into England, though only too often it came from
le roi soleil. Louis XIV's France, in these years, was the
great force, one might almost say the great fact, of Europe;
and Charles was an instrument in making it greater still. In
all conscience, he "should have marched with the Dutch
and fought the French"; and as after 1674 the Dutch were
aligned—against Louis—with the Empire, Prussia, and
Spain, had England joined them, France might have been
checked a full generation before the Marlborough wars.

But Charles hated the Dutch, and, by throwing in his lot with Louis, could attempt their ruin while furthering the cause of Rome. This is to simplify, for in that age of treacherous loyalties, had England chosen to oppose the French, Holland might well have supported them. The whole matter is less a question of political than of personal ethics: what stigmatizes Charles is that he sold his allegiance, and in the greatest secrecy. As a result, England was more or less fighting Holland even when fighting on Holland's side, and supporting France even when apparently opposing her. Wisely for his own reign, though less so for his successor's, Charles had approved the marriage of his brother's daughter to his sister's son—the marriage of the Princess Mary to William of Orange. This alliance took place in the same year presumably as the Churchills', 1677.

William of Orange's marriage was one of several things that affected Sarah's. Her husband, being a soldier, was destined to be often from home: indeed, for the first five years of their married life, John and Sarah were to have no home—when in London, they made do with John's old bachelor quarters. For five years "they followed the Duke and the drum"—John having already displayed diplomatic as well as military talents. Their marriage, secretly performed, was evidently kept a secret for a good while after: from abroad John wrote to Sarah as "Miss Jennings." And Sarah, it appears, continued to behave like Miss Jennings. In the midst of addressing her as "dearer to me than my own life" he had to protest her unfairness in doubting his love or her being afraid on her side to admit that she loved him. Worse yet, she sometimes waited weeks to write at all, though John had as much need of her letters as her love, for he was often abroad. Gazetted colonel of a new regiment, he was by the same stroke sent to Holland to confabulate—it would seem successfully—with William. Another time he went, as a brigadier of foot, to Flanders. This was not so much a military venture as a pretence of aid to the Dutch; the coming Peace, as John knew, had already been arranged.

Indeed, when John came home from his trumped-up wars it was in England that he found real violence and turmoil; for with the murder, never to be solved, of Sir Edmund Berry Godfrey, the hellish nightmare of the Popish Plot burst open. The nefarious long-chinned informer Titus Oates had only to speak—and he seems to have spoken nothing but lies—for men to be vengefully tried and convicted as Catholic conspirators. For aspersing Oates's complete credibility, members were expelled the Commons; Charles's Queen was accused of plotting Charles's murder; Pepys went to the Tower charged with Popery; the King himself said of an innocent man: "I cannot pardon him because I dare not." And despite Oates's lies and the country's madness, there was some truth to feed the flames: for example, the Duke of York's confidential secretary had written to Louis XIV's confessor that there had been no such hopes of converting the "three kingdoms" since the death of Bloody Mary.

The hysteria over the Popish Plot bore very directly on the Churchills, for John's master, the Duke of York, was in line to succeed Charles II as a Popish king. And at this turn of time, when James's religion was even worse hated than was James himself, sentiment deepened to make Charles's handsome young Protestant by-blow, the Duke of Monmouth, heir to the throne. The obstruction of Monmouth's bastardy was to be removed by asserting that Charles had secretly married Monmouth's mother. But, Monmouth aside, there was a strong movement afoot to exclude James as heir; in fact, the Exclusion Bill actually passed the Commons. Charles declared he would veto it should it also pass the Lords; but he shrewdly grasped that, even were James not denied the throne, at so ticklish a moment he should be banished the country.

Hence, in March 1679 the Duke and Duchess of York took ship for Holland, with the Churchills as part of their suite. From Holland the whole party moved on to Brussels, where they settled down to live, and were presently joined by the fifteen-year-old, stubbornly Protestant Princess Anne, along with Sarah's now-widowed sister Frances. Here, almost certainly, the friendship between Anne and Sarah ripened. Meanwhile John, whose mission was not so much to share James's exile as find ways to shorten it, went on his master's behalf to Paris and London. He was well received by French Catholics as James's agent, and by English Whigs for being a Protestant like themselves. Charles at this point fell ill, and Churchill hurried James to England. But Charles got well again and James must once more go away—this time to Edinburgh. All the way to Edinburgh, John Churchill was at James's side, but Sarah was left with Frances in Jermyn Street, for she was many months with child. In a letter to Sarah, John in due time saluted the news of the baby's birth—"Pray kiss the child once for me"—but he never saw it; it died in infancy.

From Edinburgh he wrote, much as husbands in all ages do, about family:

Jan. 15, 1680

I have received yours of the 10th with a copy of the letter you writ to my Mother, which if she takes anything ill that is in that letter, you must attribute it to the peevishness of old age, for really there is nothing in it that she ought to take ill. I take it very kindly that

you have writ to her again, for she is my Mother, and
I hope at last that she will be sensible that she is to
blame in being peevish.

Or, apropos of Frances:

Pray present my services to the widow and tell her that
I am very glad she is not married, and if she stays for
my consent [3] she never will be.

Or to Sarah herself:

I swear to you the first night in which I was blessed in
having you in my arms was not more earnestly wished
for by me than now I do to be again with you. . . .

But soon after, in February of 1680, Charles recalled his
brother; and James and John were seven months in London
and at Newmarket. During this term at Court, Churchill,
who while serving James could do little to serve himself,
tried hard for a good military or diplomatic post. Continuing in James's suite, John—without improving his status—
might easily endanger his prospects; no servant of a man
so disliked and mistrusted could hope to gain in prestige.
To be sure, James himself valued John Churchill highly;
and now that he was at the King's side again, he sought an
ambassadorship for John, to France or Holland. The appointment to The Hague got far enough for William of
Orange to approve of it and for Louis XIV to hear that he
did; but it came to nothing. For one thing, James was in
no position to advance others: he was himself being furi-
ously attacked. A new Parliament had framed a new Exclusion Bill, and by the fall of 1680 the Duke was so vio-

---

[3] She didn't: having been widowed of Sir George Hamilton, she
married "mad Dick Talbot," Duke of Tyrconnel, so devoted an ad-
herent of James as to assist his amours and share his exile.

lently unpopular that the King again ordered him away. This time James stormed and resisted: to make him go required, indeed, not the King alone, but all the King's men— counselors, statesmen, two secretaries of state. But he went at last, John (and this time Sarah) with him, over a rough autumnal sea to Edinburgh.

Back in Scotland, James began an era of infamous misrule, attempting "to demonstrate . . . the policy he thought his brother should follow in England." At one extreme he got the Scottish Parliament to pass an anti-Exclusion Bill; at the other, he resorted to torture and charged men with treason. "I have cried at some of these trials," wrote Sarah in old age, "to see the cruelty that was done to these men only for their choosing to die rather than tell a lie." There would be consequences: in 1688 lowland Scotland united without exception against James. John all the while had the task of doing everything he could to get James back to England; but whoever he approached urged him to do everything possible to keep James out of it. His was an arduous and ungrateful role, all the more as he deplored his master's conduct; but at least he had Sarah with him. Life for her, in the train of the kindly if rabidly Catholic Duchess, was much pleasanter, though scarcely gay. The fault was the land's, not the lady's: the one official Caledonian recreation was playing "goffe." The Duchess had got herself talked about for countenancing theatricals; nor did it help her that they were free from the usual bawdry. Sarah found release from so much glumness by being once more with child. She went back to London to await her time; once again in Jermyn Street with Frances, she went once again to St. James's to be with Anne. Anne, at sixteen, was by royal standards now grown up, ready for the kind of courtship that was conducted at that kind of

Court; and, indeed, a *parti* from the Continent, young Prince George of Hanover, had just arrived. Like Anne, he was a Protestant; like Anne, a great-grandchild of James I; like Anne, wholly lacking in charm. They met; he kissed her, by permission, in the presence of the full Court, and in general behaved very agreeably; but he went home again without having declared himself. At the time no one dreamed that Anne would someday succeed to the English throne; still less that George would possess it after her. Just how she took his repulse is not told; but she never thereafter had a good word for Hanoverians.

Princess Anne was summoned to Scotland by her father just before Sarah's new baby—again a girl, again named Henrietta—was born in July. Its godmothers were John's sister Arabella, now decently married to an officer named Godfrey; and Sarah's mother, now reconciled to her daughter. Indeed, the baby was left with Mrs. Jennings at St. Albans as soon as Sarah felt strong enough to set out for Edinburgh. "Do not lose a minute in coming away," John had written to her, and he himself journeyed as far as Berwick to meet her. This second Edinburgh visit of Sarah's, which lasted eight months, was a much livelier one. There were royal birthday celebrations; pastorals, masques, even another attempt at the drama, *Mithridates King of Pontus*; there were banquets tendered the Duke by the townspeople, at which pies were painted vermilion or decorated with gold fringe; and for Sarah, now, there was the daily companionship of Anne.

James's position in England, with its new party system of Whigs and Tories and its outcries against Popery, continued to grow worse. Charles dissolved the Exclusion-minded Parliament of 1680, only for the new one that convened at Oxford in March of 1681 to bear the look of civil war—the

sternly Protestant Whigs actually arriving with armed re-
tainers. They did not merely desire, they were prepared to
demand, the exclusion of James and substitution of Monmouth. When their spokesman, Lord Shaftesbury, approached the King, Charles said firmly: "My lord, as I
grow older I grow more stedfast" and promptly dissolved
this Parliament too. For the four years he had still to live
he reigned without one. Prevented from making law, the
Whigs were forced into flouting it; balked of a Parliament,
they worked clandestinely in towns and taverns, even contriving that Rye House Plot which would have done in
King and King's brother alike. But their disjointed dark
schemes miscarried, and they themselves had badly miscal-
culated. The nation recoiled from the violent cries against
Popery, and suddenly the nation's vigilantes were branded
its persecutors. The Protestants were made to drink the
medicine they had compounded for the Catholics: Essex
killed himself, Shaftesbury fled the country, Russell and
Algernon Sidney went to the scaffold. Turnabout, it appeared, was foul play: in such a seesaw of intemperance and
injustice, Papists and Protestants were in about the same
proportion punished as revenged. Politically, however, the
whole thing comes off a kind of triumph for Charles and of
tribute to his sagacity. While extremes—or at any rate extremists—met and canceled out each other's power, Charles
himself felt no touch of their violence. Profiting, unlike
George III, from Charles I's example, the second Charles
concealed his determination in the cottonwool of bland
smiles. Divine right, he was wise enough to know, could
only be sustained by exceedingly human relationships.

So peaceful indeed were Charles's last years, and so
strong was his own position, that James—and the Churchills—could return to England. John was popular with

Charles and James alike, still the Duke's man of business (and the Duke, as heir presumptive, now had a mass of it), frequently the King's tennis partner. He was given a colonelcy in the King's Own regiment of dragoons,[4] besides being colonel of a troop of Life Guards. Higher honors were by the same token denied him; hearing John talked up for minister, Charles said he was "not resolved to have two idle secretaries of state"; someone else, cutting deeper, said the rumor only started because Churchill was "learning to write." But John's footing was firm, his future sunny, and his home life much fuller and happier. For one thing, he now had a home: he and Sarah had brought out Frances's share in Holywell House, Sarah's presumable birthplace near St. Albans. Here, putting up a new house after a year or two, they settled for the greater part of their lives. And early in 1684 Sarah was brought to bed of another child, who was christened Anne.

The child was not christened Anne by accident: by 1684 Sarah's connection with the future Queen was both official and close. From childhood—at Court, at Brussels, in Edinburgh—Anne had sought out Sarah as playmate, counselor, confidante. There had been much, in a way, to counsel or confide: the question of the Hanoverian visitor; the duty of two such stanch Protestants in the household of a fanatical Catholic; the business of William of Orange, unfaithful to Mary with her best friend Elizabeth Villiers; above all, that storybook romance, with its anything but storybook ending, between Anne at seventeen and the thirty-three-year-old Earl of Mulgrave. The Earl was very dashing and

---

[4] Which aroused some rhymed resentment:

> Let's cut our meat with spoons!
> The sense is as good
> As that Churchill should
> Be put to command the Dragoons.

worldly, part of that Restoration gallery of rakes—Sedleys, Ethereges, Dorsets, Rochesters—who were also poets; and he wrote good love letters into the bargain. Anne fell in love with him, and for most of a summer they were happy together. Then: "Lord Mulgrave for writing to Lady Anne, is discharged the Court." For writing to Lady Anne, in fact, Lord Mulgrave was shipped to Tangier: all the more because Anne's father had married a commoner, Anne must not. She, for most *un*romantic reasons, must marry a prince: a Danish prince, Charles had decided: named, like Anne's first suitor, George.

So " Colonel Churchill was sent to Denmark to conduct him to England to fall in love with the Princess Anne." Dutifully, George did so; he did everything dutifully; he was one of the decentest, most obliging, most untroublesome of princes or even of men, with no vice but drink and no fault but dullness. His reward was to survive as one of the great ciphers of history: he always looked, it was said, "as if it were dinner time," and his fixed reply to anything said to him gained him the nickname of *"Est-il possible?"* To the wittiest member of Anne's family he was, understandably, a crashing bore: "I have tried him drunk," Charles declared, "and I have tried him sober; and drunk or sober there is nothing to him." But though neither the Restoration's idea of a man-about-Court nor the cinema's of a prince, George played his role unexceptionably, being, for good measure, decidedly handsome.

Prince George and the Princess Anne were married on July 28, 1683. Parliament voted Anne £20,000 a year, and Charles gave her an establishment adjoining Whitehall called the Cockpit, where during the past generation Cromwell had lived the most rigorous, and Buckingham the most riotous, of lives. Almost the first consequence of the marriage was Sarah's being appointed, with the consent of the Duke and Duchess of York, one of Anne's ladies of the bed-chamber. The emolument was £200 a year, and no doubt much welcomed, but the new arrangement came almost certainly at Anne's request, with no thought, on Sarah's part, of advancing herself. Anne was not yet formidable, Sarah's position not yet firm. If the new appointment pleased Sarah, it must rather have been on grounds of vanity than of self-interest. Anne esteemed her: "The dull dressy extravagant Princess looked up to the woman whom she was paying £200 a year." And in his turn the man whom the dull dressy extravagant Princess had married looked up to her.

III

THE QUIET times continued. "The King and the Duke of York lived snug on Louis' money with only a plot or two to break the monotony," while Sarah served Anne in an atmosphere even more unruffled. The sun shone now for all of them: John had been made a Scottish baron, James was becoming a popular heir to the throne. "Never fear," Charles had once rebutted his brother's cautions to be more careful, "no one will kill me to make you king." But it seemed certain now that, if never made king, James, from purely natural causes, would turn into one. The Whig power had been smashed, the anti-Catholic agitation smothered; everyone was weary of violence and (religion aside) James just such a sovereign as the Tories hoped for and extolled in doggerel:

The glory of the British line,
Old Jimmy's come again.

It was a season of moderation, and Charles was working
with such moderates as Halifax, the man who best understood the way of the world and hence the temper of any
particular moment, who "fought the Whigs against per-
jured testimony for the life of Stafford, and . . . the
Crown and the Tories against packed juries for the lives of
Russell and Sidney." Than Halifax no Englishman has ever
spun saner aphorisms out of riper experience—"Those
friends who are above interest are seldom above jealousy";
"Men are not hanged for stealing horses, but that horses
may not be stolen." His was an unillusioned philosophy—
he preferred retreat, it has been said, to failure—and in im-
passioned or visionary moments we turn away from it; but
Halifax was as much an idealist as he had cause to be; as
any man can be who lives among time-servers, or touches
power, or himself connives on occasion. This grandfather
of Lord Chesterfield noted the characters of men; wrote
down among others—it needs to be read entire—a most re-
markable "character" of Charles II:

One great objection made to him was the concealing
himself and disguising his thoughts. In this there ought
a latitude to be given. . . . No King can be so little
inclined to dissemble but he must needs learn it from
his subjects, who every day give him such lessons of
it . . . Men given to dissembling are like rooks at
play, they will cheat for shillings, they are so used to
it . . . His face was as little a blab as most men's, yet
though it could not be called a prattling face, it would
sometimes tell tales to a good observer. When he
thought fit to be angry he had a very peevish mem-

2*.

ory . . . the whole inventory came out, there was not a slip omitted . . . It may be said that his inclinations to love were the effects of health and a good constitution, with as little mixture of the seraphic part as ever man had . . . The King did always by his councils as he did sometimes by his meals; he sat down out of form with the Queen, but he supped below stairs . . . He had as little eagerness to oblige as he had to hurt men . . . He would slide from an asking face, and could guess very well . . .

Then, one night early in 1685, Charles, chatting, as he undressed, with his Gentlemen of the Bedchamber, talked of having a house of his covered with lead; and "God knows," one of them recorded afterward, "the Saturday following he was put in his coffin." Overnight, the victim of a stroke, he had turned "pale as ashes," and, for all his apology at being such an unconscionable time a-dying, it was only five days till he was dead.

Fifteen minutes after his brother's death, James met the Privy Council to be recognized as king. Though all danger was past, his qualms and precautions were understandable, and his first declarations to the Council, avowing respect for the laws—and the Church—of England, were notably reassuring. With Tory and monarchical sentiment just then at their strongest, with the nation enough grieved by Charles's death to lack acerbity toward his successor, James was in a surprisingly strong position; and the new, and very Tory, and very friendly, Parliament he came before and saluted with fair words, voted him, as they had never voted Charles, fat revenues for life. Then, amid so much sunlight, a shadow fell: on the second Sunday of his reign, the King went to Mass in the Queen's Chapel at Whitehall and had the doors thrown open for all to see. On this, or a like occasion, the Catholic Duke of Norfolk, carrying—as premier peer—the sword of state, stopped at the door of the chapel. "Your father, my lord," said James, "would have gone further." "Your Majesty's father," Norfolk answered, "would not have gone so far." The Protestant Court felt uneasy, the Protestant clergy alarmed. Nothing could have been less like Charles, who called for a priest only on his deathbed. Doubtless the truer Catholic could hardly help being the less successful king; and doubtless all that James forfeited through candor, Charles had only preserved through guile. But James played tricks of his own; James wooed Privy Council and Parliament alike, till he thought himself powerful enough to dispense with them. "James," as Stuart Reid put it, "had most of his brother's vices, and scarcely any of his virtues." Charles was not a good man, but he made a good companion and an engaging king. James's small talk with ladies, if we can credit Gramont, ran to hunting-field "accounts of broken legs and arms, dislocated shoulders, and other curious and entertaining adventures." James sinned sexually no less often than Charles,[1] and blundered politically much oftener. Charles's personality did much to offset his character, whereas James was cruel and sullen as well as despotic, and no more commanded loyalty than he inspired trust.

At James's accession, John Churchill was shown agreeable but not unusual marks of favor: his colonelcy in the Dragoons was confirmed, he became a Gentleman of the Bedchamber and an *English* peer, Baron Churchill of

[1] Charles remarked that James, "devout as he is," loved women even more than he did: but chose such women, said Charles on another occasion, as James' priests must have provided for penances.

Sandridge. He was not made a minister, only once again an envoy—being sent to Versailles, officially to inform Louis of the accession, but in fact to seek a larger English subsidy. But as Louis had shrewdly sent James half a million livres before Churchill arrived, Churchill on arriving could scarcely ask for more, and contented himself, if hardly his master, with the appropriate announcements and thanks. His most unofficial remark while in France was that, should the King try to change England's religion, he would "instantly quit his service."

On his return, John was able to spend a month with Sarah. Then Monmouth landed in Dorset, denouncing James as—among other things—Charles's murderer, and asserting (what Charles had always stoutly denied) his own legitimacy. Monmouth had been spurred on by the Protestant exiles he lived among, who envisaged an England quite free of the feelings that had exiled them—an England still stanchly Whig. And Monmouth, on landing at Lyme Regis, had been wildly received. During the first twenty-four hours his ranks were swelled—mostly among out-of-work miners and weavers—by fifteen hundred men. When word of the rebellion reached London, John Churchill was appointed a brigadier general and, leading his troops, sped forthwith to the West, covering 120 miles in four days. Monmouth sent a letter to John, asking his aid; John sent the letter on to the King. The King, meanwhile, had dispatched the French Earl of Feversham as Churchill's military superior, an act of possible mistrust on James's part which caused definite resentment on John's. "I see plainly," Churchill wrote, "that the trouble is mine, and that the honor will be another's." Monmouth—whose only chance lay in speed, in multiplying recruits and snowballing conquests till his cause became a crusade—bungled his strategy and procrastinated. Yet at Sedgmoor, where he was beaten, he caught Feversham so far off guard as to be asleep, with half his men stupefied from cider. It was Churchill who, while the foppish Feversham was surveying himself in a looking-glass, took command, strengthened the royal defenses, opened the victorious offensive, and in fact announced the victory. Monmouth, caught in a ditch, was conveyed to London, where he first groveled like a coward for his life, then died decently enough on Tower Hill. Feversham was awarded the Garter.

It was a decided victory for James, but one that possibly abetted his eventual downfall. It increased his already inflated self-assurance; it nourished his contempt for the wishes, which were to become the will, of the nation. Moreover, in his treatment of the rebels he showed as incredible want of heart as of judgment. Seldom, for so swiftly broken an insurrection, have so many offenders been tried or have their trials proved such unspeakable farces. The Bloody Assizes remain one of the great blots on English history, and probably a hundred people are familiar with the ferocity of the punishments for one who recalls the actual circumstances of the crimes. It is true that Macaulay, who perhaps gave the event its real notoriety, overstated its horrors: nevertheless, when the maniacally cruel Judge Jeffreys was done, at least 150 "rebels" (many of them ignorant rustics out of work) had been put to death and hung gibbeted all over the roadsides; some 800 had been sold into slavery; and many more had been flogged and imprisoned. Now James's cruelty was no secret, had it ever been. To a lady who sought an audience of him to plead for her brother's life, John Churchill, striking the chimneypiece, remarked: "This marble is not harder than the King's heart."

Nor, for James, was such harshness a purge: it was rather a stimulant. More than ever "he would make England a Catholic country and himself an absolute monarch." True, the difficulties were such as no realist would dream of combatting; the dangers so great as to make even a fanatic take thought. James took thought: recalled how, for granting concessions, his father had gone to the block; basked complacently in the knowledge that he had, just now, a Parliament more favorable to the Crown than any that had met since 1661. Hence, and every day more peremptorily, he asserted his divine right to govern wrong. Like George III a century later, James had no thoughts whatever of being commanded and only the most fitful ones of being advised. As A. L. Rowse has said, he was one of those men "who will hardly take Yes for an answer." Moreover he, unlike George III, was the actual arm of the Government, with the right to choose his own ministers and set his own policy; and understandably, as the policy he fixed on grew more misguided, such ministers as were willing to promulgate it proved more compliant.

James now attempted the Parliamentary repeal of the Test Act, whereby Catholics would no longer be debarred from office and could indeed be hoisted to power; along with the repeal of the writ of habeas corpus, whereby troublemakers could be let languish in prison. He further intended a large standing army, which Catholics would officer. Such tactics were the more ill considered in that with a little management James "could have secured every reasonable liberty a Catholic could desire"; and nowhere were James's actions more deprecated than among the old Catholic families. Parliament, meantime, was truly disturbed: the idea of Catholic officers threatened its greatest love, the Anglican Church; the much enlarged army revived its ugliest memory, the Cromwell dictatorship. James, at a stroke, had managed to alienate Whigs and Tories alike, and when the Commons most respectfully protested enlarging the army and suspending the Test Act for officers, James's answer was to prorogue Parliament. Though it was not officially dissolved till two years later, it never met again during his reign.

To compensate for the loss of support at the center, James now issued a Declaration of Indulgence that would greatly improve the status of Papists and Dissenters, and—as he supposed—rally both of them to his side. But the Dissenters, aware that they were merely being used, rejected so fraudulent a meeting of extremes; wherefore the King himself was pushed even further toward extremities. Thus, wishing to dispense with the test against Catholics in the army, James asked one of Jeffreys's henchmen whether he could find twelve judges who would sustain such an over-riding of the law. "Your Majesty," he was told, "may find twelve judges to your mind: but hardly twelve lawyers." Still James worked on, quite unperturbed, flaunting rather than masking his intentions. A large army—it totaled 40,000 men and exceeded any standing army in English history—was quartered at Hounslow, just outside London, "to keep the capital in awe." To be sure, some men out of fear and others out of ambition and love of place—mayors and justices, lawyers and lords—were converted to Rome or bribed or cajoled into silence, but increasingly, as time went on, most men grew alarmed and alienated. "I had rather," said the great Irish Protestant Duke of Ormonde, "live and die in Carolina than in Ireland."

To John and Sarah Churchill, conscious of the drift of things, these were years of growing decision. Pretty clearly John had decided from the outset to oppose as long as he could and only desert when he must, but by now the thought of desertion was neither very wild nor very horrifying. No doubt the Churchills were most influenced by their stanch Protestant feelings, but somewhat influenced also, it is not too cynical to suggest, by their knowing how stanchly Protestant the nation—and the Princess Anne— were. So far as opposing the King was concerned, it very early became necessary to take a stand: in January 1686, at the trial of Lord Delamere for complicity in Monmouth's rebellion, John—as junior baron—was forced to vote first of the thirty peers sitting in judgment; and voted, as did all twenty-nine after him, "Not guilty." But the real choice of sides and weighing of loyalties arose chiefly from their relation to Anne. They were already pledged to Anne as against her father; and between Anne and her father there was already a formidable breach. Rumors had been flying about that, would she only turn Catholic, she would be named— ahead of her sister Mary—James's successor, a proposal that angered and alarmed her. And she must have been wrought up only the more when the King refused her permission to visit her sister at The Hague. Anne's Protestantism was perhaps the stubbornest conviction of an incredibly stubborn nature; rather than change her religion, she wrote to Mary, she would "choose to live on alms." And she had bidden John Churchill write in like vein about her to Mary's husband. Then, speaking for himself, John added that as against being faithful to his religion, he set the King's favor at naught; and thereupon added to that: "I think it may be a great ease to Your Highness . . . that the Princess of Denmark is safe in the trusting of me: I being resolved, although I cannot live the life of a saint, if there be ever occasion for it, to show the resolution of a martyr." Lord Churchill knew perfectly well, of course, that this was something more than a bit of private family mail, that it embraced conspiracy and fell not too far short of treason. As a worldling, John Churchill would perhaps never have carried loyalty beyond all limits of prudence; in any case, there was toward James no deep compulsion for being loyal. The King had been kind to him, but not more; and he, toward a King whose policy he greatly opposed—and who had never, as it happens, permitted him office—need be no more than decently grateful. Without doubt the soundest course for a worldling was to keep as much as possible out of trouble's way, and John tried, among other stratagems, to be sent as a soldier to Holland. But the maneuver failed. Thereafter, when really forced to speak, he presumably spoke his mind; told James, in January 1688 for example, that he would not support repeal of the Test Act. This was sufficiently public knowledge for someone to write in a letter: "Lord Churchill swears he will not do what the King requires of him." That it should be public knowledge is conceivably what Churchill desired most.

By 1688 James had so far asserted the royal will that a Catholic admiral ruled the fleet; that—to give just one further example—James's Protestant brother-in-law Clarendon had been succeeded as Lord Lieutenant of Ireland by Sarah's Catholic brother-in-law Tyrconnel. Now James went ever farther: he issued a second Declaration of Indulgence for Papists and Dissenters, and a week later ordered the Anglican bishops to distribute it throughout their dioceses and have it read in all their churches. Sancroft, the Archbishop of Canterbury, together with six other bishops, petitioned the King to withdraw this order on the ground that it was illegal. Their petition found its way into print, whereupon James had all seven arrested, confined to the Tower, and brought to trial for seditious libel. The trial

assumed immense importance to a nation that saw in it the
handiwork of a bigot when he becomes a despot. At the
start, the packed jury disagreed; there followed a night of
waiting and tension; then came the verdict: Not guilty.
"What is that clamor?" asked James among his troops at
Hounslow. "Sire, it is nothing—it is just that the soldiers are
glad the bishops have been acquitted." "You call that,"
James answered, "nothing?"

The trial had been the more momentous for coming on
the very heels of a darker event. Married for fifteen years
to Mary of Modena, James had had no heir by her: the
children she had borne him had died in infancy, and that
there would be other children was by now despaired of.
But suddenly, during the winter of 1687–8, the Queen was
reported to be with child. The news came like a thunder-
clap: "the Catholics thought it was a miracle, and the
Protestants . . . an imposture." In June, in any case—just
two days after the bishops had been sent to the Tower—
the Queen was delivered of a son. To most of the nation,
this was news of the direst and blackest import. Knowing
both Mary and Anne to be fierce Protestants, England had
endured James's Catholicism in the belief that the thing itself would not endure; however dark matters seemed,
there was light at the end of the tunnel. But now Mary of
Modena's Catholic son, and presumably all his line, would
follow James upon the throne. Overnight the promised
happy ending—indeed, anything that resembled an ending—
was deleted from the drama.

As it happened, the Prince's birth stirred up more than
grim forebodings: it aroused peculiar doubts. With extraordinary obtuseness, seeing that even for Catholics it
resembled a miracle, the King had invited no Protestant
officials to the lying-in. Anne was at Bath at the time, and

the Archbishop of Canterbury in the Tower; and there
was present no formal representative of the Church of
England, or of Anne or of Mary; no Dutch representative of William; only a scattering of Anglicans among an
assemblage of Papists. As a result, stories soon circulated
that the Queen had never been pregnant, and that an infant had been brought to her bed in a warming-pan; or
that the Queen's own child had died at birth, and another
been substituted. Wrote Anne to Mary: "I shall never now
be satisfied, whether the child be true or false: it may be it
is our brother . . . where one believes it, a thousand do
not." Mary, in reply, taxed Anne with not giving details
enough and would have her answer some eighteen questions. This time Anne spared no details: "I never heard
anybody say they felt the child stir. . . . Mrs. Dawson
tells me she has seen it stir but never felt it." And again:
"I never saw any milk, but Mrs. Dawson says she has seen
it upon her [i.e., the Queen's] smock." In Holland, William, who had ordered a thanksgiving service when he first
heard of the Prince's birth, canceled it on hearing that reports of the birth had been greatly exaggerated. He thoroughly welcomed the imposture about an imposture, for
by this time William and his English friends were discussing
his intervention by every post. William by now had
warmed to the idea, only stipulating that he must be asked
to come—he would not invade.

The invitation he required was brought to him in July
by an English admiral who had been smuggled out of the
country as an English sailor. It had been composed the very
night—"while London was still ruddy with bonfires"—the
seven bishops were acquitted. Its seven signers included
some very great names—Danby and Devonshire, Shrewsbury and Russell, as well as Compton, the deposed Bishop

of London; and the invitation they proffered, the cool, dispassionate, businesslike document they signed, was evidence of their inner steadfastness. They could ask William to curb and very possibly depose his father-in-law in the same tone with which they might have invited him to unveil a monument. Their names were too great for Churchill's to be one of them. But John, a short time afterwards, sent William—by one of the signers—an excellent, unequivocal letter of allegiance which Macaulay has most unfairly aspersed.[2]

William, for his part, hesitated no longer. "Now or never!" he is credited with saying: whatever he said, he at once began to act. His decision, reached after much weightier deliberation than we have anywhere suggested, was taken on much larger grounds than we have anywhere set forth. William saw England in terms of all Europe; he saw James's Catholic designs as part of an increasing Protestant oppression;[3] he saw—he always saw—France, with whom James was allied, as the great villain of European drama. William "took England," Halifax would say, "on the way to France." But, beyond any growing oppression of Protestant peoples, this was clearly a good moment to get rid of a Catholic king: for (it so happened) a more powerful Catholic, Louis XIV, was badly at odds with the most powerful Catholic of all, the humane high-minded indomitable Innocent XI.

His declaration made, William sent envoys into Germany to raise troops, and acquired the support of several prince-

---

[2] In having, more than once, to take issue with Macaulay, I would not for a moment seem to belittle his *History*. His faults are every bit as grave as they are well known, but his virtues, though no longer so well known, remain incomparable.

[3] In France, for example, where the Edict of Nantes was revoked, and in Hungary and the Palatinate.

lings. Though it was possibly September before James was
sure the invitations were out, he must long before that have
scented trouble, and had begun to revise—indeed, to a great
extent reverse—his policy. In November, he announced, a
new Parliament would assemble; he removed many Catholics from office and reinstated many Anglicans; he proclaimed a general pardon. But the rumor that the Prince of
Orange was coming laid bare James's actual motive; the
people felt no need to be grateful. Besides, James's strengthening, even now, his army with Catholic regiments from
Ireland disturbed the English and angered them. The Irish
regiments led Lord Wharton to compose inflammatory
words to go with a quickstep of Purcell's—the words of
"Lillibullero." [4] "Perhaps never had so slight a thing,"
wrote Bishop Burnet, "so great an effect." Night and day
the tune was whistled and sung, by the soldiery first, then
by people of every kind.

William was everywhere rumored to be coming; yet as
the weeks—full of contrary winds—of a fateful autumn
passed, he did not come. But the "Protestant wind" blew
for him at last, blew him straight down the Channel past
the assembled English fleet, which had no way of attacking
him even had it shown the will; and on November 5, Guy
Fawkes Day, he landed at Torbay. Meanwhile, in England,
his Revolution allies had been busy raising troops—Bishop
Compton, for example, had gone North "to see his sisters."
Yet it must not be supposed that William had in any way
become a national hero: a deliverer of a kind he might certainly be, but one quite without aura or glamour.

He landed, having wisely brought his army with him,
and from Torbay he began an orderly, all-but-unopposed

---

[4] "Lillibullero" was a password among the Irish when, in 1641, they
were slaughtering Protestants.

advance. Slowly he began to collect adherents—the lords of the neighborhood first; then, by ones and twos and threes, those in the service or patronage of the King. James, who reached Salisbury after William had halted at Exeter, had vaguely counted on nonresistance. But now he must act. When the suggestion was made to him to have certain mistrusted adherents, Churchill among them, done away with —Feversham, "on his knees," had begged for it—James "could not resolve it." He could not, in fact, resolve anything. Had he agreed with John Churchill and others to move against William; had he braved the chance of rebellion among his troops, he might just possibly have staved off revolution among his countrymen. For by way of English blood being spilled, by way of Dutch soldiers killing English ones, James might somehow have wrested England's support. Having no case in logic, he must needs find his cause in emotion. But James, after much indecision, elected to retreat; and as he turned back, liegemen and luck alike turned scornfully away. By night John Churchill rode off with his brigade to join William; so did others close to James; so, only a little later, did James's son-in-law Prince George.

Soon after John's desertion, orders to arrest Sarah reached London. Anne—who had informed William at Exeter that she meant to be guided by the Churchills, and that at the right moment her husband would abandon her father—had of course known, as Sarah knew, all that was in their husbands' minds. Now, with the orders for Sarah's arrest, Anne contrived delays that effected their joint escape. Sarah spoke afterwards of having, in all that followed, "obeyed" her mistress—who "rather than see her father . . . would jump out at window." But it is quite obvious that Sarah—who, unlike Anne, was in very real danger—

had herself not only staged the performance, but also planned the show. Weeks earlier she had superintended the building of a private staircase that led from Anne's apartments to her own unguarded ones; and now the two women slipped out of the Cockpit into a murky melodramatic November night of rain. Awaiting them in the dark were the Bishop of London and the poet Charles Sackville, Earl of Dorset—Nell Gwynne's "Charles the First." The party sloshed through the wet to Charing Cross—Anne, it is told, losing a shoe en route and slipping her foot into one of Dorset's gauntlets. At Charing Cross they climbed into a coach and drove to the Bishop's, where they spent the night; at daybreak they drove to Dorset's handsome seat in Epping Forest; they drove next to Lord Northampton's, the Bishop's brother; and came at last to Nottingham, where the Earl of Devonshire had raised, and now headed, an army of wellborn rebels.

There Anne was received with rapturous devotion by the insurgents; and an impromptu—and festive Court set up. At a banquet given by Lord Devonshire, servants were scarce; and the young Colley Cibber, who to please his father had put aside his dreams of the stage and turned soldier, now turned footman as well. He wrote, long afterwards, in his *Autobiography:*

> The post assigned me was to observe what the lady Churchill might call for. Being so near the table, you may naturally ask me what I might have heard to have passed in conversation at it; which I should certainly tell you, had I attended to above two words that were uttered there, and those were "Some wine and water.". . . . Except at that single sound all my senses were collected into my eyes, which . . . wanted no

better amusement than . . . the delight of gazing on
the fair object so near me. If so clear an emanation of
beauty, such a commanding aspect of grace, struck
me into a regard that had something softer than the
most profound respect in it, I cannot see why I may
not without offense remember it; such beauty, like the
sun, must sometimes lose its power to choose, and
shine into equal warmth the peasant and the courtier.

This early tribute to Sarah's beauty coincides with her
first real triumph of stage-management. Here, in the flight
she had arranged and which affected her own safety so
much more than her mistress's, Sarah's great influence over
Anne for the first time occasioned fateful action. The flight
itself now turned into something more like a progress: from
Nottingham Anne and her court moved, with enough state-
liness to require a purple flag, to Leicester; thence to War-
wick; and at last to Oxford, where Anne was reunited
with Prince George. From all the real turbulence of these
decisive indecisive weeks Anne and Sarah were comfortably removed. James, following his decision to retreat, had
returned to London to find Anne departed and cry out:
"God help me! Even my children have forsaken me!"
While presumably treating with William, the King spirited
the Queen and baby Prince to France, then himself sought
to follow after, throwing the Great Seal, as he went, into
the Thames with a mind to clog and halt the wheels of
Government. But certain sailors on the ship he boarded
were suspicious of who he might be, and forced him back
into his own kingdom. Unfortunately, by the time he returned to Whitehall, William had reached Windsor. The
situation itself had pretty much reached a resolution; and
James was hardly more now than William's prisoner,

though given every encouragement to escape. His guards looked almost ostentatiously the other way, and this time, having been moved from London to Rochester, James had not far to flee. On the 22nd of December, attended by the Duke of Berwick—the son borne to him by Churchill's sister—James stole out of England forever. Not till he was gone for a few days from London did Anne—and Sarah with her—come back to it and straightway appear at the playhouse decked out with orange ribbons. And now John, to reassemble his Life Guards, and then William, at the head of his army, arrived in London also.

IV

IT had proved a far more sweeping victory for William than any he could have logically hoped for. He had come presumably not to supplant, but merely to intervene; to demand, first and foremost, a free Parliament—a Parliament that should determine the order of succession and the legitimacy of the infant Prince. It had not been on the cards that anything so ticklish should come off so triumphant; that it did required a positive genius for blundering in James. James at the start had refused to treat with William at all, or to advance to fight him either; nor—while William remained on English soil—would he summon a Parliament. When, later, he had sent commissioners to parley with William at an inn, they brought back, despite William's vastly improved position, terms as moderate as the original ones. James did not need Divine Right to hold his throne; mere reasonableness would have been quite sufficient. Instead, some convulsion of perversity led him to put greater trust in France than in England, and to suppose he could inculcate a sense of firmness through the example of taking flight. That the Revolution proved so bloodless and hence so Glorious is owing most of all to a bungling monarch who threw away the loyalty of his subjects.

John Churchill's loyalty he had lost earlier, however—and in view of John Churchill's importance to our story, we must needs examine the personal morality of his decision. It was a decision that Churchill had to make in company with a great many other Englishmen, and in the clear light of history, even in the murkier light of his own age, it proved to be the right decision. James was a bad king; his sincerest quality—his fervent faith—produced bigotry, intolerance, and a determination to impose that faith on the nation; had the nation sanctioned James's claim to divine right, they must have either had to keep James in power or involve themselves in a bloody civil war.

Whether John Churchill reached the right decision for entirely right reasons is more arguable; and whether, once he came to it, he ought to have gone on pretending loyalty to James is more arguable still. Sir Winston Churchill contends that in the 1680's one could not merely "resign" or go into retirement as one would today: cut off from Court, one had no possible career. Nevertheless, John owed a great deal to James both before and after he became king; his relation to James was peculiarly close, and in any relationships so close there cannot but be some stigma to one's dissembling. John Churchill's position was the kind that is almost made to be moralized about; and it so happens that in John Churchill's case the two most celebrated verdicts are also the two most extreme—the utter condemnation of Macaulay, the substantial vindication of Sir Winston. To any one open-minded, it has been clear for a century that Macaulay—with his brilliant incapacity ever quite to assemble the truth; with his need, which John Churchill satisfied, for a large and lordlike villain—must himself be condemned. Plainly Macaulay is out for blood; but Sir Winston is out—for blood—as well. Writing as a descendant, he proves uncommonly judicious; all the same, that is not equal to writing exclusively as a historian. He is at the same pains to ascribe creditable motives to John as Macaulay was to introduce base ones; and hence, like Macaulay, seizes on trifles for far more than they are worth. He is a tremendously cogent attorney for the defense, but in a situation where what history requires is a wholly disinterested judge.

Exactly what went on in John Churchill's mind, let alone his heart, we can never know; but in view of his own declarations, and his particular dilemma, and his turnabout violent age, it is not too presumptuous to speculate. Doubtless, no man can be fully summed up in a single word; but if any man can, surely it is Marlborough, who was in every sense a worldling. He was not base by nature, nor by inclination either; but virtue hesitated as soon as ambition beckoned; it beckoned, with some need for deceit, at stage after stage of his career; and, despite what he might fancy, he was no more martyr than saint. In most big crises of his life he was guided, as are all but a few people, by self-interest. Had he been as steadfast as the bishops, he would have taken the same dangerous risks. Had he been as honest as a Clarendon, he would have ventured the same downhill road. He was not of their fiber—as they in turn were not of his mold. John Churchill was everywhere regarded as the courtliest man of his age; suavity was his hallmark, diplomacy his forte; and plainly in such a man there will as soon be something treacherous as trustworthy. One's mind will not let go an anecdote of John during his great warrior years, when he met abroad an exiled Jacobite nobleman and showed him very marked attentions. "At dinner," wrote the nobleman, "sitting by me, he would continually take me by the hand, but politicly (at which he was a great master), putting his hand under the napkin."

Churchill's new master in any case now held the field— the burning question being, by what title? Although, strictly speaking, no Parliament could meet, since a sovereign was needed to summon one, yet "an election was held and a body assembled"—a Convention, as it styled itself; a Convention Parliament, as it is styled by history. It met on the 1st of February 1689, and required just three weeks to effect, or validate—or in a way prevent—a revolution. Naturally, it could not assert William's position until it had decided on James's. The King had definitely gone away: the question was whether he should simply be marked "absent," or of his own volition had withdrawn, or deserved to be expelled. The Whigs were for clearly expelling him, thereby affirming that the Crown was held through the consent of the people as vested in the authority of Parliament. But the Tories, who had helped effect the Revolution without in a sense espousing it, desired nothing so drastic. What they wished for was an absentee king and an active regency, and it was by only two votes that the regency proposal was defeated. In the end, James was said to have abdicated, and the throne was declared to be vacant.

It was as well that the Convention rejected a regency, for William had point-blank refused to be regent. During a long, difficult period of deliberation, he had brilliantly kept silent, and when he spoke out at last it was not, he remarked, to dictate terms to the Convention; it was only to make clear his own. He would not be merely a regent, nor would he, again, accept a lower rank than his wife's. A maneuver of Halifax's to make him sole monarch failing ignominiously, he insisted upon the Crown during his lifetime—jointly with Mary, as long as she lived, but for himself alone, should she predecease him. Mary—who when told she was to marry William had "wept all the afternoon and all the following day"—would seem with the years to have fallen in love with him, and now gave him unqualified support from The Hague. The Convention and the country were of no mind to dispute it; they were much more concerned with restoring order in England than with worrying whether the sickly William might outlive his healthy wife. So Mary crossed over from Holland, and on February 23 her husband and herself jointly accepted the throne—he to possess the executive power—and accepted along with it the Convention's restrictive Declaration of Rights. Divine Right had departed, with James, from England forever; and the people's sovereign should from henceforth be its servant.

William's terms fell hardest on Anne, who would now succeed to the throne only on the death of both her sister and her brother-in-law. This setback for her proved no less a setback for the Churchills, since their future was bound up in hers; yet in the end it was John who urged Anne to acquiesce. When the Convention first met, John had favored a regency, but once William's ideas transpired, he would not so much offend William as to vote for one, and in fact did not vote at all. He did later vote for James's having "deserted" rather than "abdicated" the throne, but once abdication became a condition for making William and Mary joint sovereigns, he assented to it. And when he saw that William must perforce be king, he persuaded Sarah—who was strenuously against Anne's lowering her position—to urge Anne to change her mind: after all, what chance had William of outliving his wife? William in turn agreed that Anne and her children should possess the throne before any children of his that were not Mary's.

Thus the new King had every reason to feel kindly toward Churchill, who had now favored him over James and Anne alike. And he was not slow to reward him. At the Coronation he made the obliging baron a belted earl—Earl of Marlborough.[1] He made him also a Gentleman of the Bedchamber. He gave him a place on the Privy Council. He virtually created him commander-in-chief of the English army. To be sure, the famous Marshal Schomberg enjoyed higher rank, but served largely as William's deputy, and assented generally to whatever Marlborough proposed. But, for all such royal favor, William showed no liking for John or Sarah, least of all for their helping to bring round Anne. For when Lord Halifax had named Churchill as someone who might influence her, William had retorted that "Churchill could not govern him nor his wife as they [sic] did" Anne and Prince George. And William, as John knew, distrusted him; the beneficiary of double-dealing is no less aware of it than the victim. Nonetheless, John was far better off under William than he had been, or had like to be, with James. He was an earl instead of a baron; he was a commander who, instead of suddenly having any Feversham put over him in battle, had no one but a complaisant Schomberg over him at all. Under William, moreover, there was every chance to rise in the world, including a virtual guarantee of immediate war. On the other hand, had James remained king and John remained Protestant, he would have been fortunate not to have lost ground.

[1] The name Marlborough was taken from a recently extinct earldom belonging to a remote connection of John's.

As for Sarah, she was now reinstalled with Anne at the Cockpit. Their long intimacy had grown greater through the crisis they had endured together. If it by no means represented a true meeting of minds, it expressed something quite as uncommon. Despite appearances, it was not the meeting of someone with no mind of her own and someone else who had mind and to spare. Anne had very much a mind of her own without in a sense having any mind at all. She either entreated to be led or refused to be, was all compliance or all opposition. The true interest of their relationship lay rather in how much Anne doted on the woman she should so much have resented. This dull dumpling of a princess adored Sarah for her looks, her quick mind, her unfettered personality; this inveterate stickler for form would put aside for Sarah the one great advantage she possessed, her rank. When Anne was twenty, and just beginning marriage with Prince George, she had set about dispensing with all ceremony. As Sarah described it,

She grew weary to be treated by me with the form and ceremony due to her rank; nor could she bear from me the sound of words which implied in them distance and superiority. It was this turn of mind which made her one day propose to me that, whenever I should happen to be absent from her, we might in all our letters write ourselves by feigned names, such as would impart nothing of distinction of rank between us. Morley and Freeman were the names her fancy hit upon, and she left me to choose by which of them I should be called. My frank, open temper led me to fix upon Freeman, and so the Princess took the other, and from this time "Mrs. Morley" and "Mrs.

Freeman" began to converse as equals, made so by affection and friendship.

In this play-acting, Prince George agreed to become Mr. Morley, and John Churchill Mr. Freeman. Moreover, Anne urged Sarah to

> let me beg of you not to call me your highness at every word, but to be as free with me as one friend ought to be with another. You can never give me any greater proof of your friendship than in telling me your mind freely in all things, which I do beg you to do.

For Sarah, there could scarcely have been a more coveted or, in the long run, a more costly gift: Sarah had not quite ascended to being Anne's equal but only to play-act at being. For the lesser distinction there were doubtless, from Anne's point of view, good reasons enough. Anne's mother was dead; her stepmother, though kindly, was Catholic; her sister lived at a distance, and had never been close. And more even than her dispensing with rank offered evidence of love, it offered evidence of seeking it.[2]

[2] The nature of Anne's feeling for Sarah is too intense to ignore, yet not altogether easy to define. For it is complicated by the whole atmosphere of Anne's girlhood. Her sister Mary, for example, was involved in a friendship with Frances Apsley in which Mary acted the wife and Frances the husband, and in which Mary wrote to Frances as follows:

> I have sat up this night . . . to tell my dear dear dear dearest dear husband . . . that I am more and more in love with you every time I see you, and love you so well that I cannot express it no way but by saying I am your louse in bosom and would be very glad to be always so near you.

At exactly the same time Anne played husband to Frances's wife. Some of this derives from the way very young girls of the period—and very young princesses even more—were kept apart from men, and hence given to inventing a life with them. Often, too, they played male roles in Court theatricals (Anne and Frances addressed each other by names taken from Lee's *Mithridates*.)

Sarah, Duchess of Marlborough

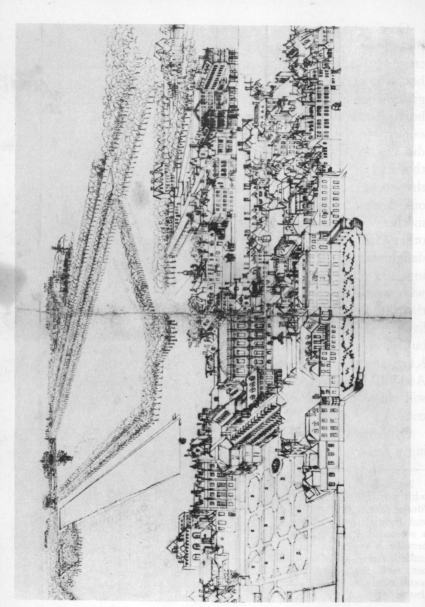

Whiteball Palace, c. 1694

On Sarah's side, all this just now must have been very
pleasant and exhilarating: she had in Anne an exalted mistress who delighted to honor her, who craved to be with
her, who chose to drop down to her: Anne was at once a
great benefactress and a kind of toy. True, Anne must have
bored Sarah by now, if indeed she had not from the very
outset, but Sarah's role did not bore her, and certainly life
did not. And though the two women were very unlike,
they had things in common which were most uncommon in
the world they inhabited: both of them were highly virtuous, both of them happily married. Both, besides, were
mothers of numerous children, and godmothers to each
other's. Sarah, in this spring of 1689, could boast three
daughters and a son; Anne, what with frequently miscarry-
ing, and children dying in infancy, had only a daughter,
who would die the next year. And in this spring both of
them were with child again. Sarah, in the summer, was delivered of a fourth daughter; Anne, much more impor-
tantly, of a son who was named William in honor of the
King, and ennobled by the King as Duke of Gloucester.
As William and Mary, after many years of marriage, were
still childless, Anne's baby was very much in line of succession.

Of Anne's baby Anne's sister the Queen grew exceedingly fond, but from Anne herself drew farther and far-

---

So much might be no more than adolescent transferences coupled
with period romanticism. Yet almost three years after her marriage at
fifteen, Mary still could write to Frances protesting Frances's inconstancy,
and urging her to "take heed . . . for 'tis dangerous to vex a lover and
a woman." And a grown-up Anne writes, from time to time, with
peculiar intensity to Sarah, displaying more than ordinary affection.
Indeed, Anne's attitude toward women was remarked upon soon after
her death. Allowing for the current tendency to ferret out and stress
sexual abnormality, one still has a sense of something in Anne's emotions
that suggests the abnormal.

3

ther away. They had never really been close; only when cast, for a term, as Goneril and Regan had they found a vital tie. And now events in which Sarah played a considerable part were to alienate them the more. While still in Holland, Mary had been cordially enough disposed toward Sarah, though she must have known how decisive an influence the Churchills exerted over Anne. But she had reason, just then, to approve of it, for it was exerted in William's behalf. Once Mary was in England, however, Sarah's hold over Anne became something to resent—and to resent all the more because it so vastly exceeded her own. Soon cool in her relations with Sarah, Mary grew with every day colder.

For one thing, relations grew worse as time went on between Mary and Anne. Doubtless Anne was touchy, but her position was decidedly ticklish. She had behaved well toward William in relinquishing her place in the succession, and he, surely, might act generously toward her. Yet, quite beyond his habitual sullenness, he proved deliberately uncivil. He and Mary ignored Prince George as a man, and snubbed him when he sought to enter their service, whether on land or sea. They made the Prince and Princess of Denmark no more noticeable a part of the Court than of their own more intimate circle; and they acted very meanly indeed in the matter of Anne's allowance.

On becoming king, William had been granted a Civil List of £600,000, out of which Anne's allowance was presumed to come. In her father's time she had received £32,000; now, by virtue of her being heiress presumptive, of her having the Duke of Gloucester to provide for, and of her subordinating her claims to William's demands, she might reasonably expect something far handsomer. But William, never very generous at best, deemed it pointless to expend money on a sister-in-law he merely disliked as against a France he judged his mortal enemy. Even had William been openhanded, Anne would have still been his official dependent; when he proved niggardly, John and Sarah proposed carrying the matter of Anne's allowance to Parliament. Such a proposal William and Mary strongly deprecated: it challenged their power quite as much as it proclaimed their snideness. One night, at a Drawing Room, Mary brought up the matter with Anne. Her friends, said Anne, felt that her status ought to be clarified. "Pray," asked Mary, "what friends have you but the King and me?" Anne did not answer, but she felt deeply affronted, and when she reported the conversation to Sarah, Sarah but felt the more militantly aroused. Anne, it was determined, should ask for £70,000 a year. To be sure, she could not ask for it just yet, since William had dissolved Parliament, and in the interval before Parliament reconvened, William and Mary sufficiently acknowledged Sarah's influence to send emissaries to her, entreating that she entreat Anne to drop the idea. The emissaries were not above reminding Sarah of her own well-being and advising caution. But Sarah, her sense of justice almost as much aroused as her sense of power, refused to shift ground.

William and Mary thereupon sent a much more formidable—which is to say a much more charming—envoy, that Earl (and future Duke) of Shrewsbury who bore the nickname "King of Hearts." He promised that Anne, on the word of the King, should have £50,000 a year; if William broke his word, he would not serve him, Shrewsbury vowed, an hour longer. Sarah replied that if William broke his word, she did not see what it would avail Anne that Shrewsbury quit his service. The King of Hearts went back empty-handed to the King of England, and the matter of

Anne's allowance was carried in due time to Parliament. Parliament gave her, by right, the £50,000 the King might have been pleased to bestow through kindness.

Sarah was victorious and her mistress grateful. "I have had," Anne wrote to her dear Mrs. Freeman,

> something to say to you a great while, and I did not know how to go about it. I have designed, ever since my revenue was settled, to desire you would accept of a thousand pounds a year. I beg you would . . . never mention anything of it to me; for I shall be ashamed to have any notice taken of such a thing from one that deserves more than I shall ever be able to return.

Sarah writes in her Memoirs that, though "the circumstances of my family at this time were not very great," she felt some scruple about accepting Anne's offer. She accordingly sought the opinion of Lord Godolphin—already something of the very great friend he would increasingly become—who felt "that there was no reason in the world for me to refuse it." She might well, in view of how she had incurred her sovereigns' displeasure, find very good use for it.

William had "taken England on his way to France." It was from a Dutchman's point of view, which is to say a European's, that he treated the situation in England, that he deplored James's subservience to Louis XIV. For a generation, indeed, England—sometimes covertly, sometimes openly—had been the ally of France. Beginning now with William, she would far oftener be the enemy.

William III—of Orange and of England alike—has almost precisely the opposite appeal of a Charles II. Where Charles went furred with charm, and like a conjuror diverted the eye from what his hand was doing, William walked forth in armor and chilled men into silence and submission. He has something dramatic about him, as there is about a dour landscape, as have all those, too, who brood and bide their time. Even his incivility, however displeasing, is peculiarly vivid.

Born in 1650—the same year as John Churchill—William was the son of Charles II's sister and of the Dutch Stadtholder, William II, who died a week before his birth. He was denied his father's title and passed a sickly childhood fighting for it, his own misfortunes mingled with those of his kinsmen, the exiled Stuarts. All this bred one of those indomitable weaklings, those defrauded potentates, whose will to power comes to know no bounds. When he was acknowledged Stadtholder at last, he was full-grown into the role of a patriot warrior; and indeed his entire career was a kind of Holy War to stifle the pretensions, to crush the power, of the ruinator of the Dutch Republics, Louis XIV. When he married his cousin Mary, it was not for love of the bride, any more than Charles sanctioned the match for love of the bridegroom. To William, seeking to demolish Louis, an English alliance raised hopes of powerful support; to Charles—a secret Catholic in Louis's pay—a Protestant alliance might throw his subjects off the scent. Toward Mary, William almost certainly never felt any amorous emotions. Her friend Elizabeth Villiers was his mistress as long as Mary lived (honoring his wife's final wishes, he broke with her after Mary died), and there were, besides, the strongest indications that William was homosexual. His feeling toward his wife was further complicated by her prior rights to the English throne, which must eventually make him, at The Hague, so inferior a sovereign as to seem her mere subordinate. Demonstrating for once that a busybody can prove a blessing, Bishop Burnet one day asked Mary what she would do if called to the throne of England. She answered that her husband was her lord, and that "she had no higher wish" than to be his subject. Burnet lost no time relaying this to William, who from then on gave her his full confidence and, increasingly, his devotion.

Becoming King of England satisfied both a strong personal and a strong political ambition in him, but England itself he always disliked—English lords might stand behind his chair at dinner, but it was Dutchmen who actually dined with him, and he was only happy when he could be at The Hague. Nor did England like him any better. He was from first to last, of course, a sick man while there, dwarfish and slightly hunchbacked, suffering from weak lungs, from asthma, from hemorrhoids—and the rides that relieved his asthma made the hemorrhoids a torment. With such ailments, he could never live comfortably in London, while living away from it did not endear him to his courtiers and estranged him from everyone else. Not only had he a forbidding air and a murderous temper; his manners were often utterly boorish (the most famous anecdote about him tells how, one day, when Anne was dining with him and the first green peas of the season were put upon the table, he snatched every last one for himself). In addition, he was by nature anything but a sound constitutional monarch—"no British sovereign," Keith Feiling has said, "ever so prized the royal prerogative as did the Liberator"; and though it was the Whigs who made him King, it needed their great historian to make him Whiggish. But Macaulay notwithstanding, William saw himself as not a Whig, but a warrior, while history sees him as primarily neither, but as a ruthlessly astute and patient politician, a master manipulator of persons and situations alike. He was always his own prime minister. Of no mind to defer to others, of no temperament to trust them, yet knowing when and how to praise or punish or fling them aside, he had the brilliance not to seem brilliant. On a purely practical plane, in a purely practical sphere—for he had neither personal charm nor humane ideals—he was indisputably great.

War against France began in the very first spring of William's reign, and in two places—Flanders, whither Marlborough was sent to lead the British troops, and Ireland, where James II had arrived as "deliverer" and reigned as king. In the Flanders campaign, Marlborough served under William's friend, the Prince of Waldeck. He had first to drill the miserably disorganized English troops, and by dint of his "meticulous housekeeping," his constant concern for their comfort and health, he enabled them to play a decisive role at the battle of Walcourt in August. For his part in this victory, which included his adroit maneuvering on the spot, John won Waldeck's praise and hence William's, who honored him with a colonelcy in the Royal Fusiliers.

Schomberg, meanwhile, had been sent with inadequate arms to Ireland, where James commanded 100,000 Catholics; but himself in no shape to attack and his forces attacked by disease, Schomberg, as the months passed, found his plight alarming. To relieve it and run the show, William went to Ireland himself, leaving England in the hands of Mary and a council of nine. Marlborough was one of these, and served also as commander-in-chief. William was scarcely gone when news arrived of a French naval victory over the Dutch and English fleets off Beachy Head (July 10, 1690), in which the English played so ignominious a role that the Dutch were said to have the honor, the French the advantage, and the English the shame. The

English might also have the anxiety, for the way now lay open for a French invasion of England—an invasion it would be Marlborough's task, with a kind of home-grown army, to repel. Fortunately, the day after Beachy Head, William defeated James at the Boyne (where old Schomberg was killed) and sent him flying out of Ireland; more fortunately still, when James asked Louis for an army to invade England, Louis refused.

There being no invader to hold off, Marlborough himself had thoughts of invasion. He asked to take an army to Ireland, and, though the Council refused his request, William on hearing of it approved. For all that, there were delays; what might have even proved disastrous ones, and Marlborough at length was given, not the English troops he asked for, but a mixture of Huguenots, Dutchmen, and Danes. And not quite given them, either, for the Duke of Württemberg, who arrived at their head, now pressed, on the score of higher birth, for a higher command. A bad compromise was finally reached of having the two men command on alternate days; and here the diplomatist in Marlborough who so notably assisted the general had one of his earliest successes. Marlborough, on the first day, chose "Württemberg" as the password; a much mollified Württemberg, on the second, chose "Marlborough," and thereafter virtually left John to manage what proved a brilliant campaign. Cork fell, and then Kinsale, greatly impeding French aid for the Jacobite forces. Curiously enough, John fought an army commanded first by his brother-in-law Tyrconnel; then, when Tyrconnel ran off to France, by his nephew Berwick. By October, Marlborough was back in England, where William received him with the proper compliments—said indeed that no one who had seen such little service was "so fit for great commands." But there was lacking on William's part a certain warmth.

William, who had always in English eyes been much more of a necessary evil than a popular choice, was now becoming rather generally unpopular. And the feelings of the nation at large toward William were much intensified among the people about him. Beyond that, this was for the great world the age of the trimmer, of two-faced allegiance, of hedging one's bets:

The times are so ticklish I vow and profess
I know not which party or cause to embrace—
I'll side with those, to be sure, who are least in distress,
Which nobody can deny.

Hence, within a shockingly short time, a great many bigwigs—Marlborough among them—were corresponding with James at St. Germains. Anne also was in touch with him; it was through persuading her to write, in fact, that John got from James the pardon he wished for. In Marlborough this was pretty clearly an attempt to stand in well wherever he could, a prudential need to take thought of the morrow. But John also had by now a real sense of disappointment and disapproval toward William. John's services in Ireland had gone entirely unrewarded: William had granted him no place in the Government, had rejected his application to succeed Schomberg as Master General of the Ordnance, had refused Anne's request that he be given the Garter. From pique, no doubt, Marlborough went on to disparage what he might well have disparaged from principle: William's favoring, in his English army, Dutchmen over Englishmen. In fact, John lubricated the general discontent among English officers, as he helped fabricate the opposition in Parliament. And clearly from pique John used

3 ˣ

highly injudicious language about William's Dutch favorites, while perhaps applying to William himself some of the epithets in vogue with Anne and Sarah: "Caliban," "the Dutch monster," "the Dutch abortion." No smallest part of this, whether disloyal or merely discourteous, escaped William's notice; while William had resented from the first how intimate and influential John and Sarah were with Anne. Nor was this mere pettiness on William's part: it was quite possibly Protestant Anne rather than Catholic James who would become the rallying-point of any concerted movement against William and Mary—Anne, whom the Marlboroughs so palpably dominated. To Caliban, John and Sarah were the powers behind any throne-to-be.

Owing largely to the Marlboroughs—not least in the matter of Anne's allowance—relations between Anne and Mary were already sorely strained, and it was Mary who now took action. Early in 1692 she sent for her sister and ordered her to get rid of Sarah. Anne refused. Mary enlarged on all Sarah's misdeeds. Was it to this troublemaker— a troublemaker married, moreover, to a traitor—that Anne was giving a thousand pounds a year of her Parliamentary grant? But Anne—an Anne big with child—remained inflexible. The Queen, by now infuriated, threatened to deprive Anne of half her grant. But Anne was not, was indeed never, to be bullied; she held her ground, and the two sisters, parting in heat, were condemned ever after to coldness.

Anne would not dismiss Sarah, but the very next morning William dispensed with John. Two hours after Marlborough, as Gentleman of the Bedchamber, had handed the King his shirt, he was himself handed an order dismissing him from all his employments and forbidding him the Court. No official reason was given, nor need be: John

must have long since counted the cost of speaking out
against William [3] or of writing to James. Sarah, unlike
John, was not specifically forbidden the Court, for the
good reason that William and Mary could never have
dreamed she would appear there. But that is precisely what
she did. "Being turned out," she observed, "is something
disagreeable to my temper." So on the 4th of February,
which was Anne's birthday, she went with Anne to Kensington Palace: Anne, with Sarah and a sense of righteous-
ness at her side, could always be brave. On their arriving
at the palace, the Queen showed as great control as did the
courtiers amazement. There was not the slightest hint of a
scene, and at the end of the evening Mrs. Morley and Mrs.
Freeman went home, Sarah flushed with a sense of victory.
Next morning came a letter to Mrs. Morley from the
Queen:

> I hope you will do me the justice to believe it is
> much against my will that I now tell you that after
> this it is very unfit Lady Marlborough should stay with
> you since that gives her husband so just a pretence of
> being where he ought not.
> I think I might have expected you should have spoke
> to me of it. . . . But seeing you was so far from it
> that you brought Lady Marlborough hither last night,
> makes us resolve to put it off no longer but tell you she
> must not stay, and I have all the reason imaginable to
> look upon your bringing her as the strangest thing that
> ever was done. . . .
> But now I must tell you it was very unkind in a
> sister, would have been very uncivil in an equal, and I

[3] William regarded Marlborough's behavior as so intolerable that,
as he told those about him, but for being a king he would have called
John out.

need not say I have more to claim which though my
kindness would make me never exact, yet when I see
the use you would make of it I must tell you I know
what is due to me and expect to have it from you. 'Tis
upon that account that I tell you plainly Lady Marlborough must not continue with you in the circumstances her lord is. I know this will be uneasy to you
and I am sorry for it. . . .

This was peremptory enough. Yet Anne still chose to
defy her sister and defend her servant—her answer read in
part: "As I think that this proceeding can be for no other
intent than to give me a very sensible mortification, so there
is no misery that I cannot readily resolve to suffer, rather
than the thoughts of parting with her." (How part, indeed,
with a woman who helps one compose such letters?) Anne's
reply—her uncle, Lord Rochester, having refused point-
blank to deliver it—went off to the Queen by a servant.
Swiftly by the Lord Chamberlain came back the Queen's
answer: Lord and Lady Marlborough were to leave the
Cockpit at once. Now indeed had the crisis come, and
Anne was everywhere advised, admonished, entreated, beseeched (Prince George alone abstaining) to part with
Sarah. Sarah herself urged it, only to bring Anne to the
verge of hysterics, imploring Mrs. Freeman never to speak
of parting again. The whole thing, for Anne, was an opportunity to affirm her devotion to Sarah, to maintain—
which, spite of her dowdiness, she always did—her high-
held dignity. Very well: if the Marlboroughs must leave
the Cockpit, so would she. She at once borrowed Sion
House at Brentford from the "Proud" Duke of Somerset,
and at once moved in. The King and Queen were incensed,
and tried, vainly, to have the proud Duke expel the dis-

obedient Princess. While Sarah accompanied Anne to Sion House, the Court and the town buzzed and tittered with gossip. Some of the gossip concerned the pettiness of the King and Queen, who now refused Anne a guard of honor, deprived her of salutes and other marks of rank, and would later, when Anne visited Bath, decree that she be shown no official courtesies. It was thought that Mary, turning her sister out of her house so soon after sweeping her father off the throne, was not conspicuous for family feeling. And indeed only once more while they lived did the two sisters meet. When, in April, Anne's labor began, she followed protocol and sent her sister word of the approaching event, adding how very ill she felt. Mary took no notice; the child died at birth; but this fact too, in accordance with protocol, Anne conveyed to the Queen. Mary did now, in her own good time, come to Sion House, but no more to be sisterly than condole. "I have made the first step by coming to you," announced the Queen, "and I now expect you should make the next by removing Lady Marlborough." Anne in a weak sick voice refused, and Mary swept from the room, quite ignoring Prince George, who toddled after her.

Anne grew very feverish and ill after Mary left, but was most concerned about Sarah's leaving. "If you should ever do so cruel a thing," she informed her, ". . . from that moment I shall never enjoy one quiet hour. And should you do it without asking my consent . . . I will shut myself up and never see the world more." And a little later, after further entreaties: "If it be possible I am every day more and more yours."

Anne had need of such tenacity, and Sarah of so much tenderness, for on the 5th of May, Marlborough, together with several other known or suspected Jacobites, was suddenly arrested on a charge of high treason and committed to the Tower. This resulted from the forged testimony of one Robert Young, who concocted a letter—in which John offered James help in regaining his throne—and had it placed in a flowerpot at the Bishop of Rochester's. (Fortunately, the flowerpot was near the servants' quarters and the letter could not be found when first searched for.) At once Sarah hurried from Sion House to London, using every possible resource to have John freed. Failing, she was only dissuaded from a vow to share his imprisonment on the ground that by remaining free she could more quickly end it. And in the midst of these anxieties came news that the Marlboroughs' younger son, Charles, had died.

Anne, however indignant, was powerless to help. Her letters of sympathy to Sarah even suggest that she and Prince George were themselves in some danger. She fussed over Sarah's health: "For God's sake have a care of your dear self. . . . I fancy asses' milk would do you good." And, hoping it might somehow help the Marlboroughs' cause, she wrote a conciliatory letter to Mary. Back came an icy one:

> I have received yours by the Bishop of Worcester and have very little to say to it since you cannot but know that as I never use compliments, so now they will not serve. . . . You know what I required of you. . . . You can give me no other marks of it that will satisfy me.

It was his very accusers who proved a source of help to John. Robert Young—and his accomplice Blackhead— were hauled up in June before the Privy Council. Blackhead confessed that at Young's bidding he had hidden a paper in the Bishop's flowerpot, and though Young denied the story, he had already confessed to being an expert forger who had obtained John's signature by writing to him about the character of a servant. On June 15, Marlborough was released from the Tower on a writ of habeas corpus. Among the sureties for his £6,000 bail were Shrewsbury and Halifax, whose names were promptly stricken off the Privy Council. By an oversight, Marlborough's remained on it till it was noticed sometime later.

The Marlboroughs were now able to join Anne and Prince George at Berkeley House in Piccadilly, where they had removed from Brentford. It was not a very gay period for any of them—though on one occasion Anne required "half a dozen boats" to go by water to the playhouse. John had not been cleared, but was merely out on bail; and Parliament, which must clear him, would not meet again till autumn. Anne was generally cold-shouldered by society; Sarah had "one day what she called the spleen, and the next the vapors." John himself, however—though to establish his guilt there was certainly no need to fabricate it—remained unruffled, changing so little as to go right on communicating with King James. No less did he go right on opposing King William, and when Parliament finally convened in November, he at once laid his case before it. Support for him came readily: it was argued in the Lords that to retain bail for Marlborough after the charges against him had been dropped was an infringement of privilege. Noisy speeches were delivered on both sides; and William, visualizing a *cause célèbre* he was not at all anxious for, now used the royal prerogative to set John free. He was free at last of what might have proved a very costly, a perhaps even fatal, predicament. Had the letter that the forger's accomplice deposited in the Bishop's flowerpot been discovered when first searched for, so very clever was the forgery, so very plausible the charge, so possible the corroboration of it by others—and so inflammatory would have been the whole atmosphere of the trial—that Marlborough, and the Bishop with him, might all too conceivably have gone to the scaffold.

V

JOHN was now free, but the Marlborough fortunes took no great upward turn: he had lost all his employments, and Sarah served a Princess with so little footing at Court as to be shunned for the most part by courtiers. That summer Sarah went to Bath with a convalescent Anne, who, while there, was at the Queen's express desire shown every possible discourtesy. Back again in London, Anne assigned the Marlboroughs handsome quarters at Berkeley House and offered John, who had no other post, a thousand pounds a year to be an officer in her household. He declined the offer and used his enforced leisure, instead, to intrigue with James. Indeed, during 1694 he possibly—in the matter of the Camaret Bay letter—committed his most indefensible act. He has been charged with sending information to James concerning the proposed English attack on Brest. That John had any genuinely treasonable intentions has long been discounted: at worst he was relaying information already known to be in James's hands, and it now seems far more likely that he wrote no letter at all. The actual expedition, with the French howsoever forewarned, proved a disastrous failure.

Life at Berkeley House proved almost as quiet as at St.

Albans—whither John and Sarah went when they could, to
be with their children, and where sometimes Anne went
with them. At Berkeley House there were few visitors, but
they were of such sort at least as to flout the royal ban or
even serve as reproofs of the royal behavior. But Berkeley
House was nothing in the least resembling a rival court,
was nothing suggesting, indeed, a life for courtiers. There
may well have been the games of cards to which Anne was
always addicted, or visits to something of Congreve's or
Purcell's. Or Anne and Sarah might work a quilt together;
a quilt at any rate survives that they are said to have done
jointly.

This uneventful but by no means reposeful two-year
spell was jolted suddenly by news of the Queen's illness.
At first all was rumor without—and understandably, since
all was speculation within. It was known that the Queen
had suffered a shock when an archbishop died at the Palace
in the midst of officiating; it was given out besides, by the
doctor in attendance, that Mary had measles. Only after
a day or two did it become plain that she had smallpox in
its most virulent form. Anne sent to inquire and to ask
that she might attend upon the Queen. Next day, at the
King's command, Lady Derby wrote back that the Queen
needed the utmost quiet, and that it was hoped the Princess would put off her visit. Lady Derby then scribbled a
postscript to Anne's lady-in-waiting: "Pray, Madame, present my humble duty to the Princess." Sarah leaped upon
the postscript, shrewdly inferring, "more than if the College of Physicians" should inform her, that the Queen was
doomed. In less than a week, during which time Anne
never approached her sister's bedside,[1] Mary was dead.

[1] Once, when Anne's sympathy was conveyed to the Queen, Mary
answered, simply: "Thanks."

Mary's death, as Lady Derby had surmised, meant a very real change in Anne's fortunes. It was not so much that, Mary dying without issue, Anne became heir (on William's death) to the throne. It was rather that until now, however matters fared for the sickly William, there had been every prospect of long life for Mary. Now sickly William survived, and at any time—next year, three months, three weeks from now—Anne might succeed him. And at her side as Queen would be the Marlboroughs. The Marlboroughs, and the woman they served, were not insensible of the change; they scarcely could be. There was a sudden, fulsome procession of courtiers to Berkeley House, so much of one that a half-witted peer won a smile from Anne when he said: "I hope Your Highness will remember that I came to wait upon you when none of this company did."

William could not be insensible of the change either, nor of what it might betoken. As Sarah remarked, he was "well aware that everybody who had a mind to show they did not care for him" would pointedly do so by making their court to Anne. He therefore—at any rate after a nudge from Lord Somers—agreed to a reconciliation with his sister-in-law; sent her a civil message; and when she came to wait upon him, told her that St. James's Palace was at her disposal. All William's civilities, however, were no more than what we should nowadays term public relations. Certainly they represented no change in private feeling. The cold, brilliant King could never abide a Prince and Princess who were on every score such dullards; a boor toward the most exhilarating of his subjects, he was not one to be courtly toward the most exhausting. On William's and Anne's side alike one encounters a complete rebuttal of all one's romantic conceptions of royalty. An animosity that should have been a blend of delicate intrigue and stylish insult was prolonged between a sovereign who must have seemed graceless in Academe and a matron who would have been thought deadly in Suburbia. Yet not this is the real irony, but rather that in all ways that count—of stubbornness and stolidness; of fixed purpose to level France or raise up Anglicanism—both were redoubtable monarchs. What they lacked was the mien, or glitter, or panache of countless figureheads.

The civility that William showed for a time, extended even to Sarah. Once, she records, he went out of his way to speak to her—true homage from a man who did not speak to most people he walked squarely by; once he even asked Sarah's opinion of Lady Albemarle, the Dutch wife of Dutch Keppel, adding brusquely: "Don't flatter her." But Sarah was not to be misled, and rightly did not feel flattered in turn. Caliban soon wearied of being amiable toward her or Anne; inside a year or so, he was no longer even polite. After his victory against the French at Namur, Anne wrote him—on the advice of several lords, but against the wishes of Lady Marlborough—a letter of congratulations. To this letter, which Sarah thought it "unbecoming" in Anne to write, William returned not the slightest answer, nor any more of one when asked had the original letter miscarried. He behaved even worse toward Prince George, who, being in mourning for the recent death of his brother, the King of Denmark, sought leave to wear black when he should come, on William's birthday, to wish him joy. He was told that he would not be received unless he came in colors— which he did, though with "great uneasiness." Anne herself sometimes gave William birthday balls at St. James's; of their gaiety we know nothing, but it is recorded of one of them that not for years had there "bin seen so much fin clothes and rich liveries"—His Grace of Southampton wore black embroidered with silver, His Grace of Norfolk black embroidered in gold. Eventually, however, William's palace at Whitehall burned to the ground, a work of spiritual arson in a King who hated London and now could spend the time at Kensington, Windsor Castle, and Hampton Court.

Though England and Holland were at war with France, Marlborough had been denied all military office no less after William became reconciled to Anne than before; as late, indeed, as 1696 he was being implicated—this time by a defendant in the assassination plot on William's life—in Jacobite activities. The whole past few years in England were everywhere sulphurous with Jacobitish fumes. And John seems, in these years, to have been discredited by loyal Tories as a conniver with St. Germains and distrusted by loyal Jacobites as conniving for Anne rather than James. It was not till more than four years after Marlborough's release from the Tower, not indeed till after the Peace of Ryswick in 1697, that he was granted employment by the King. Through the efforts of several friendly and influential statesmen, John obtained from William the post of governor to Anne's son, the Duke of Gloucester. The Duke—whom Anne always spoke of as "my boy"—was now almost nine years old, and had need of an establishment of his own. William proved gracious in making the offer: "My lord," he is reported to have told John, "teach him but to be what you are, and my nephew will never want for accomplishments." At the same time William restored Marlborough to his old rank in the army and to the Privy Council, and John's twelve-year-old son was appointed Master of the Horse.

John's appointment was, of course, extraordinarily congenial to the Duke of Gloucester's parents, for in the matter of upbringing and education Anne and Prince George saw eye to eye with the Marlboroughs. William, however, was of no mind to let his sister-in-law hold the reins too tightly. "The Princess Anne," he muttered, "shall not be Queen before her time." But in practice he made few changes in Anne's household list for her son, the chief one being to appoint Bishop Burnet, whom Anne loathed, as the Duke's other governor, or spiritual guide. The "blabbing" Whig bishop and the suave Tory Marlborough got on, as it turned out, very well—well enough, in fact, for Burnet to rewrite the portions in his *History* involving John's desertion of James. Unhappily, he neglected to destroy the earlier version, which, being unearthed, had repercussions. It fell upon Burnet also to superintend the Duke's education, and it is thought that he proved too severe a taskmaster. Trying to make a prodigy of learning of the high-strung, delicate boy—who, like all Anne's children, suffered from water on the brain, and had so large a head that it was hard to fit with a peruke—the Bishop rammed down him hunks and chunks of constitutional history and Gothic jurisprudence and feudal law, and very possibly helped bring about his death just after his eleventh birthday. There is a last night-etched scene of John riding beside the child's coffin as it is carried by torchlight from Windsor to Westminster.

It was during these same years that the two oldest of Sarah's daughters were married. The eldest, Henrietta, made one of those youthful love matches that are happy family alliances as well: at eighteen she married twenty-year-old Francis Godolphin, the son and only child of the man who was all his life the Marlboroughs' greatest friend and ally. The bridegroom's father could not contribute greatly to the young couple's fortune, but the Marlboroughs gave Henrietta £5,000 in dowry, and Anne gave the same—she wished to give a "mite" of £10,000, but John and Sarah would not permit her. Anne, Sarah's second daughter, made a marriage of greater consequence. Her partner was Charles, Lord Spencer, a widower from an important family, and the most Whiggish—and priggish—of men. An able mind and an avowed republican, he had denounced his unprincipled opportunist father in the House of Commons, and he professed to believe the worst republic superior to the noblest monarchy. Whatever Sarah's feelings, John did not much favor the match. On the worldly side there could be no question of its excellence: Charles Spencer would one day be very rich, and his father, who had stopped at nothing for power under James, was influential now under William. But John was not happy marrying off a favorite daughter, who by all accounts was a very superior girl, to a man of both rigid personal and rash political tenets. Sarah finally won John over, and once again parents and Princess alike provided £5,000 in dowry. It is from this marriage—as the family name of Spencer Churchill bears witness—that the Marlborough blood and titles have descended.[2]

In 1698, when William went off to Holland, Marlborough was named to serve on the Council of Regency. And from then on, William "used in peace the soldier he had neglected in war." Late that year, enraged over Parliament's ousting his Dutch soldiers,[3] he was to confide in Marlborough his resolve to abdicate, a decision that John

---

[2] The Churchill half of the name was restored by law in 1817.

[3] William's marked preference (on both personal and national grounds) for the Dutch continued to be a sore point with the English, not least for his grants and gifts. The King's gifts to his favorite, Lord Portland, "recalled in lavishness those of Edward II."

almost certainly opposed. At this juncture, when no Act of Settlement yet existed, an abdication might have done many other things than set Anne on the throne. For the next three years, at any rate, the King and his general, though in their relations neither close nor candid, were often of one mind, and shared in particular the same feeling about France. John remained in essence a Tory, where his sovereign was in practice a Whig, but in this early dawn of the party system, the nature of William's sovereignty created party ambivalences. The Tories cherished the idea of a king, while disliking a foreign one; the Whigs welcomed a foreign one for thus having less aura of kingship. Hence—as the Whigs would usually back the Tories when the Tories were at odds with William—the King, as the century closed, was in a very unstable position, and republicanism never stronger. The Duke of Gloucester's death in July 1700 made momentously vexing the whole question of the succession after Anne should die. There was the very real possibility indeed, William himself entertained it—of recalling James II's son from St. Germains. There was the more remote possibility of giving the crown to a prince of Savoy, a grand-nephew of Charles II. There was James I's granddaughter Sophia, the Electress of Hanover. And there was the possibility of a republic.

Fortunately, all Protestant England, Tories as well as Whigs, was concerned for what lay ahead; and by the next year, 1701, the Act of Settlement had come into effect,[4] ordaining that, should both William and Anne die without surviving issue, the crown would pass to Sophia, the nearest possessor of Stuart blood who was also a Protestant. By the

[4] The sovereign, the Act stipulated, must belong to the Anglican Church; could not leave the country without the permission of Parliament; and must be advised by the whole Privy Council and not by secret counselors.

terms of the Act, James II and his descendants were clearly excluded. In that same year, as it happened, James II died, and a high-handed act, at his death, on Louis XIV's part— his proclaiming James's Catholic son the King of England— virtually assured the outbreak of a long-brewing and full-scale European war. War clouds had been gathering for years round the stormy question of the Spanish succession —just what, on the death of Charles II of Spain, was to be done with the Spanish crown and with Spain's territorial possessions had long disturbed and divided Europe. Two treaties had sought to partition Spain's crown and colonies, first among Austria, France, and Bavaria, then between Austria and France. But on his deathbed the feeble-minded Charles bequeathed the realm to Philip of Anjou, a grandson of Louis XIV. The balance of power in Europe could exist only if France and Spain were separate, hence this bequest augured serious danger. The one solution was for Philip to rule over a Spain totally independent of France. But Louis took something more than family pride in his grandson's inheritance; he took a personal hand. He would not reassure the Dutch that their trade and military rights in the Spanish Netherlands would be respected; nor was he at all diplomatic with the Austrians, who already were spluttering over how much France stood to profit, and they to suffer, from Philip's accession. It was Louis's plan, in fact, to gain military supremacy throughout Europe before his adversaries could successfully unite, and by virtue of his connections he seized a number of strategic garrisons along the Dutch frontier—a sort of eighteenth-century occupation of Belgium. But once Louis's intentions became plain, all Europe was aroused, and in September of 1701 England, Holland, and Austria formally banded together to oppose an amalgamation of the French and Spanish thrones.

It was at precisely this moment that Louis chose to recognize James II's son as King of England. Such insouciance was able to unite even Whigs and Tories, and to reconcile all England to the necessity for war. William, knowing war to be inevitable, had earlier begun preparing for it, and had reached now the crucial—in a sense, the crowning—moment of his reign. But, chancing at this very turn of time to ride at Hampton Court, he was injured when his horse stumbled and fell; and was in such miserably poor health as not to survive the injury. The wariest and most implacable of Louis's adversaries must leave the struggle to a different— an untried and female—monarch, and even as William lay dying at Kensington, some of those who stood about him were privately and callously speeding bulletins of his condition to Anne at St. James's. The Jacobites, alluding to the occupant of the molehill that had caused William's horse to stumble, might toast, at William's death, "the little gentleman in black velvet." But the great mass of his more faithful subjects was not likely to toast William's memory.[5] Few kings have died so little regretted of their countrymen; though, to be sure, these were not his countrymen.

---

[5] One engraved goblet to his memory toasts "Good King William, who freed us from Pope and Popery, Knavery and Slavery, Brass Money and Wooden Shoes."

PART TWO

COUNTRY OF
TIGERS

Be careful of your behavior, for you are
in a country amongst tigers and wolves.

JOHN TO SARAH

VI

ANNE'S reign began (as it ended) on a Sunday—a clear bright day, that "sunshine day" for which she once told Sarah she could wait with patience. Her old antagonist Bishop Burnet hurried to St. James's to fall at her feet with the news. She could scarcely lament the death of one who had treated her so often without courtesy, had shown her husband an almost studied contempt, had put Marlborough in prison and driven Godolphin from office. In the course of that Sunday she received the Privy Council, whom she told in her clear and melodious voice that she stood for safeguarding the Protestant succession and combatting the power of France. In the course of that Sunday, the Houses of Parliament assembled, each to recognize her title, to vote her an address of loyalty, and to make explicit its desire for a vigorously prosecuted war. Crowds, too, in the course of the day, formed outside the palace, and courtiers milled within—among them Anne's Jacobite uncle, Lord Clarendon, who, when asked what he desired, demanded curtly: "Admittance to my niece." Told to "go first and qualify himself"—by taking the Oath of Fealty—"and then she would be very glad to see him," he left the palace, nor ever attempted to see her again.

On the Wednesday she met the Houses of Parliament, saying much what she had said to the Privy Council, but adding: "I know my own heart to be entirely English." If these last words gave offense to William's particular followers, they pleased and impressed the nation at large. So too did her appearance: in wearing, besides her crown, gorgeous royal robes of red velvet, ermine, and gold, she was said to have chosen a portrait of Queen Elizabeth for her model, and there were soon murmurs of a second Elizabeth and of a glorious epoch opening.

All the more as she so wholeheartedly declared herself, the nation rejoiced in its Queen and closed ranks behind her. She was Protestant, she was Stuart, she was English; and, being gracious in manner, solidly against France, and at least outwardly against Divine Right, she bespoke all her country's principles and desires. In the matter of France, moreover, she acted with tremendous dispatch. Just forty-eight hours after she came to the throne, she gave Marlborough instructions as her Ambassador Extraordinary to Holland, whither he was to proceed at once, to inspirit England's allies and map out the spring campaign. At the very end of William's reign, John had come to stand very high: the sick King had every way taken him into his confidence, had set about making him—no less in political and diplomatic than in military matters—his successor; and during William's last months as King, John achieved, in terms of a most delicate and urgent diplomacy, some notable successes. He, for one thing, so prepared the treaties of the Grand Alliance as to have Parliament freely assent to them —a most important feat, since to be at odds with the Commons was always dangerous, and could now be fatal. Thus, as concerned the actual numbers of English troops, John made no commitments to the Allies: he saw that a Parliament not allowed to determine this would disallow much else. While in William's service, John also dissuaded

Charles XII of Sweden—in return for English money—from supporting France and from hindering Denmark's support of the Allies.

In terms of position, John had thus finally come into his own: he was no less the dead King's heir than the new Queen's favorite. On Anne's first entrance into Parliament, with Prince George and Sarah as her personal attendants, it was John who carried the Sword of State before her. And she made him Captain General of the British armies abroad; and gave him, on the fifth day of her reign, what she could not make William give him—the Garter. As for Sarah, it was hardly less a sunshine day to Mrs. Freeman than to Mrs. Morley. Anne was scarcely Queen before Sarah was made Groom of the Stole and Mistress of the Robes and Comptroller of the Privy Purse; very soon after, Anne wrote that she was minded

> to ask dear Mrs. Freeman a question . . . if you would have the Lodge [i.e., the Rangership of Windsor Park] for your life, because the warrant must be made accordingly; and anything that is of so much satisfaction as this poor place seems to be to you, I would give dear Mrs. Freeman for all her days.

In addition, both Sarah's married daughters were made Ladies of the Bedchamber. From the various posts Anne had conferred on her, Sarah's emoluments came to some £7,500 a year; and Anne begged Sarah to accept besides a £2,000 annuity. This Sarah refused. She was flushed, just now, with success; and indeed sat high. As the royal favorite and confidante, she was besieged by all who sought royal favor or outright rewards; lacking her approbation, as she put it, "neither places, nor pensions, nor honors were bestowed by the Crown." She held, in fact, a court of her own, and on occasion interceded with Anne in behalf of Anne's own relatives: she, Sarah—who hated Lord Rochester—got his daughter-in-law, whom Anne disliked, made a Lady of the Bedchamber. Sarah's reasons were characteristic:

> There was, in truth, a particular pleasure in serving my Lady Hyde in this instance . . . for in my life I never saw any mortal have such a passion for anything as she had to be in this post. While the thing was pending, she had so much concern upon her, that she never spoke to me upon the subject without blushing. And after it was granted, she made me more expressions of gratitude than ever I had from anybody on any occasion.

At the time Anne became Queen, nothing that distinguished Sarah from Anne by way of character and temperament had in any way imperiled their friendship. The differences between them were, however, numerous and great, and extended even to politics. Where Anne and Marlborough were politically much akin, both being Tories, though he a more moderate one, Sarah was from the outset a Whig. In religion, again, where Anne and Marlborough were both devout Churchmen, though he less High, Sarah was at heart little better than a freethinker. Socially the differences between the two women were no less marked. Anne was "slow," even for a queen; "though"—as Trevelyan says— "she could read a speech well in public, [she] could not carry on a conversation." What might have made Anne resentful of Sarah—that while the Queen sat silent at Court, or labored to bring forth commonplaces, the favorite rattled wittily on—was prevented by the fact that the Queen maintained no Court. Anne reserved Sarah's darting chit-chat and stinging comments for herself alone; her pleasure

Princess Anne and William, Duke of Gloucester, c. *1695*

GEORGIUS, PRINCEPS DANIÆ,
DUX CUMBRIÆ,
ARCHITHALASSUS ANGLIÆ.

George of Denmark

was to sit listening eagerly to Mrs. Freeman, rather than look stolidly at Court ladies and gentlemen. There was Anne's constant ill-health to excuse (and often justify) her dispensing with Court life, and those who attended the few receptions she gave, and sat "for a quarter of an hour about the Queen in dead silence," must have rejoiced at her delicate constitution. Certainly no one not commanded into the Queen's presence ever disinterestedly sought it out. People even did their fawning and their place-hunting through her servants; while Anne herself wanted no visitors, "having little to say to them, but that it was . . . hot or cold." She liked dice and cards [1]; she liked horse races; she liked to go hunting in a chaise; on occasion she went driving or attended reviews of her troops; and more and more—her religious devotion intensified by the deaths of all her children —she read works on religious subjects. Besides the consolations of religion, there were the pleasures of the table; with Anne, indeed, gormandizing was next to godliness. Whether, as came later to be rumored, she drank heavily out of a teacup—whether she deserved the title she acquired, of Brandy Nan—is more moot. In a Post-Revolution jingle, her husband and not she had the name—

King William thinks all,
Queen Mary talks all,
Prince George drinks all,
And Princess Anne eats all—

and Sarah absolved her of such "libels": "I believe . . . she never went beyond such a quantity of strong wines as her physicians judged to be necessary for her"; as, after her death, did Roger Coke, the brother of one of Anne's cour-

---

[1] Sarah, in later years, was to sniff at Anne as "a little card-playing automaton," but this, surely, was the spade suit calling the club suit black.

4

tiers. The rumors, in his view, arose from her having "light cooling things in her closet" which some from ignorance, and others from malice, supposed were "strong waters." What her doctors prescribed, however, was perhaps not entirely negligible.

Speaking of her presumed influence over Anne, Sarah remarked that "It will be a surprise to many . . . that the first important step which her Majesty took after her accession to the Government was against my wishes and inclination: I mean her throwing herself and her affairs almost entirely into the hands of the Tories." But there was good reason, of course, why Anne should elevate the Tories, even against the wishes of her favorite: "from infancy," as the favorite elsewhere acknowledged, Anne had been made to feel hostile toward the Whigs. They sought to lessen the power of the Crown, and were not vigilant for the Church; indeed, Anne usually called the Tories—what indeed the Tories often called themselves—"the Church party." Beyond that, Anne and Prince George had both been ill-used during William and Mary's Whiggish reign. It was consequently well for the Marlboroughs'—and the country's—fortune that John and Godolphin were both mild Tories, for in granting them so much power Anne was as much actuated by conviction as by friendship. Sarah, however, was no more stopped in her Whiggishness by John than by Anne. From the outset of the reign she was determined to make the Queen feel friendly toward the Whigs, and though "at first" she did not get very far, she could claim—while Anne was bringing Tories into Government and Court—to have kept at least a few Whigs in office. But Anne, as Sarah herself confessed, was in no wise drawn to the Whigs. And in the same letter in which Anne calls Sarah her "dear, dear Mrs. Freeman," and is " most passion-

ately hers," and would not have the two of them "differ
. . . in the least thing," she yet differs forcibly enough:
"Upon my word, my dear Mrs. Freeman, you are mightily
mistaken in your notion of a true Whig; for the character
you give of them does not in the least belong to them, but
to the Church." Sarah, informed that she was "mightily
mistaken" about a true Whig, might perhaps begin to
wonder whether she could not also be mistaken about a
true Queen.

And indeed—at a time when the sovereign still made his
own choice of Cabinets, and Cabinets as yet bore no strong
party stamp—Anne set herself about with Tories, and with
such Tories as might easily dispute Marlborough's (and
Anne's own) policy toward the war. And where Whigs
who shared John's views were not, like Somers and Halifax,
excluded for having been William's friends, they might, like
the rakish Wharton, be dismissed for their wicked morals.
In the first summer of her reign, indeed, Anne dissolved the
existing Whig Parliament: the new election returned a Tory
majority to the Commons, though the Whigs still controlled
the Lords.

Months before—on St. George's Day, April 23—Anne,
amid great rejoicing, had been crowned, being carried in a
sedan chair, around eleven in the morning, from St. James's
to Westminster Hall, and thence—when the procession
formed, with Prince George walking before her as Generalissimo of the Forces—to the Abbey. She was crowned
around four in the afternoon; coronation medals were
thrown to the highborn inside the Abbey, and money, outside, to the mob. The Queen herself was so crippled with
gout as to be unable to walk and as to find the ceremonies
and the ceremonial banquet that came after them—where
Her Majesty's champion entered Westminster Hall in full

armor on horseback [2]—an ordeal. In the evening she came home to St James's exhausted. George, on the other hand, was in high spirits and in no mood—as the Lord Chamberlain ventured to suggest—for proposing to the tired Queen that they go to bed. *"I propose!"* cried George—"I cannot, I am Her Majesty's subject and shall do naught but what she commands." "As that is the case," said Her Majesty, "I command you, George, to come to bed."

While John was briefly in Holland as Anne's ambassador, the hostile influence of her uncle Lord Rochester began asserting itself at home. The great arch-royalist Clarendon's son, the great arch-bigot James II's agent, this High-Church, High-Tory Lord Lieutenant of Ireland seized the opportunity of being in London—and of John's being out of it— to gain the Queen's ear. As a result, he effected a number of Court appointments that were uniformly Tory, often anti-war, and sometimes unfit for office. Soon after, he published the first volume of his father's *History of the Rebellion*. Though the *History* was rightly to become a great classic, the publication of the first volume was a calculated piece of propaganda, inciting resentment against Nonconformists as the Puritans' heirs, and against Whigs as the Roundheads' successors. In his preface, Rochester even railed openly against sending an army to the Low Countries. Marlborough was to judge Rochester the greatest obstacle in England to his plans for crushing France; should Rochester and his group, John wrote next year to Sarah, become strong enough to determine the course of the war, "they may ruin England and Holland at their pleasure."

Rochester even aspired to be Lord Treasurer, but here

[2] To proclaim that, should anyone deny the sovereign's right to the Crown, he was prepared to defend it.

John pressed home his influence; unless he had someone he
could count on for money and supplies, he could not succeed in the field. The necessary man was Godolphin. From
far back he had been Anne's true friend as well as the Marlboroughs'. He had supported Anne "when Rochester would
not even carry her letter to Queen Mary." He had done his
utmost to prevent William and Mary from reducing Anne's
Parliamentary grant; he had been at her side and remained
of her circle despite William and Mary's ban on it. He had,
indeed, so special a place in her thoughts, or feelings, that
he was "Mr. Montgomery"—as the Marlboroughs were
"Mr. and Mrs. Freeman"—to her "Mrs. Morley." Moreover,
he was nominally a Tory and a man long experienced in
office, particularly at finance. He was skillful, adaptable—in
all, marvelously competent. His first master, Charles II, had
said of him that he was never in the way and never out of
the way; the usually slanderous Mrs. Manley called him
"the greatest genius of the age with the least of it in his aspect." For all his having voted to exclude James II from the
throne, he became—after James ascended it—his minister.
He had, in turn, served William, being, like John, simultaneously in communication with St. Germains. Yet he had
never seemed devious, nor aspired immoderately to office.
Some offices, indeed, he refused; and others he resigned
from.

In personal life he was "of slow speech" and "a very
black and stern countenance," but in his inclinations gay.
What he loved was gambling and sport, what he doted on
was that blend of the two, horse-racing.[3] His place of ref-
uge and seat of bliss was Newmarket, and it is as much perhaps with Newmarket as with Whitehall that he must ulti-

[3] He had come to love it in an era when the horses bore such names
as Sweetest-when-Naked.

mately be identified. It was his son who brought to England the most wonderful horse, it may be, outside mythology—the Godolphin Arabian, that chief of three stallions from which descend in direct male line the whole race of English thoroughbreds.

The ties between Godolphin and the Marlboroughs were strong ones: Godolphin had befriended and bestirred himself for John and Sarah—and even had asked William for leave to retire—when they were in disgrace, and his son had married their daughter. For John, embarking on so great and hazardous an assignment, having Godolphin as Lord Treasurer—at a time when the office signified First Minister—was essential. For John knew what he must contend with, quite beyond the power of France: "he knew," says Sir Winston, "the Queen; he knew the Dutch; he knew the German Princes; he knew the English Parliament." Without a Lord Treasurer he could absolutely count on, whether in the matter of armies or munitions or supplies, "he would not mount his horse." Marlborough wanted Godolphin far more, in fact, than Godolphin wanted the job. He would rather not, he said, take office—and this office least of all. John had to urge him again and again, had again and again—before Godolphin. would yield—to insist it be a team or nothing.

The Queen had now her soldier and her paymaster, her field marshal and her prime minister. She, and John hardly less, still needed in Parliament a firm hand that would be also a friendly one. Parliament itself was a jumble of party maneuverings and intra-party factions, of partisanship at the cost of patriotism, and Jacobitism as a threat to security. If what John needed called for the wisdom of a statesman, it also—and more immediately—demanded the wiles of a politician. Fortunately a man with something of the stamp of both was already Speaker, was indeed leader, of the House: Robert Harley.

Like Godolphin—though they were very unlike also— Harley had almost every political merit but stature. Like Godolphin, too, he would be engagingly remembered for something outside politics: in its way, the Harleian library is as celebrated as the Godolphin horse. Harley's books have indeed a luster that the man who collected them quite lacks. The man was on the one hand too devious and shifty to seem properly statesmanlike, on the other, too practical, sensible, moderate ever to become intellectually vivid. He loved tricks, it was said, even when there was no need for them; and himself said that he would "howl with the wolves, and . . . call black white and white black." If he had almost no principles, he had almost no prejudices. His sanity assailed Whigs and Tories alike for the madness of faction; it extended to all lack of illusion concerning the glitter of office; and the fact that no one ought to have trusted him never prevented his enjoying almost everyone's confidence. He must have managed well who could advocate Anglicanism and remain a Nonconformist; begin as a Whig and wind up a Tory leader; wind up a Tory leader without losing Whig support; be opposed to war, yet find logic in a war against France; stutter and stammer out an oracular jumble of sentences and yet control the Commons. Furthermore, it was he whom Marlborough and Godolphin urgently wanted and needed during this spring of 1702; the three men became, and were indeed referred to as, a triumvirate, with Harley able to control the party and to anticipate the moods and sway the deliberations of the House. Under William, he had gained great prestige with the Tories by twice refusing a secretaryship of state. Good-natured "Robin the Trickster" was called "the most moder-

ate man in the Tory party"; and if he was one of its poorest
speakers—"huddled," as Pope said, "in his thoughts"—his
convoluted stammerings yet played their part in making
him the enigma he aspired to be.

As for Whigs and Tories, Anne's reign saw a kind of
codifying of party principle, an intensifying of party zeal.
Though on this head or that their beliefs might alter and
even reverse themselves, the Whig and Tory [4] badges of
Queen Anne's reign roughly persisted into Queen Victoria's. The Tories were the landed interest and the Church
party; the Whigs—though in their heyday enormous landowners—were the moneyed interest and the party of toleration and Dissent. Two seemingly ill-assorted groups formed
the backbone of Whiggism—Nonconformists and patricians. The largely Baptist, Calvinist, and Quaker Dissenters,
at this time mostly tradesmen, artisans, merchants and sea-
faring men, were townspeople predominantly, Londoners
most of all. If excluded by rank or religion from political
life, they were understandably, indeed necessarily, politi-
cal-minded—supporting Parliament as against the Crown
and backing the Whigs on grounds of trade as well as of
faith. Under Anne even the pacifist Quakers had to support
the Whigs, though they were the war party, since the Tories constantly hunted Quakers down. Being, so many of
them, well-to-do, the Dissenters had votes out of all proportion to their numbers. The Whig aristocrats whom the Dissenters backed were almost never Dissenters themselves, but
were tolerant believers—or unbelievers: often boasting
Roundhead blood, they too were for Parliament as against
the Crown; for trade and (partly for trading reasons) for

---

[4] Both names originated in the seventeenth century as terms of abuse,
Whigs signifying Scotch Presbyterian rebels; Tories, Irish Catholic
bandits.

war against France. It might almost be added that they were
for brains as against mere blood; and with their huge ability
to reward and advance the capable, they won adherents
from a great variety of lawyers and army and navy men.
Though much less homogeneous than the Tories, the Whigs
under Anne were far more unified; for on vital issues—war
with France, union with Scotland,[5] toleration for Protestants, and the Hanoverian Succession—they were in the sol-
idest agreement. The Tories, on the other hand, saddled
with High Church bigots and fanatical Jacobites, were
often fiercely divided where they had most need to stand
together.

The war, moreover, enriched the commercial-minded
Whigs and bled the land-captive Tories. In Parliament the
Whigs scoffed "at the corn-dealers and sheep breeders who
thronged the Tory benches," and who could no more quote
the classics than understand high politics. Under their famous Junto, the Whigs were more firmly organized and
more ably led. Of the five members of this inner Whig
council, one—the least important—was Admiral Russell, Earl
of Orford, splendid at sea but neither liked nor trusted on
land. One, Lord Somers, had been the Lord Chancellor and
stood forth an esteemed interpreter of constitutional law.
Somers and the arrogant Lord Halifax,[6] a financial genius
who had founded the Bank of England and established the
national debt, were *novi homines*, men of title for having
proved men of talent. The remaining two Junto members
were Sarah's son-in-law, the honest, bad-mannered, bad-
tempered, unpopular Sunderland, and Lord Wharton, hu-
manly the most fascinating of the group—devoted to parlia-

[5] Which was achieved in 1707.
[6] Not to be confused with The Trimmer; this is Pope's "full-blown
Buffo," the patron of Congreve, Addison, and Prior,
Fed with soft dedication all day long.

4*

mentary government and religious toleration, the party's
leader in the House of Lords, and perhaps its best vote-
getter as he tirelessly bowled up and down the country. On
the theory that the way to a man's vote was through his
gullet, he sometimes, in his whirlwind way, singlehandedly
got thirty Whig candidates elected. He is best known to
posterity as one of the greatest of English rakes, "abhorred
by Heaven and long since due to Hell"; he was also one of
the blandest of English liars; and Dr. Johnson's "detestable
Wharton" too, "who was not above drunken profanation of
churches." He would seem to have been of that race boasting also Charles II and Charles Fox, a race of charmers.

The groundwork for war, and for prosecuting it, having
been carefully laid, the time had now come to declare it.
The matter was not altogether simple. At home only Godolphin and the Queen knew that John had solemnly bound
England to declare war on France (simultaneously with the
Empire and the Estates General) on May 4 (O.S.). Not
only must the covenant have Parliamentary sanction; but
England's exact role in the war had still to be worked out.
In terms of land war, was she to be a full or only a limited
partner? On this head, there was Rochester's desire for a
limited partnership—and Rochester's influence on the Queen
—for John to combat. Luckily, John held a trump card: he
had persuaded the Allies to denounce the Pretender's claims
to the English throne, to make this purely English bone of
contention a *casus belli*. Certainly England, in return, could
not assume a merely secondary role. As Allied rejection of
the Catholic Pretender's claims had originally been one of
the Tories' conditions for fighting—their thought being
that the Catholic Emperor would never agree to it—they
were trapped by their own strategy. Hence, with no need

for Anne to throw her weight toward Marlborough rather than Rochester—which, in a pinch, she must surely have done—England elected to become a full belligerent. On schedule, Garter King of Arms rode through London on the 4th of May proclaiming, while trumpets blared and the populace cheered and shouted, that England was at war with France.

Though, war having been declared, the people cheered, there had earlier been, not just with High Tories but, in the nation generally, a decided anti-military sentiment. Some of this went all the way back to Cromwell, some had grown up with the advance in popular government, some was connected with the state of soldiering itself. The militia aside, a soldier's was a lifetime profession, as often dedicated to a foreign country as to his own; most of the great national armies of the day were both polyglot and polylingual. Only among the French and English forces was there much national feeling, for one thing because countries like Germany and Italy were not really nations. In England, though press-gang tactics might help man the navy, there was as yet no way of mauling or manacling people to serve the Queen on land. There was only enlistment, with each colonel having to handle his regiment's enlisting. Thus recruiting officers—as well-spoken, it is to be hoped, as Farquhar's Serjeant Kite [7]—were sent about the country; with "bounty-jumpers," men who took the Queen's guinea and quickly deserted, as their most frequent recruits. The whole business struck a decidedly unheroic note:

[7] "If any gentlemen soldiers or others have a mind to serve her Majesty, and pull down the French king: if any prentices have severe masters, any children have undutiful parents: if any servants have too little wages, or any husband too much wife: let him repair to the noble Serjeant Kite . . . and they shall receive present relief and entertainment."

We then shall lead more happy lives
By getting rid of brats and wives
That scold and brawl both night and day [8]
Over the hills and far away.

The warfare was even more unmodern than the soldiering. Old-fashioned cavalry charges with pistols rather than swordplay were just going out of style, though even during the Marlborough wars battles were lost by the "cavalry halting to fire." Marlborough, indeed, was possibly the first commander to forbid cavalrymen to fire at all. Where French infantrymen fired by ranks, the English fired far more accurately by platoons: marksmanship with Marlborough was so vital as to become a prime activity in winter quarters. John himself, moreover, even though commander-in-chief, often rode out with each of his associates to illustrate his orders; this habit of personally shifting about the furniture of combat was one reason for his extraordinary success; he very truly

. . . *taught the doubtful battle where to rage.*

John also braked the unruliness of his men; the English soldiers who had previously plundered Dutch villages (it was said that "if God Himself were a soldier, He would pillage") were turned into well-liked and respected regiments who, by 1704, marched with decorum halfway across Europe.[9] But if John disciplined them into decency, if his camps were described as "the best academy in the world

---

[8] But frequently soldiers' wives went with them to war and in a sense kept house for them; cooked, washed clothes, fetched fuel. Mistresses and wenches also abounded.

[9] On the march to Blenheim, the *enemy* country of Bavaria was, to be sure, ravaged mercilessly, even the church bells being broken up, and most things burned or destroyed that could not be carried away. But Marlborough controlled all the men who were "immediately under him."

to teach a young gentleman wit and breeding," it was through showing a special concern for their welfare. They were well fed and well clothed and, for their day, well cared for when sick or wounded; and never subject, so long as Marlborough was in command, to the atrocities of the period, the "ceremonial lacerating of their flesh." Besides frequent executions, there were commonly in armies inhuman floggings: consider, in *Tristram Shandy*, the grenadier so bestially whipped that he "begged to be shot outright"; or —if fiction seems untrustworthy—take fact, take a guardsman who, for killing his colonel's horse, was ordered 12,600 lashes, and received 1,800 "of which he nearly died." (If the lasher did not lay the stripes on hard enough, he was liable to the same or to double the number of them.) In the navy, things were not appreciably better—"Pox above board," wrote one man, "plague between the decks; hell in the forecastle, and the devil at the helm." It was a "pinch-gut world" whose mercenaries not necessarily even "saved the sum of things for pay," for often as not they went unpaid. Officers might fight one war without having been compensated for the previous one; there were even such instances as a military governor who, in 1689, had lost his wife, children, and fortune during a siege, and who, still trying to collect his salary in 1704, was the State's prisoner for debt because the State would not pay its own debt to him.

War, in those days, followed a kind of protocol. Professional armies were a novelty, and cost so much that nobody wanted to send them into action. The most approved usage was to invade a country and try to live off it while the opposing armies sat "looking at each other" for months on end. If one army got up and moved, the other discreetly followed, only for them to sit down somewhere else and look at each other again. Sometimes a fortress garrison could be weakened, and the fortress then besieged; sometimes a fortress would be threatened to make it strengthen its garrison—and weaken its army in the field. Pitched battles were rare; [1] a cease-fire for the winter months was mandatory. What with bad drainage and bad roads and a consequent problem of supplies, armies fighting in winter would have perished of dysentery and exposure; and in any season battles were fought, wherever possible, in rich, fruitful plains, near navigable rivers and canals. It was because, as Fortescue says, the Spanish Netherlands met all these requirements that it proved a favorite *mise en scène:* the ground was so familiar that every move and gambit was foreseeable while the many invested fortresses held out and surrendered almost on schedule. Louis XIV delighted in such gentlemanly sieges, and imported to the neighborhood his whole retinue, including a Court painter and a theatrical troupe. And since France set the tone for everything, even war, the rest of Europe contentedly followed suit.

But not so Marlborough. He had no mind to subsist lazily off the enemy; he wanted to smash it. He wanted first to trounce the French in the field and then march straight on Paris, not (as he was advised) capture French and Spanish colonial possessions or, at most, invade not France but Spain. For any conquest of Spain, John knew, besides being proverbially difficult, could never prove decisive, never fully humble France. But to get to Paris, John saw, was also difficult: he must advance through the Moselle valley while wresting from the French the whole extent of the Rhine from Coblenz to the Dutch frontier.

---

[1] But what battles there were could be indescribably concentrated, fierce, and bloody: "Sometimes 200,000 men fought for an afternoon in a space no larger than the London parks . . . and left the ground literally carpeted . . . and in places heaped with maimed or slaughtered men."

On the 23rd of May (N.S.), just over a week after England had delcared war, John sailed from Margate for The Hague. Sarah came to see him off, and as his ship moved from shore he looked for her "for a long while, with the perspective glass . . . in hopes I might have had one sight of you," and then sat down and wrote her a love letter. "I would have given my life," he told her, "to come back." Reaching The Hague, he was detained there by a variety of diplomatic and military matters, and it was a good month before he could take up his command (a command reluctantly granted him, for he had yet no great Continental reputation) in the field.

A great commander of those days was much more than a military man. If only because he had so many illustrious, and even royal, personages in his army and on his staff, he must needs become a personage himself. In the thick of conducting a campaign, he had to set up a Court. He, and what might well be called his guests, did not feed; they dined—profusely, and off silver. Howsoever the battle fared, the food and the salvers, the wines and the wine-coolers, had to be watched over and counted up, and packed and moved, at huge cost in beasts and men. Marlborough brought with him his coach-and-six; and in public wore scarlet and gold lace; and was surrounded not just by staff officers and aides-de-camp, but by stewards and secretaries. If he received, by established custom, a percentage of the army's bread contracts, he had in turn to pay for intelligence out of his own pocket. Thus, though his emoluments were huge—some £50,000 a year, or a couple of million dollars in present money—his disbursements were commensurate; notorious penny-pincher though he was, he must on countless occasions part with great numbers of pounds.

For two centuries John has been assailed for an immoderate love of money. And he did love money, strove to amass it, shrank from disbursing it. He earned, as a result, the intense ridicule of his contemporaries; and though, for being so miserly, he undoubtedly had many tales of miserliness thrust upon him—so that any single anecdote may be questioned—his behavior has been only exaggerated, not misrepresented. One can easily enough believe that he owned but three coats, or would walk miles through muddy streets—once walking home after *borrowing* coach fare—just as one can doubt that, to save ink, he never dotted his *i*'s (indeed, Horace Walpole tells the same story of Sarah) or that, when a messenger arrived in camp by night and John learned there were no papers to read, he said: "Put out the lantern." [2] But certainly, in an age when great generals lived as sumptuously as they could manage, Marlborough lived as simply as he dared. He had no food wagons, no retinue of courtiers or hangers-on. He may well not have cared for such flourishes; he certainly did not care to pay for them.

Miserliness is in reason so hard to account for at all that there is no real accounting for it in John during an age that particularly exalted the lavish gesture and made fun of the closed palm. Sir Winston points to John's childhood, with his hard-pressed family's galling dependence on a grandmother's generosity; he points to the contrast between John as a Court page and the richly dowered youths he lived among; and to his soon seeing—the more so as he fell in love with a girl hardly better off than himself—that acquiring money was the surest key to a large career. It is a fair point. The only trouble is that John suffered not just

---

[2] But Lord Acton records that once when this story was repeated "an officer present stated that he was the visitor whom the duke had treated so parsimoniously."

from penny-pinching, but equally from greed. He did not simply fear poverty or strive after independence; he inordinately craved wealth. Amid all the uproars over how moral was his conduct, what must at least once be pointed out is how unspiritual, how entirely materialistic, was his nature.

When finally, late in June, John took command in the field, French and Allied detachments sat eying each other on the Scheldt and along the Upper and Lower Rhine; but the main French army—60,000 men under Marshal Boufflers—was eating off Prussia in the Prussian dependency of Cleves. On June 10, Boufflers had made a dash to cut off the Dutch commander—who sat twenty miles away—from his central fortress at Nimeguen, and the Dutch commander had saved himself only by headlong retreat.

All Holland was quaking when John reached Nimeguen on July 2. He collected 60,000 men of his own and advanced to within two leagues of Boufflers, but the frightened Dutch insisted on delay, and it was not till the 26th that John took the offensive and uprooted his adversary. A week later John was superbly situated for an outright attack, but the Dutch—after first consenting to it—again restrained him, and Boufflers escaped into Belgium. Then, by a ruse, John tempted Boufflers out into the open and, with the French at his mercy, prepared for the kill. But again Boufflers was saved because again the Dutch refused to move, and they refused again the day following. The inaction by which Marlborough was crippled (instead of Boufflers crushed) hung on a Dutch constitutional proviso that two members of the Government must accompany the commander-in-chief on all military operations, and must assent to all major ones. This assent withheld, the Dutch forces were immobilized, and a Marlborough so angered that it took all his self-command to remain outwardly calm, and so outraged that he apologized to the enemy for not fighting, could only alter his tactics and go fortress-hunting along the Meuse. Having captured a number of fortresses, John decided to take Liége, only to have the Dutch refuse, for the fourth time, to send out their armies. It was only because Boufflers at length fell back that John was empowered to go forward and Liége won at last after a bloody siege. It was now the end of October and time to go into winter quarters. Thanks to the Dutch, John, by his own reckoning, had during this first year's campaign heart-breakingly failed, but by the reckonings of his age he had achieved a "glorious victory."

Painfully little as expelling the French from the Maas and the Lower Rhine might seem to him, to others—and notably the Dutch—it seemed spectacularly much. Athlone, John's own second-in-command, who had opposed John's getting the captain-generalcy because he wanted it for himself, was filled with praise: "The success of this campaign is solely due to this incomparable chief. . . . I opposed in all circumstances his opinions and proposals." In returning by water to The Hague, the incomparable chief narrowly escaped capture. Raiders stopped his boat at night; Marlborough lacked a passport, and, had not his clerk, in the darkness, slipped into his hand one made out in the name of his brother, General Charles Churchill, he would probably have been taken prisoner.[3] Rumors indeed were circulating that he had been captured, and his entry into The Hague in the rumors' wake created tremendous jubilation.

From The Hague, John returned for the winter, "in

[3] Was John recognized? The passport—it was customary for the opposing generals to provide passports for one another—was out of date;

strict privacy," to England, being met by Sarah at Margate. In London he was thanked by that tremendous Tory, Sir Edward Seymour, in the name of the Commons "for retrieving the honor of the English nation"; and on December 2, very soon after he had arrived, Anne made public her desire—already broached in private—to offer him a dukedom.

Though flattered and, as is plain, enormously tempted by the proposal, John felt—or at any rate fabricated—certain qualms: he could not feel his financial position equal to maintaining the dignity of such high rank, and could not but wonder whether the honor should not be deferred until after the Peace (on which reasoning, as it happens, he would never have received it at all). Heinsius, the Dutch Grand Pensionary, thought John's accepting it would benefit the Queen "with all the Princes abroad." "I urged upon him," wrote John by way of answer,

> the trouble it might bring upon the Queen by several families pressing to have the same title . . . that I should make a worse figure in England for being a Duke than as I am, till I had an estate for it. He said the Queen's kindness was such that I need not doubt a fortune, and that whatever was done at this time . . . would be without envy, since all the people were pleased with what I had done. He farther urged to me that it was not reasonable to expect ever to have so much success in any other campaign as in this. . . .

The Queen was more than eager to confer the title; indeed, in first broaching the matter—as it happens, to Sarah—she had deplored having no better way to express

---

and it may be that for once John did not practice his usual thrift. And, whether or not he bribed the raiders, he rewarded the clerk with £50 a year for life.

her gratitude, particularly at a time when John "deserves all that a Rich Crown would give, but since there is nothing else at this time, I hope you will give me leave as soon as he comes to make him a Duke"—even though she knew that Mrs. Freeman "does not care for anything of that kind."

Sarah most assuredly—if we are to accept her own words at face value—did not care for it. She recorded that when she first read Anne's letter "I let it drop out of my hand, and was for some minutes like one that had received the news of a death of one of their dear friends." And all it came down to, she added, was a matter of precedence—of how one should go through a door, "and when a rule is settled, I like as well to follow five hundred as one." As she liked to follow nobody, this last statement, at least, was truthful enough.

John was more eager in the matter, or more honest. He bade Sarah "say all you can to the Queen for her extraordinary goodness to me," but adding that he had "a mind to nothing, but as it may be easy with you" and agreeing with his wife that "we ought not to wish for a greater title, till we have a better estate." But he had a feeling that the Queen's "goodness" would not confer the one without the other, and he got Godolphin to point out to Sarah that ducal rank would be of use to him in his dealings with England's difficult allies. In face of such arguments, Sarah gave way; and on the 14th of December John became Duke of Marlborough.

The Queen at once saw to it that he should be able to sustain his new rank. She sent the Commons a message announcing an annual grant of £5,000 from the Post Office revenues "for the support of his title," and asking of Parliament a grant that might descend, beyond her lifetime, to John's heirs. But to this, for all John's popularity, there was strenuous opposition. It was Tory policy—lately it had more than once been Tory practice—to oppose long-term diversion of public revenue to individuals. Seymour, so lately gracious, led the attack, and one of John's own subordinates carefully itemized his huge emoluments from Dutch and British sources. Godolphin sought guidance from Harley of how to avoid a humiliating Parliamentary refusal, and, though surprised and vexed, Marlborough agreed there must be no vote. He accordingly had the Queen inform the Commons that he would refuse the arrangement she had proposed.

Relieved now of any need to act, the Commons offered a glowing résumé of Marlborough's services, along with deep regrets that it could not further reward them. Anne, smarting from the Commons' rebuff, wrote to Sarah that she wished her "dear Mrs. Freeman and Mr. Freeman" to accept £2,000 a year from the privy purse, "besides the grant of the five. This can draw no envy, for nobody need know it. Not that I would disown what I give to people that deserve . . . but you may keep it a secret or not, as you please." The Marlboroughs refused the offer. John, however graciously Parliament might voice its regret, was "a little chagrined"—and a little disconcerted, for he had agreed to a dukedom on the understanding that it include what befitted a duke; that, should he be killed, or a kind Queen die, or a new sovereign prove unfriendly, there need be no dimming of the Marlborough luster.

In the midst of all this came genuine tragedy. The Marlboroughs' son Lord Blandford, this winter, was sixteen years old, and had gone from Eton to Cambridge—though he had rather have entered the army to serve under his father, who desired to have him. But Sarah would not hear of it, and Blandford, for the moment, did no more than in-

trigue, together with a friend, for a cavalry commission.
John's heir had grown, by all accounts, into an attractive
youth; one biographer deduces, or opines, that he united
"his mother's abilities and his father's sweetness." Certainly
he was at times in his mother's black books: "I would have
writ to my mama," wrote Blandford to his father in the
summer of 1702, "but that by what she said to me in her
letter I am afraid she will never thoroughly forgive me,
which has grieved me so much that I cannot tell how to
write till I have some hopes of being friends with my dear
mama." And he hopes that his "dear papa" will "be so kind
as to intercede" for him.

While at Cambridge during the following autumn Blandford paid a number of visits to Godolphin when the Lord
Treasurer was at Newmarket hard by. Thither, when smallpox broke out at Cambridge, Godolphin bade the boy come
to escape the epidemic. An apprehensive Sarah wanted the
boy to come home, but Godolphin deemed Newmarket,
with its bracing air, safer. The boy remained in Godolphin's
house till after Christmas and then went back to Cambridge.
In January he took sick, and it was soon plain that he had
smallpox in a most virulent form.

Sarah raced to Cambridge to nurse him; the Queen had
her own doctors follow after in her own royal coach. John
remained behind, restless and—as the boy grew constantly
weaker—more and more distressed. "If we must be so unhappy as to lose this poor child," he wrote at length to
Sarah, "I pray God enable us both to behave ourselves with
that resignation which we ought to do." And: "If this uneasiness which I lie under should last long, I think I could
not live." By the time this came to Sarah, there could be no
hope, and John was summoned to Cambridge only in time
to watch his son die and see him buried in King's College

Chapel. The father, already overdue in the field, could not linger, and after making a new will, which had to be sent after him to sign, he sailed early in March for Holland. After so great a loss, he told Ailesbury at The Hague, he might better retire than "toil and labor for I know not who."

The loss to both parents, it is clear, cut terribly deep. It constituted the losing of a child; of an only son; and, further than that, of an heir: their name now could not be straightforwardly passed on.[4] John controlled his grief, as he controlled emotion always, and, by going off to war, was driven to divert his thoughts. But Sarah, in the short while John was with her at St. Albans, and much more afterwards, was wracked by suffering. There were, at first, outbursts of weeping so violent and prolonged that people feared for her reason. She would not see the Queen: "It would have been a great satisfaction to your poor unfortunate [5] faithful Morley if you would have given me leave to come to St. Albans, for the unfortunate ought to come to the unfortunate. But since you will not have me . . . God Almighty bless and comfort my dear Mrs. Freeman."

After John sailed for Holland, Sarah shut herself up, refusing to see anyone, even her favorite daughter, Anne. She went at last to London, but only to remain alone and to spend hours, dressed meanly in black, in the cloisters of Westminster Abbey. Then she was back again at St. Albans, as deeply secluded as ever. "There is but one stroke

[4] Though John still hoped for a male heir. "Pray let me have . . . an account of how you do," he wrote to Sarah. "If it should prove such a sickness as that I might pity you but not be sorry for it, it might yet make me have ambition." ("What then," inquired Trevelyan, "is ambition if Marlborough lacked it?")

[5] Anne had actually introduced this adjective—which became traditional—into her correspondence with Sarah after the death of her own son three years before.

of fortune," she wrote in answer to a message of con-
dolence, "that can be more severe and after naming it I can
say no more." She seemed so distraught, she looked so un-
well, that Godolphin wrote anxiously about her to Marlborough. "If you think," John wrote to Sarah, "my being
with you can do any good, you shall quickly see you are
much dearer to me than fame or whatever the world may
say." There had been, briefly, that hope that her want of
health might mean another child, but by now the hope had
vanished. By now, too, the soreness of Sarah's grief had
begun to heal. But as her tears dried up, so did one of those
few jets of tenderness and affection within her; and she
was to emerge from seclusion to resume, with an unprece-
dented vehemence, the game of politics and power.

VII

IN a worldly sense, what with the titles and revenues conferred upon her, and with John's triumphs abroad that
had meant a dukedom at home, the year of Anne's accession had proved almost fairylike for Sarah. And beyond
what she herself was pleased to enjoy, there was the power,
now, of granting enjoyment to others or of taking it from
them. She could reward; she could punish; she could meddle—already sometime back she had noted that "Statesmen . . . ran to open doors" for her. Among the many
things she had seen to was that the young daughter of a
ruined merchant uncle of hers should be helped. Abigail
Hill, who went about mousily with downcast eyes in her
colorless face, had of necessity become a noblewoman's

chambermaid. Just before the accession, Sarah, after taking her into her own home, had got her made Anne's bed-chamber woman.

Yet the event that showered Sarah with such large and declarative benefactions was by fine degrees to impair her position as well as enhance it. Sarah, thanks to the accession, had become the Queen's favorite, but Anne had become the Queen. Anne, like Victoria a long while after, was almost immoderately domestic and middle-class, but she had, like Victoria also, a royal will. And like Victoria she was both filled with virtuous desires for her country's and her subjects' welfare and actuated by irrational and petty motives. Anne had something of that stupidity, that failure to understand, which so often imparts authority and re-sembles grandeur; she had all of that infrangible obstinacy which can take on rocklike strength. When her fan went up to her mouth, Keith Feiling has said, ministers knew that her mind had snapped shut. Indeed, she wrote once to a minister who had flouted her: "I desire you would not have so ill an opinion of me as to think when I have determined anything in my mind I will alter it." Much of the time—with her own life full of unhappiness, and her husband's in the public sense a misfortune—she wanted an arm to lean on. But though on a thousand occasions she might choose to follow, she would never against her will be led. There was nothing patrician in her manner, only much that was regal in her blood; and from having been ill-treated by her prede-cessors on the throne, she was all the readier to occupy it with the utmost assertiveness. Thus she revived a custom of Charles II's, of attending important debates in the Lords—but not as he did, because hearing himself de-nounced "was as good as a play."

In consequence, the grander favorite had now a grander

mistress. Gone was the adversity that had done so much to unite them; and Anne was not only Queen, but much loved. It was not really that her feelings for Sarah had changed; and with John so gloriously proving his mettle in the field, she was all the more in a mood to be kind. But there were little things. Earlier, what with their domestic ties and private griefs and public humiliations, there had been less to alienate Sarah and herself in the way of Whigs and Tories. About religion, to be sure, even in the old days Sarah had struck Anne as all too offhand; whatever she might feel for the Churchills was as nothing to what she felt for the Church.[1] In the old days, however, Anne had defended her against the world, had even insisted to her sister Mary that no one more than Sarah had "better *notions* of religion." But now, as the reign opened, the shadows of religion and politics grew increasingly ominous. There was Sarah's habit—which Anne would reprove—of whooping up the Whigs, and her more recent habit of crying the Tories down. Political differences had once been merely personal differences; now what Anne felt had immense public importance. Sarah was no longer differing with Mrs. Morley; she was at variance with the Crown—and often as the champion, and even the very voice, of the commander-in-chief.[2] All this went on, moreover, in the teeth of a political crisis involving religion. To enable Dissenters to hold office, there had arisen a practice of Occasional Conformity, of their now and then taking the sacrament according to the Established Church. Anyone who,

[1] Anne was even an exception to Charles II's remark that all the Stuarts could sleep through a sermon.

[2] Sarah's Whiggishness, though based on convictions, was intensified, as time went on, by her realizing that the Whigs were the real supporters of John's war policy and the one key to his staying in power. And John's interests—however much she might endanger them—were always her prime concern.

having taken the sacrament, "reverted" stood to be prohibitively fined, though in actual practice prosecutions were rare.

To deprive the Whiggish Dissenters of office, the Tories now introduced a bill outlawing Occasional Conformity. Anne so much approved of the bill as to get her occasional conformist of a Lutheran husband—whom the new law would debar from public life—to vote for it in the Lords. (While voting with the Tories, the obedient George told the Whig teller: "My heart is vid you.") Marlborough and Godolphin, perhaps from devotion to the Queen, plainly from fearing Tory opposition to their war measures, supported the bill in public while privately helping to kill it. It passed the Commons with ease, but eventually failed because first the Lords so much reduced the fines as to render them meaningless, while next the Commons reared up that the Lords should dare usurp the Commons' age-old powers over money. With the milder Tories in the Commons abstaining, the bill as finally rewritten failed to pass.[3]

Sarah, unlike John, had loudly and publicly opposed the bill. She had no sympathy, she wrote long afterwards in her

[3] The Bill lives on for inspiring one of the most famous of all literary anecdotes, for being the engine that catapulted Defoe into a sea of troubles. He first angered his fellow Dissenters by denouncing Occasional Conformity as an ignoble practice. He next, with his *Shortest Way with Dissenters*, so brilliantly travestied High Church fanaticism as to be supposed an inspired High Church writer. When it came out that he had written the pamphlet with bitter irony, the Tories became enraged and insisted he be punished. Tracked down, Defoe was sentenced to stand three times in the pillory and to go to prison. In Newgate, he was bitterest about his fellow Dissenters' abuse and most aggrieved that the Tory ministry should so persecute him when it was only Tory fanatics he had meant to ridicule. "Thus," he commented, "like old Tyrell who shot at a stag and killed the King, I engaged a Party and embroiled myself with the Government."

But in the pillory he became a hero to the populace; a martyr in the eyes of a mob that pelted him, not with rotten eggs, but with flowers.

Memoirs, with "High Church nonsense of promoting religion by persecution," and indeed saw the whole thing as tending much less to serve the needs of the Church than to enhance the voting strength of the Tories. In all this Anne was very particularly grieved to find dear Mrs. Freeman differing with her. Fortunately, about now, Sarah—on a matter even closer to the Queen's heart—could display gratitude and affection. Anne wanted Prince George to have his own income—£ 100,000 a year for life—and some permanent state offices. The chief of these, Generalissimo of Her Majesty's Forces by Land and Sea, was one that would take George to neither battlefields nor warships, that indeed would not even require him to give up drinking.[4] Over this and the large State income, neither House raised any objection, but over perpetuating the income for as long as George might live, they raised considerable. Recalling all the foreigners William had ranged about him, particularly after Mary's death, Parliament wanted no George who should outlive his wife to swell the large ranks of financed foreigners under the Hanoverians. Mainly through the efforts of the Marlboroughs, the income-for-life bill was ratified by one vote, but leading all its opponents in violence was the Marlboroughs' son-in-law Sunderland. (Sarah was furious. While she sought to show Anne what good friends to monarchy the Whigs could be, her extremist Whig son-in-law was violently opposing what lay closest to the monarchical heart.)

Gratefully—not least for Sarah's rage in her behalf—Anne wrote to Sarah that she was "sure the prince's bill passing after so much struggle is wholly owing to the pains

---

[4] Anne really desired much solider offices for George: not only the commander-in-chiefship over British and Allied forces (which the Dutch would not consent to) but also the rank of Consort (which Parliament would not even consider).

you and Mr. Freeman have taken" and that "neither words
nor actions can ever express the true sense Mr. Morley and
I have of your sincere kindness on this and on all other
occasions," and was, to her "last moment . . . most passionately and tenderly yours."

In certain small ways, at least, Sarah could assist the
Whigs without too dangerously antagonizing the Queen.
Thus, when the Occasional Conformity Bill was defeated
and the Tories—as an alternative way of strengthening their
ranks in the Lords—had Anne create four new peers, Sarah
managed to coax a Whig peerage out of Anne also. At first
the four Tories refused the honor if a Whig was to share it,
but unless he did, Sarah told John and Godolphin, she—
having vouched for it—could not show her face in public.
And though neither John nor Godolphin desired a peerage
for Mr. Hervey, and the Queen and most of the Government heartily disliked one, Sarah had her way. Whether
she personally next managed to soften Anne's views on
Occasional Conformity is not clear, but she must have
played a part in the Queen's later urging both Houses
against reintroducing the measure. As it happens, Anne did
not prevail, but this time, when the bill was introduced—
and again defeated—Prince George stayed away. Indeed,
so rancorous now were the Tories' feelings generally, so
dangerous their maneuvers—in Government they were advocating a purely defensive war in the Netherlands—that
Sarah's fierce espousal of the Whigs had a certain real political value, a certain genuine effect on the policy of the
Queen and the conduct of the war. Thus, when the Tories
drummed up their mere defensive war, Sarah could con-
front John and Godolphin with the fact; she could warn
them of the consequences; she could wave them toward
the Whigs for support.

This was the more important in that, for all her pleas to
the Queen and the Queen's own distressed reactions, Sarah
could not budge Anne's official position: the High Tories
remained at the helm. And this did much more than outrage the Duchess of Marlborough: it gravely impeded the
Duke. John's position on the Continent was often at the
mercy of the political climate at home, a climate insalubri-
ous for its intra-Tory heats as well as Whig-and-Tory tem-
pests. The High Tories were not only so violent about
Occasional Conformity that, as Swift remarked, people
"out of zeal for religion have hardly time to say their
prayers"; the High Tories equally—as harshly taxed landowners, or diehards, or Jacobites—wanted the smallest-sized
war they could get. They naturally assailed John for his
conduct of a war that in its second year was proving disastrous. More, noting his large pay from the Dutch and his
ambitions in the field, they could find his motives for grand-
scale combat more dubious, even, than his management.

The Whigs supported the war firmly enough—but they
too were disturbed by the disasters, and much irritated besides for having no place in Government. As a result, the
Junto lords decided to assail the Ministry from which they
were excluded, which meant attacking Godolphin as Lord
Treasurer and John as commander-in-chief. Previously
they had supported both, but John, now, was to be ad-
judged incompetent in the field, and he and Godolphin
alike viciously wasteful of subsidies and indifferent to aims.
And he and Godolphin alike were to be attacked for twice
voting for the Occasional Conformity Bill. Thus, on
grounds of "principle" among High Tories and of party
maneuvering among the Whigs, John and Godolphin came
alike under fire. Being in England, Godolphin bore the
brunt of it and was the more eager to cry quits. He kept

urging Marlborough to let him resign, and when Marlborough refused, even relations between the two stanch partners grew strained.

In the outcry raised by the High Tories, the Queen herself was not spared, so that she gradually turned away from them—but not, for all Sarah's insistence, to ally herself with the Whigs. Her choice, in the coming Cabinet crisis, was the moderate Tories, whom their higher-flying brethren called Sneakers. When Anne overrode the High Tory Nottingham's objections to this, he resigned, and Harley, while remaining Speaker, replaced Nottingham as Secretary of State.

In the face of reverses and Dutch shackles abroad and of censure and bombardment at home, John increasingly came to share Godolphin's wish to retire. Sarah now, in her unavailing efforts to convert Anne to the Whigs, used the two men's dissatisfaction as a trump card. She read the Queen a letter of John's in which he spoke of resigning, adding that she and Godolphin felt quite as John did. The Queen rose to the bait. "It is no wonder at all," she wrote to Sarah,

that people in your posts should be weary of the world, who are so continually troubled with all the hurry and impertinences of it; but give me leave to say you should a little consider your faithful friends and poor country, which must be ruined if ever you put your melancholy thoughts in execution. As for your poor, unfortunate, faithful Morley, she could not bear it; for if ever you should forsake me, I would have nothing more to do with the world, but make another abdication; for what is a crown when the support of it is gone? I will never forsake your dear self, Mr. Freeman nor Mr. Montgomery . . . We four must never part till death mows us down with his impartial hand.

Sarah, seeing the Queen sufficiently alarmed to make concessions, urged John to rid himself of his Tory obstructionists, but he was of no great mind to shift from a Tory to a Whig alliance. "I think both parties," he wrote to his wife, "unreasonable and unjust"—and counseled moderation. As always, the vast problem of war in Europe had to be set against remaining at peace with Sarah at home: "I hope in God this will agree with what you desire and then I can have no uneasiness."

Meanwhile the war went on, not very happily for England. An unsuccessful English expedition against Cádiz in 1702 was, to be sure, redeemed when the English, in returning home, captured part of the great Spanish fleet at Vigo Bay and sufficiently regained prestige for Portugal to join the Allies.[5] In the East, the Allies fared badly: Louis XIV's ally, the Elector of Bavaria, seized Ulm and opened communications with the French on the Upper Rhine. Then, in a surprise dead-of-winter move, France's great general Villars crossed the Rhine, captured Kehl (the key to southern Germany), and by spring had traversed the Black Forest and joined up with the Elector on the upper Danube. So matters stood when Marlborough, grieving over the loss of his son, returned to The Hague in the spring of 1703. He found nothing to inspirit him among the Dutch who, obstructive as usual, spiked his proposal for countering Villars by attacking Antwerp and Ostend. They merely

[5] England's Methuen Treaty with Portugal, in May 1703, proved epoch-making. By giving England free use of the great harbor of Lisbon, it helped forge England's permanent strength in the Mediterranean; by letting England sell cloth to Portugal, on an exchange basis favorable to the Portuguese, it made port the great eighteenth-century English wine and condemned the wellborn Englishman to gout.

John Churchill, Duke of Marlborough

Anne crowned

allowed him to capture Bonn [6] and forced him to fight not
the French, but themselves. For eighteen days he was
within striking distance of the French, who sat waiting for
something to happen and were amazed when nothing did;
on all eighteen days John sought leave to attack, on every
one he was refused it. And now, in the East, Villars and the
Bavarians defeated the Austrians near Höchstadt—so that
France and Bavaria controlled the Danube from Ulm to
Linz; had support, under Tallard, on the Upper Rhine; and,
helped by Hungarian rebels, threatened desolation "almost
to the walls of Vienna." The situation—though eased by the
Elector's quarrels with Villars (which led Villars to throw
up his command)—was acute. For even if John got Allied
consent to besiege Paris—which was doubtful—he could
hardly attack before 1705, whereas, were Austria not
helped, Vienna must fall in 1704 and, by falling, ruin the
Allied coalition.

The high peril in which Vienna now stood roused the
Emperor to urge a major Allied campaign on the Danube.
He was assisted in this by Wratislaw, his able envoy in
England, and by the celebrated Prince Eugene [7]: the three
of them felt, moreover, that with the Dutch so terrified of
an offensive, and with the Allies' Rhine commander, Louis
of Baden, so totally lacking in drive, Marlborough might
prove receptive to the plan. And indeed, despite his own
Moselle project, John was. "Receptive" is the proper word,

[6] The capture provides a fine instance of John's parsimoniousness.
Writing to Sarah, he hopes the Queen "will excuse my not putting her
to the expense of an express to bring the news of Bonn being taken."
Bonn, Huy, and the fortress of Limburg were all that Marlborough
won during 1703; the Dutch were delighted.

[7] A French-speaking prince of Savoy, Eugene was brought up at the
court of Louis XIV and afterwards felt the strongest desire to humble
him. Louis, he felt, had behaved badly toward his parents and not much
better—by insisting that a young man who yearned to be a soldier

for, contrary to common belief, it was not John who first thought up the march to the Danube; his sole merit lay in carrying it out.

The Danube decision was, all the same, long in coming. It was only after countless discussions with his Dutch and other allies, it was only as a result of Wratislaw's constantly insisting that Vienna, unhelped, must fall, that John agreed that the Moselle must give way to the Danube, and Vienna be saved rather than Paris assaulted. Fortunately, since Allied troops were already massed on the Rhine, John could weigh one plan equally with the other; and when one had finally been chosen, could still use the other as a blind. Never, certainly, would the Dutch consent to any campaign involving the Danube. Indeed, before John had quite decided for it, it was with the utmost reluctance that the Dutch would accept the Moselle. John came away depressed; and in his deciding for the Danube, Holland's attitude counted almost as much, perhaps, as Austria's plight. It was probably sometime in March of 1704 that Wratislaw finally gained John's consent, probably early April before they had planned the campaign. The plan involved moving Eugene from the War Office to become John's brother commander in the field—along with Louis of Baden, who was not wholly trusted, and who was expressly made Eugene's military inferior. The whole scheme was worked out in the greatest secrecy and so kept. Only John, the Em-

---

should instead become a priest—toward himself. In any case, Louis helped make of Eugene an implacably hostile soldier who would dispute his ambitions to be master of Europe. Eugene went in time to Vienna, entered the Imperial army, and became a field marshal by the age of thirty. Having no wife, no home, no country, he made soldiering his whole existence. By now the most famous general in Europe—notably for conquering the Turks—on the threat to Vienna he was recalled from fighting in Italy to become what amounted to head of the War Office. John, though he had never met Eugene, greatly admired him.

peror, Wratislaw, and Eugene can with certainty be said to have known of it. Queen Anne and Godolphin very likely knew (and approved) that Marlborough would lead the English in some kind of campaign in behalf of the Empire. The French and the Dutch must at all cost be kept from knowing; nor did Sarah know.

Before setting out on what was to become the most famous of all his exploits, John returned to England and spent happy days at St. Albans with Sarah. But while in London just before he sailed, he fell foul of his wife's terrible, jealous rage. The episode, involving an unidentified woman, springs into fierce life in a handful of John's letters—letters, all save one, directed to Sarah herself.

> When I do swear to you as I do [John wrote to her] that I love you, it is not dissembling. As I know your temper, I am very sensible that what I say signifies nothing. However, I can't forbear repeating what I said yesterday, which is that I have never sent to her in my life, and may my happiness in the other world as well as in this depend upon the truth of this. . . . You say that every hour since I came from St. Albans has given you fresh assurances of my hating you, and that you know I have sent to this woman; these two things are barbarous, for I have not for these many years thought myself so happy by your kindness as for these last five or six days, and if you could at that same time think I hated you I am most miserable. . . .[8]

> Saturday
> . . . As for your suspicions of me as to this woman, that will vanish, but it can never go out of my mind

[8] John was so distressed as to write about Sarah to Godolphin, and of "how unhappy her unkindness makes me. I would have seen you this morning, but that I am not fit for any company."

the opinion you must have of me, after my solemn protesting and swearing, that it did not gain any belief with you. This thought has made me take no rest this night, and will for ever make me unhappy.

. . . If the thought of the children that we have had, or aught else that has ever been dear between us, can oblige you to be so good natured as not to leave my bed for the remaining time, I shall take it kindly to my dying day, and do most faithfully promise you that I will take the first occasion of leaving England, and assure you, that you may rest quiet that from that time you shall never more be troubled with my hated sight.

My heart is so full that if I do not vent this truth it will break, which is that I do from my soul curse that hour in which I gave my poor dear child to a man that has made me of all mankind the most unhappiest.

The final reference, as Sir Winston remarks, "cannot refer to any one but Sunderland," who, presumably, had carried a story to Sarah or found some way to alarm her. What truth it contained, if any, is past knowing, but that there was any deep basis in fact can, I think, be doubted. Sarah, with scarcely a year gone by, had lost her son, found her hopes dashed of bearing another, and very possibly begun to suffer a change of life. Her mother's grief, and her subsequent woman's agitation led her to think, not just that John had been unfaithful to her, but equally—and certainly unfoundedly—that he "hated" her.

When he sailed from Harwich in April, Sarah saw him off, but the wound had not healed; in the very moment of parting, she handed him a paper that confessed her feelings and brought up painful charges. From The Hague on April 29—by which time she had written in kindlier vein—

John wrote: "I do own to you that I have had more melancholy thoughts and spleen at what you said in that paper than I am able to express but was resolved never to have mentioned it more to you after the answer I gave to it, which I hope is come to your hand."

A few days later John had from Sarah a "dear letter of the 15th." He would feign not burn it, but would "have it in my power to read this dear letter often, and that it may be found in my strong box when I am dead." She had so far relented as to propose joining him; but though this was impossible, for he was "going up into Germany" where she could not follow him, her letter has "preserved my quiet, and I believe my life."

In this spring of 1704, when John returned to the Continent, the French were very close to European domination and world power. Vienna was almost within their grasp, Italy in the gravest danger, and, for all John's Lowland victories, the Spanish Netherlands remained in Louis's hands. And so hampered was John by the Dutch that, save Vienna or not, he must seek any real victories at a distance. And real victories were needed now in terms of morale, as they were needed no less in terms of John's own command; for, lacking success in the field, the Godolphin Ministry must fall.

So far from acquainting the Dutch with his Danube plans, John had to plead with them to let him conduct the Moselle campaign in person; and then was allotted only 15,000 men. At this he sent the Dutch an ultimatum: he was marching off all his English troops. The ultimatum succeeded: the Dutch gave him many of their own men, and under such generals as were particularly congenial to him.[9] And once the Dutch gave in—and saw (as he had prophesied) that

[9] He took no native Dutch troops, only foreign ones under Dutch command, and thus got rid of the Dutch government deputies.

when he left the region, so did most of the French—their good behavior continued, even when they found out where he was headed.

By May, John had assembled near Cologne an army of 40,000 men; additional troops would join him as he marched. On the 19th he began his famous series of movements, going up the Rhine to Coblenz. The very first day of the march, the Dutch implored him to come back, while Louis of Baden, scenting trouble close by, beseeched him to hurry forward. He sent reassuring messages to them both and marched undeflectedly on. Much foresight and feeling was shown for the marchers. The army would set off at three a.m. and reach the day's camping-ground, while it was still cool, around nine; and, the Commissary having gone before, "the soldiers had nothing to do but to pitch their tents, boil their kettles, and lie down to rest." On May 29, John came opposite Mainz, where he made some ostentatious feints to suggest designs on the Moselle: then, with speed his prime concern, he dashed south and east across the front of the French army, to pass out of striking distance of it. Yet even when it became clear that the Moselle had been a mere blind, John's real destination was thought to be Alsace. Only when John's own troops reached the Neckar near Heidelberg, whence they wheeled sharply eastward, did they—or John's own soldier brother— know where they were heading. On the 9th of June, Marlborough halted at Mundelsheim to let his infantry come up, and here, for the first time, he met the gaunt, intense, dynamic Eugene. Here too, three days later, arrived Louis of Baden. Here it was decided that Eugene—who was deeply impressed by the quality of John's hard-worked horses and long-marched men—should take over Prince Louis's role on the Rhine; Louis, entrusted with Eugene's

Austrians, would stay with John and—though rather on a
titular than a quite actual basis—share the command with
him on alternate days.[1] "It was as though Fabius," says
Fortescue, "should command on alternate days with
Scipio."

The march was resumed on June 14 under heavy rains
along water-soaked mountainous roads, with "cursing men
and sliding horses." But despite bad weather there was much
to raise the soldiers' spirits, and Marlborough's too: castles
and Rhine wine and girls and admiring villagers. And one
by one, now, the German princes were let into the Danube
secret, as Holland had been early in June, and Heinsius
much earlier. On the 22nd of the month Marlborough
joined up with Prince Louis; three days later their united
forces were so near Ulm that the Elector of Bavaria—who
needed Tallard's army, a month's marching distance away—
had to withdraw to a strong point on the Danube between
Ulm and Donauwerth.

It was Donauwerth, which would give John a vital
bridgehead over the Danube and a storehouse for arms, that
he from the first had aimed at. With its steep bell-shaped
fortress hill, the historic Schellenberg—that battleground of
half of Europe's wars—Donauwerth was not easy to capture, but John saw that it must be taken at once ("Every
hour we lose will cost us a thousand men"), before the pursuing French armies could catch up with him. Seeing John
advance, the Elector strengthened the Schellenberg, though
he so little feared an actual attack that an officer was given
leave to see his lady-love in Munich. Despite how invincible
the hill might seem and how fagged out from marching
were the men who must storm it, John—who commanded,

[1] Much confusion exists over the exact nature of the alternation, as
well as over who "commanded" when.

despite historical controversy as to whether it was his turn
to command—started an advance on Donauwerth before
daybreak of July 2, and a before-nightfall-or-never attack
on the Schellenberg the same afternoon. The attack began
badly and threatened to turn into a rout, but enough English soldiers did reach their goal to raise "a hoarse"—and
inspiriting—"hurrah"; the tide turned, and before dark it
proved a rout for the enemy. The whole battle, though very
costly in men, was little less than a triumph: Donauwerth
was surrendered and the Elector's crack regiments were
ruined. The Allies gained immensely in prestige. All Europe heard and applauded, and in England John re-enlisted
the Whigs.

John himself now crossed the Danube and, halting opposite the enemy at Augsburg, blocked the road to Vienna.
To be sure, the enemy, having entrenched itself, could not
be attacked; on the other hand, it might well be starved
out, and for three weeks Bavaria was systematically de-
spoiled of its foodstuffs. Then, on the 6th of August, the
French came up with Eugene's men right behind them; and
if the Allies were not to lose the Rhine—which Eugene had
had to leave unguarded—there must be instant action. On
the 9th, Louis of Baden, who had grown jealous of the
Donauwerth success, was sent—mainly to get him out of the
way—to besiege Ingolstadt. He had hardly set forth when
the united French and Bavarian armies were seen marching
upon Eugene's isolated (and inferior) force. Next day the
enemy crossed the Danube, but made no attack; and now
John inside twenty hours moved twenty-four miles—over
bad roads and three rivers—to unite his whole army with
Eugene's. By sending out "deserters" to announce his immi-
nent retreat, John next day kept the French from attacking
his tired men. That day, August 12, John and Eugene rode

out and examined the terrain. They discovered the enemy
extended for four miles along a ridge, with its right on the
Danube banks near a village called Blindheim, since better
known as Blenheim.[2]

The enemy's forces were not only well placed; they also
outnumbered John's—ample reason for John, now, to
abandon the Danube for the Rhine. Very early the next
morning, however, his men were to be seen advancing, eight
columns strong, straight at the French. Though astounded,
the French and the Bavarians were in no way discomposed,
and proceeded to draw up their battle lines. For the Allies,
Eugene commanded the right, Marlborough (on the Blenheim side) the left; their total forces were 52,000 men and
52 guns against 56,000 men and 92 guns—poorish odds for
launching an unprecedentedly bold offensive.

It was actually the French who, at eight in the morning,
opened fire. With Eugene's guns not yet in place, the Allies
spent the morning in a reading of prayers and with John
riding back and forth to rally his men. At last, shortly after
noon, Eugene was ready, and the Allied attack—at John's
end, a surprise attack—began. For what John did, so as to
split the enemy, was to hurl his cavalry over marshlike
ground that seemed insuperably wrong for it, and to throw
men straight at the village of Blenheim. This led the frightened French commandant to pull back into the village—as
John had hoped he would—all the men stationed outside.
The Allies now made a furious rush at Blenheim, and lost
heavily: wave after wave was repulsed till John at length
immobilized his men on dead ground in front of the village,
with orders to keep up a steady fire and to make feints of
advancing. Now, with the enemy inside Blenheim intent

---

[2] The French army was divided in two and kept so because horse-
sickness was raging in one of the halves. There was also a Bavarian army.

5*

on the Allied forces without, John started his main army advancing on a much wider front—advancing under such heavy fire and with its center so hard pressed that John had to borrow cavalry of Eugene. Its arrival helped keep the enemy at bay by the same kind of feints as were making at Blenheim. Then, at four o'clock—having tied up large enemy forces on two other fronts, and having massed his own cavalry with strong infantry and artillery support behind it—John began what had been his aim from the outset, what was to be the real battle, the grand assault at the center. Even so, the French infantry reserves stood their ground, and a sharp countercharge of horse might yet have carried the day. But the French cavalry hesitated and hung back, and as it did the tide of battle turned. The French themselves were now charged instead, and this time gave way, and Marlborough's horse swept superbly on, riding down the French foot as well. With Eugene pinning down the Bavarians, and other reserves penned up inside Blenheim, the routed French could but briefly rally here and there, only to flee when pursued and drown by battalions when pushed into the Danubian marshes. Marshal Tallard was captured, and his army fell apart; the other French army was, in company with the Bavarians, in headlong retreat and only not cut to pieces from being mistaken, in the dusk, for Eugene's men. Blenheim alone was left; and, though surrounded and once again attacked, for a time held out. But with its houses bursting into flames and news of overwhelming disaster seeping through, it agreed to parley—and accepted the bold English announcement that all further resistance was useless. More than twenty-seven battalions of dragoons, many of which had not yet fired a shot, laid down their arms.

Blenheim was something more, even, than a great military

triumph: it constituted a turning-point equally in the affairs of Europe and in the art of war. John and Eugene had dared such risks as would have appalled almost all other commanders of their day. Yet every risk had been most astutely calculated. And in crushing the enemy,[3] John and Eugene had shattered the French dream of dominating Europe, the French design of a vast empire beyond the seas. France so reeled from the defeat that, by proclamation, even to speak of it was made unlawful.

Before the day quite ended, John—who had been seventeen hours in the saddle—scribbled a few lines of what had happened, addressing them not to the Queen, but to his wife:

> I have not time to say more, but to beg you will give my duty to the Queen, and let her know her army has had a glorious victory. M. Tallard and the two other generals are in my coach, and I am following the rest. The bearer, my aide-de-camp, Colonel Parke, will give her an account of what has passed. I shall do it in a day or two by another more at large.[4]

Colonel Parke, a Virginian, dashed across Europe, reaching Sarah in London inside ten days' time. She in turn sent him galloping with John's message to the Queen, whom he found playing dominoes in a window bay at Windsor. It was customary to give the bearer of victorious tidings £500: Colonel Parke asked rather for a portrait of the Queen, which he presently received set in diamonds, and

[3] The Allied losses were over 14,000 killed and wounded; the enemy's, upwards of 30,000, plus 15,000 prisoners and 3,000 deserters.
[4] Writing to Sarah in greater detail next day, John said: ". . . I can't end my letter without being so vain as to tell my dearest soul that within the memory of man there has been no victory so great as this . . . Had the success of P. Eugene been equal to his merit, we should in that day's action have made an end of the war."

£1,000 besides. Within hours the tremendous news, already boomed and clanged about London, was being hallooed throughout the country: there were everywhere bells and bonfires, street crowds and tavern invasions, pious thanksgiving and widespread alcoholic salute.

VIII

WITH the French retreating after Blenheim all the way to Alsace, and John pursuing till, early in September, he crossed the Rhine near Philippsburg, the war ended in Germany. For John on the Continent there were tributes and honors: the Emperor made him a Prince of the Empire (a title still held by the Marlborough dukes) and conferred on him the tiny principality of Mindelheim (a possession later restored to Bavaria). But there had also been tension and strain. A few days after Blenheim, John wrote to Godolphin of being so "disordered . . . that if I were in London I should be in my bed in a high fever." And now there were problems and tasks. Louis of Baden—furious that being sent to Ingolstadt had really meant being sent to Coventry— ruined the Moselle campaign that opened in September. For his larger operations ahead John had need of military help from Prussia and the German states; and the conqueror of Blenheim, weary from months in the field, set forth in a lumbering coach to conquer Frederick I of Prussia. The recalcitrant Frederick, harkening "to a voice which offered threats and bribes with equal smoothness," in time gave John what he had come for, and honors and diamond hatbands besides. And by assenting, Frederick increased throughout Europe the belief in John's miraculous powers. Then, lumbering on to Hanover, John was shown new honors and achieved another triumph. Here there were peculiar difficulties, for the Electress Sophia craved an invitation to the country that, should she outlive Queen Anne, she would one day rule, while Anne—to whom Sophia signified her own death warrant—would under no circumstances invite her. John, in consequence, had to charm the tough, outspoken old Electress out of her desire to go. He showed her "a deference which surpassed all the customary forms of the German Courts"; and she, who not too long before had disparaged him to her resident philosopher, Leibniz, now called him as skilled a courtier as he was brave a general, and presented him with a piece of tapestry.

At length, in December, he reached The Hague and saw now, in triumph, the States-General, which at last sight he had foxed. Holland gratefully gave him a basin of solid gold and quickly approved the treaty he had made with Prussia. But it had qualms in the very moment of its exultation, pleading with him never to go such distances, never to court such dangers, again. Then, after an eight months' absence, John set out for England, bringing with him on a royal yacht Marshal Tallard and other illustrious prisoners of war, whom soon after the Marlboroughs "nobly entertained" at St. Albans.[1]

At home, meanwhile, there had been rejoicing and other honors. To be sure, the Tory politicians who had been croaking disaster over Marlborough's daring Danube campaign—and were all ready to impeach and perhaps even im-

[1] In the matter of prisoners of war, everything was very ceremonious; high-flown compliments extended even to men in the ranks. "With many men like you," said John to a captured private, "the King of France would soon be victorious." "It is not," the soldier answered, "men like me he lacks, but a general like you."

prison or behead him for it—now resented his triumph. Sarah commented that one would have thought Blenheim was a victory over the Church of England rather than over the armies of France. But the nation generally felt great need of celebrating so glorious a victory, and on September 7 there was a splendid thanksgiving service at St. Paul's, with first a stately procession through flower-strewn streets: Knights of the Garter and Yeomen of the Guard, lords and ladies, grenadiers and trumpets, and at length a coach of state in which sat the Queen ablaze with jewels and—at her side, in "plain garments" and no jewels at all— the Duchess of Marlborough.[2] God having been thanked, Who had matched them with this hour, the whole nation yet desired to remember the Duke in a more substantial way. There were various proposals. A first thought was to clear a large London area, turn it into a square bearing Marlborough's name, erect twin statues of John and the Queen, and build him a magnificent town house looking out on it all. Godolphin deprecated this, thinking it questionable to set any subject on an equal footing with his sovereign, and suggesting—as also much less expensive—an annual thanksgiving service. In time the Queen herself was asked to name a suitable testimonial; who, after taking thought, proposed that the Royal Manor and Park of Woodstock—that pleasaunce of "Saxon, Norman, Plantagenet and Tudor kings"—be conveyed to the Duke and his heirs forever. An act was quickly passed to this effect: it conveyed some 15,000 acres worth about £6,000 a year, and Parliament also authorized a grant of £5,000 a year

---

[2] After John's return, there was a great pageant—a procession, while cannon boomed and crowds cheered, from the Tower to Westminster Hall, bearing the enemy's flags and standards (which became one of the sights of London). Anne, this time standing aside, watched the show from the windows of St. James's Palace.

during the Queen's lifetime. Nor would the Queen, in munificence, fall short of the country. She would build at Woodstock, at her own expense, a commemorative palace to be called the Castle of Blenheim. Such honors, such acquisitions, pleased John tremendously, appealing not least to his dynastic sense. Woodstock and Blenheim would create a noble setting for his posterity, and, as the most illustrious of his posterity has remarked, John "regarded the raising of his family to the first rank in England as second only in importance to raising England to the first place in Europe."

Meanwhile, for all the political wrangles and release of party venom, Sarah gained generally in power and scope. John's military successes could not but further, in the April elections of 1705, the Whigs' political fortunes. Even before the elections Sarah had finally persuaded John himself to intervene with Godolphin in the Whig interest. "I have writ," he informed Sarah while still on the Continent, "to my Lord Treasurer as you desired concerning 19 and 55"— the cipher names for Buckingham, the Tory Sarah wanted dismissed, and the Whig Duke of Newcastle she wished to supplant him. And in due course Buckingham—who in unhappier days as the Earl of Mulgrave had befriended and courted Anne—was dismissed as Lord Privy Seal; as, soon after, was the Lord Keeper, Sir Nathan Wright. Wright's successor, the able, high-minded Cowper, was chiefly Sarah's work also, as his own diary attests: "In the evening visited . . . the Duchess of Marlborough who declined all acknowledgment I offered of thanks for my advancement."

As a result of Tory bungling, the Queen herself was now to feel kindlier toward the Whigs. When the 1705 elections gave the Whigs a majority in the Commons, the Tories cooked up a scheme to embarrass them. They would sound a view halloo that the Church was in danger and advocate inviting the Electress to come from Hanover and defend it. Knowing that Anne would violently oppose such a project, they felt they would have the Whigs in a trap: for, should they also support the proposal, they would ruin themselves with the Queen; and, should they not—which would seem to impugn the Succession—they would compromise themselves with the nation.

The Whigs brought an easy sanity to such Tory madness. They arranged for the Queen to be present at the debate so she could hear the Tories engagingly insinuate that she might any day turn soft-brained,[3] while to attest their support of Hanover the Whigs introduced a Regency Bill for upholding the Succession should time elapse between Anne's death and her successor's arrival in England. Not only did the Tory ruse fail; it also incurred the Queen's not easily dissipated resentment. So much so that at last—and at just the moment when relations between Anne and Sarah were a little strained—it softened the Queen's feelings toward the Whigs.[4] As her dislike of them was a prime cause of discord with the Duchess, Anne was very glad that she could be at peace with Sarah:

> I believe dear Mrs. Freeman and I shall not disagree as we have formerly done, for I am sensible of the services those people have done me that you have a good opinion of, and will countenance them, and am thoroughly

[3] All during Anne's reign there was much maneuvering (often at Anne's expense) because her ailments suggested that she had not very long to live.
[4] The helpless High Tories could only go on chanting their favorite tune of "the Church in danger":

> When Anna was the Church's daughter
> She did whate'er that mother taught her;
> But now she's mother to the Church
> She leaves her daughter in the lurch.

convinced of the malice and insolence of them that you have always been speaking against.

Thus, for a time, the Groom of the Stole and Keeper of the Privy Purse was once again something like the favorite of the Queen. She had seldom sat so high or, in natural consequence, been so busy. She was deeply wrapped up in Whig affairs; there were her Court duties, exacting, however dull; there was that cursed concomitant of sitting so high, the endless procession of place-seekers moving upward toward one. There were family matters also—Sarah's two older daughters had for some years been presenting her with grandchildren; and now her two younger daughters were married off. Her third child, Lady Elizabeth, married the Earl of Bridgewater; her youngest, Lady Mary, Viscount Monthermer. To each of these, as earlier to their sisters, the Queen gave £5,000 in dowry.

Besides all this for Sarah, there was now the matter of the palace that Anne was building at Woodstock. The architect was to be Captain John Vanbrugh, whose *The Relapse* and *The Provoked Wife* had in years gone by adorned the declining London stage. The choosing of Vanbrugh—beyond his being of the Board of Works, from which the choice would come—has only recently been explained. For so lordly a monument the obvious, the virtually predestined, architect was Sir Christopher Wren. Though Vanbrugh in his youth had been sent to France to study "house building," in 1704 he was known to the public as a playwright. In 1704, however, he was also Comptroller at the Office of Works and rather a favorite with the Whigs, and though Wren might anyway have been passed over as too old or too old-fashioned, it was Vanbrugh's Whiggishness that—a little indirectly—proved decisive. For Vanbrugh, as a member of the great Whig Kit-Kat Club, had apparently talked so well there about architecture, and made line drawings so uninhibitedly splendid, that his fellow member Lord Carlisle had commissioned his building one of the vastest domestic piles in the history of England, Castle Howard—and had recently got Vanbrugh made a herald—Clarenceux King at Arms—for good measure.

According to Sarah, in a document newly unearthed, it was John's man of business, the elder James Craggs, who suggested Vanbrugh for Blenheim. And according to Vanbrugh himself, in a second document newly unearthed, John and Godolphin soon afterwards came to see his model of Castle Howard; and as the creation at Woodstock was meant to be fully as vast, the scheme of Castle Howard carried the day. Castle Howard, with its immense central portico, its great sweeping pavilioned side wings, and its massive hundred-foot-high dome, marked the advent of a fearless unforeign baroque that, if often imperfect and not notably consonant with home life, had yet an indisputable grandeur. It brought high rhetoric in stone to a nation that had always treasured it in language. Just why a playwright with a publicly expressed contempt for heraldry should have been created a herald is doubtless a little obscure, but it was at least fitting that a herald be the architect of Blenheim, which might seem built to the sound of trumpets.

Actually it was to be built to sounds far less elevating, though on occasion no less loud. Sarah disliked Vanbrugh's scheme from the outset: she thought it far too vast ever to prove comfortable, or even to be finished in time for John to enjoy its discomforts. Vanbrugh sought to vindicate the grandness of scale by saying that this was not to be just a nobleman's mansion, but a great nation's tribute, and thus needed "the qualities proper to such a monument, viz.

Beauty, Magnificence and Duration." Agreeing with Vanbrugh that, so considered, Blenheim could not be too grand,
John and Godolphin overruled Sarah's protests, but she
continued to put "usefulness and convenience" above "show
and vanity" and to disparage, as a dwelling-place, something that was to cover three acres.

In June 1705, Vanbrugh, having asked for "some visible
authority," was appointed by warrant Surveyor "for and
on behalf of" the Duke. This was part of a curious arrangement for building and financing Blenheim, which, though a
gift from the Queen, was to be paid for by the Government. There were no set terms: large sums would periodi-
cally be paid the Duke by the Treasury, which the Duke in
turn, building as he chose, would pay to the workmen. Nine
days after Vanbrugh became Surveyor, the foundation
stone of Blenheim was laid by Vanbrugh himself

> and then seven gentlemen give [sic] it a stroke with a
> hammer, and threw down each of them a guinea.
> There were several sorts of music, three morris dances
> —one of young fellows, one of maidens, and one of old
> beldames. . . . From my lord's house all went to the
> Town Hall where plenty of sack, claret, cakes etc.
> were prepared for the gentry and better sort; and un-
> der the Cross eight barrels of ale, with abundance of
> cakes . . . for the common people.

Vanbrugh with—as Laurence Whistler puts it—"his infallible sense of scenery," had placed the palace on a broad ta-
bleland toward one end of the park. To the north stood the
half-ruined old manor of Woodstock, where the Black
Prince had grown up; while hard by was the Bower where
Henry II lay with Fair Rosamond "whose skin was so delicate . . . that the blood could be seen sliding in her veins."

Of the palace Vanbrugh was building, "a very large, exact and intelligent model" had been set before the Queen for her to observe and pass on at her leisure; and, according to Vanbrugh, she confessed herself "extremely pleased with it . . . and required no sort of alteration." The work, once started, went briskly forward. Wren, after a visit to Woodstock, had estimated a cost of £100,000 for no more than what Vanbrugh called "the magnificent part": for what else he envisaged, by way of courts and gardens, of causeway and lake, certainly another £100,000 would be required. All England was combed for contractors and master masons, and while they—and Vanbrugh's architectural blood brother, Hawksmoor—were hurrying to Woodstock at Vanbrugh's behest, a Mr. Boulter was hurrying there at Sarah's, to keep Vanbrugh in check. The first winter brought the first griefs: frost cracked the local stone; and walls, while Sarah rumbled, had to be new built. Then, finding that stone brought from a distance ran into money, she rumbled again. And she rumbled once more when, as time passed, she found that "though nothing had been finished, nearly everything had been begun." Vanbrugh tried to explain the situation: if trees, for example, were later to afford the maximum pleasure, they needed to be planted early, while walls were going up. And walls indeed went up, and after a while the eastern wing could even boast a roof.

But, though Sarah might differ with the Queen's architect, her differences with the Queen were now healed and her relations with the Whigs wonderfully satisfying. In December 1705 her notoriously uncourtly son-in-law Sunderland could write from The Hague concerning all the political "good news" from England and congratulate her upon it, "for I am sure nobody has contributed more to-

ward it than you." And as she could gratify the Whigs, so
on occasion she could discompose the Tories. One of them,
coming to Hampton Court to see the Queen, observed the
Duchess of Marlborough looking upon him "with anger"
and forthwith retired to his country seat—with, as one commentator rather boldly hazards, "a nervous breakdown."

Other Tories manifested a different homage; in the form
of lampoons. At Sarah's nod, they said, the Queen should
deny her friends and kindred,

> *her Church and God*
> *And Anne shall wear the crown but Sarah reign . . .*
> *Churchill shall rise on easy Stuart's fall,*
> *And Blenheim's tower shall triumph o'er Whitehall.*

"Queen Zarah," as the Tories called her, not only sat high
enough to reign; she also descended low enough, putting it
mildly, to electioneer. When a Mr. Gape was elected M.P.
for St. Albans, one Henry Killigrew accused him of bribery—only for Gape's counsel to accuse Sarah, who had
backed Killigrew, of ill practices. Against Gape the bribery was proved; the evidence against Sarah was legally less
damaging, though morally no more exalted. She had summoned various citizens to Holywell House "for a little
friendly political conversation"—to tell Charles Turner, for
example, that "such men as Mr. Gape would unhinge the
Government" and that "Papists' horses stood saddled night
and day"; or to ask a Mr. Miller could he be for men who
opposed the good of the nation; or to read Jeremy Hop-
kins a speech of Charles II's. And to a Mr. Crosfield she definitely gave twenty guineas, though with no mention—as the
money actually changed hands—of politics. Though bribery could not be laid against her, a number of Tories—during the ensuing House debate—attacked her in blistering

terms. Theirs now was a real animosity, for it was she, more than anyone else, who had piloted the Queen toward the Whigs. In such a moment Sarah's biography palpably merges with her country's history.

Biography and history were most one, indeed, during this year of 1705. It was a period for Sarah of political ascendancy. The Whigs, whose cause she had so vigorously espoused, had won success at the polls and favor with the Queen, and were in process of winning the allegiance of the Duke and Godolphin. And Sarah enjoyed, beyond the gratitude of the leading Whigs, the deference of such Tory-ish aspirants to power as Harley and brilliant young Henry St. John. And most of all she had now the ear, as she had much regained the heart, of the Queen: though Anne might on occasion write about her to Godolphin as "my dear un-kind friend," the first adjective still took precedence of the second. Nor could Anne as yet have any real sense of her dear friend's unkindness. Politics and religion alone had thus far divided the two, with Anne much more put off by Sarah's actual attitude toward Whigs or the Church than by her imperious way of manifesting it. Nor, even on such occasions as she might find Sarah a bully, could she surmise how endlessly Sarah found her a bore. One of Anne's doubt-less most maddening habits—particularly when she was cor-nered in an argument or in the grip of a strong prejudice—was not really to answer, but simply to intone, over and over, a set phrase. "I often," wrote Sarah of times when she stood high in Anne's favor, "I often spent hours in talking to her when I would rather have been in a dungeon." Soon Anne could not help being piqued to find Sarah constantly absent from Court; soon Anne must resent Sarah's way—when her royal mistress bumbled or prated—of answering,

in a kind of yawn of words, "Lord, madam, it must be so!"
And if Sarah—as is extremely likely—found something physically distasteful in her more and more ungainly and oftener
and oftener ailing mistress, Anne must have grown aware
and resentful of this fact also. For in giving Anne her gloves
or a fan, Sarah would turn the other way "as if the Queen
had offensive smells"; and there are less credible stories of
the same sort. A less credible story of a different sort has
Sarah spilling water over Anne's dress from sheer spite—
which inspired Scribe's historically jumbled drama *Le verre
d'eau*.

It was during this period of ascendancy, and in something
like this mood toward Anne, that Sarah set about having
her son-in-law Sunderland, whom Anne detested, made
nothing less than one of the two Secretaries of State. Sunderland would not only supplant a Tory whom Anne liked,
but also would constantly, by virtue of his office, have to
come into her presence. And Sarah, in terms of Sunderland,
did not simply nag and press and pester the Queen; she
campaigned with other people, she conspired generally. She
pelted John, fighting a Continental war, with letters demanding support for her own battle at home. For a while
she failed, if only because John was too busy fighting. But
in England her nagging reluctantly won over Godolphin—
if only because the Whigs eventually made Sunderland's
appointment a condition both for their supporting the war
and for their keeping Godolphin in office. Then John, too,
however unhappily, backed the appointment.

Anne, for whom the winning of the war was paramount,
found herself in a situation she could only loathe and resent.
"Making a party man Secretary of State," she wrote in August 1706 to Godolphin,

. . . is throwing myself into the hands of a party, which is a thing I have been desirous to avoid, and what I have heard both the D. of Marl. and you say I must never do. . . . All I desire is my liberty in encouraging and employing all those that concur faithfully in my service, whether they are called Whigs or Tories, not to be tied to one or the other; for if I should be so unfortunate as to fall into the hands of either, I shall look upon myself, though I have the name of Queen, to be in reality but their slave.

Amid all this Sarah wrote officiously, and, what proved worse, not very legibly, to Anne. She prayed that, in the Sunderland affair, Anne might recognize her "errors as to this notion before it is too late." The Queen read "notion" as "nation," would not deign to answer, and spoke indignantly of Sarah's letter to Godolphin. He spoke regretfully of Anne's indignation to Sarah; who wrote again to the Queen, with no great increase in tact. Anne's reply was reasonably conciliatory, however, and wound up:

Now that you are come hither again, I hope you will not go to Woodstock without giving me one look, for whatever hard thoughts you may have of me, I am sure I do not deserve them, and I will not be uneasy if you come to me; for though you are never so unkind, I will ever preserve a most sincere and tender passion for my dear Mrs. Freeman.

To this Sarah replied in her finest vein. She not only seized Anne's olive branch and immediately wielded it like a birch rod; she also confessed: "I cannot for my life see any essential difference betwixt these two words"; and ended up proclaiming that, long-drawn-out as her letter was, it would prove less troublesome to Anne than (despite Anne's specific invitation) coming to see her would be. All this time, moreover, the general pressure on the Queen continued, but she still would not give way. She apparently understood the consequences of capitulation as what a later age would term the dangers of appeasement. "They desire this thing to be done," she wrote to Godolphin,

> because else, they say, they can't answer that all their friends will go along with them this winter. If this be complied with, you will, then, in a little time, find they must be gratified in something else.

But she was more than willing to compromise, and proposed, in the same letter, a Privy Councilorship for Sunderland—this, she said, would make her "quite easy." And "why, for God's sake," she bursts out, "may I not be gratified as well as other people?" Sunderland insisted, however, on a high administrative post, even appealing to his father-in-law for support. And in the thick of waging war, John wrote to Anne as persuasively as he could, but without effect. The truth, it is plain, was that beyond the degree of her dislike for Sunderland, and of having her hand forced by the Whigs, she had by now found other friends and was responding to other pressures. As Sarah more and more kept herself scarce and made herself unsympathetic, that cousin whom she had brought into Anne's service as a waiting woman, Abigail Hill, was more and more shown royal favor. And Abigail, as it happens, was Harley's cousin as well as Sarah's, and when the Queen retired to her private apartments at Kensington, Abigail would have Harley wait at a back entrance, to be smuggled upstairs to Anne. It was the beginning of one of the most momentous backstairs maneuverings in all history; Harley from the outset was offering political counsel, and he and Abigail were involved in a palace plot.

Whether actually aware or not of this closet drama, the Marlboroughs and Godolphin had begun to feel that Harley and St. John were moving away from them into a clandestine alliance with the Tories. Harley had openly informed Godolphin that the Whigs would stop at nothing, and Sarah felt that, in part through Harley's influence, Anne had gone over to the Tories also. She presumably even broached her suspicions to Anne as a possible basis for John's and Godolphin's retirement. Anne, in reply, maintained her dignity and continued to show affection. As for the two men's retiring—

> Can dear Mrs. Freeman think that I can be so stupid as not to be sensible of the great service that my Lord Marlborough and my Lord Treasurer have done me, nor of the great misfortune it would be if they should quit my service? No, sure, you cannot believe me to be so void of sense and gratitude. I never did nor never will give them any just reason to forsake me, and they have too much honor and too sincere a love for their country to leave me without a cause. And I beg you would not add that to my other misfortunes of pushing them on to such an unjust and unjustifiable action.

As for Sunderland, the business—which had raspingly persisted through so many months—was swiftly, in the late autumn, concluded. John came home from war, exercised his personal magnetism over the Queen, and, perhaps by also delivering some kind of ultimatum, got her to acquiesce. On the 3rd of December (1706) Sunderland became a Secretary of State. It was a coup for the Whigs and a great

coup for Sarah, who had been implacable in bringing it
about. But in a sense, from the resentment it bred in the
Queen, it had given their own tottering friendship the *coup
de grâce*.

Actually the battle for the Secretaryship has even greater
historical importance than biographical interest, for, though
it marked a crucial stage in Anne's relations with Sarah, it
constituted a kind of turning-point in the English sovereign's position in the state. What Anne was battling for—
far beyond her dislike of appointing a particular man to a
particular office—was the right to choose her ministers as
she pleased, and what her capitulation confessed to was that
she really lacked that right. For John and Godolphin were
forcing Anne's hand from having their own hand forced;
they were quite as much the targets of an ultimatum as the
transmitters. The Whigs, in truth, were not soliciting Sunderland's appointment; they were demanding it, as their
price (which they thought moderate) for supporting the
war. They felt that by controlling the Commons they held
title to control of the Cabinet, and in making their demand
they raised an enormously vital—and then undetermined—
issue: were ministers in the service of the Crown, or in the
service of Parliament and the Parliamentary group in
power? Sunderland's appointment plainly went far toward
supplying an answer.

It was indeed a historic collision, but it survived very particularly as a personal resentment. Anne not only felt that
the Whigs had made outrageous demands; she was bitter
over how much her friends had abetted the outrage. It not
only cost Sarah what was left of Anne's friendship; it cost
Godolphin what was left of her favor. Sarah, as it happens,
had made the whole situation not better for herself, but
worse, by assuring Anne that her zeal for Sunderland was

not at all for his being her son-in-law. Anne would have
minded Sunderland's appointment less as a very great favor
to the Marlboroughs than she did as a pistol-at-her-head
capitulation to the Whigs.

The Sunderland affair, it is true, came at a very ticklish
period in the relationship between Sarah and Anne, and perhaps as much for that reason as in itself had so decisive an
effect. For Sarah had come by now to offend Anne for the
things she failed to do even more than for the things she
did; for her studied neglect of the Queen, her continual absence from Court, her ceasing to show any affection in the
face of so much preferment, any solicitude in the presence
of so much distress. For it was affection and solicitude that
Anne needed and craved, and it was overwhelmingly out
of this need and craving that she drew close to Abigail
Hill. She did not so much turn from Sarah to Abigail as
she discovered Abigail waiting when Sarah was not to be
found.

No doubt the peculiarly fictional nature of the situation
helped create the flamboyantly fictional consequences.
Even now, even to us, it all seems too much in the flashy
traditions of the theater to have happened in real life. As
well expect this dowdy waif slinking past great ladies to win
the love of a dashing prince as the bosom confidences of a
violently undemocratic queen. Even more out of the theater is Abigail's overthrowing the kind cousin, the very
Lady Bountiful who had first brought her to the Queen's
notice; and melodrama itself might shrink from making
Harley Abigail's cousin also. It must have seemed fantastic
to Abigail herself; to Sarah it was all so utterly inconceiv-
able that it never once occurred to her. Only long afterwards could she grasp what at the time had seemed merely
"unaccountable." "Being with the Queen," Sarah wrote,

(to whom I had gone very privately by a secret passage, from my lodgings to the bedchamber) on a sudden this woman, not knowing I was there, came in with the boldest and gayest air possible, but, upon sight of me, stopped; and immediately, changing her manner, and making a most solemn courtesy, "Did your Majesty ring?" And then went out again.

But in 1707 the situation had to be rammed home to Sarah by an outside hand. And even then, when a bedchamber woman—who imagined she was dying—sent for Sarah to inform her that Abigail was conspiring against her, Sarah seems to have only half believed it, for, to judge by his answer, she wrote about it quite offhandedly to John.

But now—and as Abigail rather pointedly kept out of Sarah's way—another, and odder, story reached Sarah's ears: that Abigail, this summer, had been secretly married to Mr. Samuel Masham, one of Prince George's bedchamber grooms, who, said Sarah, was "always making low bows to everybody and ready to skip to open a door." Not to have been told the news by the bride did seem to Sarah rather surprising, but hardly sinister. "I went to her," Sarah wrote,

and asked her if it were true: she owned it was, and begged my pardon for having concealed it from me. As much as I had to take ill this reserve in her behavior, I was willing to impute it to bashfulness and want of breeding rather than to anything worse. I embraced her with my usual tenderness, and very heartily wished her joy.

More than that, Sarah offered to get Abigail better living quarters and to acquaint Anne with the news and gain her approval for an event that had really required her permission. Over this Abigail first stammered and then was silent, only to admit at last that she thought the Queen's bedchamber women had informed her of the fact.

This, Sarah felt, was much more serious: that Abigail should not mention her marriage to Sarah counted far less than that Anne should not:

> I went presently to the Queen and asked her why she had not been so kind as to tell me of my cousin's marriage. All the answer I could obtain from Her Majesty was this: "I have a hundred times bid Masham tell it you, and she would not."

Sarah set out to learn more. Gradually she learned a good deal more: that Anne had herself been present at Abigail's wedding, stealing down at night to the apartments of her physician—the Dr. Arbuthnot of Pope's *Epistle*—where the ceremony was performed; that Anne had given as a marriage portion a large sum of money she had requisitioned of Sarah herself from the Privy Purse. Most of all, Sarah learned that this was no mere sudden royal show of favor, but that Abigail had for a long time—during the afternoon while Prince George slept—spent hours with the Queen. She had kept Anne company, had listened, sympathized, played the harpsichord. And she had brought into the royal presence her cousin Mr. Harley, who, while Abigail rendered at the harpsichord, also sympathized with the Queen —in the matter of the Church, in the matter of the Whigs, in the matter of being "Queen, indeed." He did more, it would seem, than sympathize; he advised, he suggested; and a stupefied Sarah was left to conjecture how far things had gone, and in what degree the poor relation now surpassed her benefactress.

Sarah's anger and indignation were to be vented about equally on the woman she had so ill-fatedly been kind to and on the Queen who had so long been kind to her. She was perhaps most incensed that *Abigail* had replaced her in a role that, however much it might bore her, no one else could possibly fill. It was outrageous enough that Anne should not rest happier in Mrs. Freeman's neglect than in anyone else's solicitude, but it was beyond belief that it should be this dust-broom's solicitude Anne craved, and that this dust-broom should now stand higher with the Queen than she did!

From Woodstock, Sarah wrote to Anne, upbraiding her for disloyalty. "You are pleased to accuse me," Anne wrote in reply,

> of several things in your last letter very unjustly, especially concerning Masham. You say I avoided giving you a direct answer to what I must know is your greatest uneasiness, giving it a turn as if it were only the business of the day that had occasioned your suspicion. What I told you in my letter is very true and no turn, as you are pleased to call it.

Meanwhile Abigail kept studiously out of Sarah's way, merely writing to her at Woodstock a letter (thought to have been composed by Harley) in which she denied all double-dealing. And to Harley himself Abigail wrote:

> . . . I waited; and in the evening about eight o'clock a great lady came and made a visit [to the Queen] till almost ten. I was in the drawing room by good luck, and as she passed by me I had a very low curtsey, which I returned in the same manner, but not one word passed between us, and as for her looks, indeed, they are not to be described by any mortal but her own self. Nothing but my innocence could have supported me under such behavior as this.

Sarah's curt answer to Abigail's letter had suggested a meeting as soon as she should return from Woodstock to town.
But the meeting was slow in coming. Sarah for a while
heard nothing from Abigail, and then only a roundabout
inquiry by way of maidservants. When she complained of
the "ridiculous" roundaboutness to Anne, the Queen upheld Mrs. Masham, not once but several times. Then Mrs.
Masham called on Sarah when she knew Sarah would not be
at home, and Sarah, quite on to the maneuver, gave orders
that she would not be at home should Mrs. Masham call
again. The comedy was finally wound up with Abigail
writing to request an interview, which, being granted, became the occasion for Sarah to tell her

> that it was very plain the Queen was much changed
> towards me, and that I could not attribute this to any-
> thing but her secret management; that I knew she had
> been very frequently with her Majesty in private, and
> that the very attempt to conceal this by artifice from
> such a friend as I had been to her, was . . . enough to
> prove a very bad purpose at bottom.

To this Abigail "gravely answered" that she was sure the
Queen, who had loved Sarah extremely, would always be
very kind to her.

The thunderstruck Sarah, hearing words of such insolence from a woman she had "raised out of the dust," could
only denounce her for ingratitude and for conspiring to
undermine the Marlboroughs and Godolphin. Abigail answered that she never discussed business with the Queen,
only brought her such petitions as she was sure Sarah "did
not care to be troubled with." After this exchange, the two
women "sat awhile silent," and then Abigail got up to go,
saying she hoped Sarah would allow her to call from time

to time to inquire after her health. But "she never once," Sarah rather delightfully remarked, "came near me after this"; though when Abigail's marriage was made public, Sarah called upon *her*—"out of respect to the Queen, and to avoid any noise."

The impact of Sarah's collision with Abigail was afterwards felt most sharply in her already much-blighted relations with Anne. At moments, to be sure, Anne would write to Mrs. Freeman that "whatever opinion she may have of me I will . . . always be her faithful Morley." And for form's sake Anne went farther still. When Sarah, pricked by Anne's displeasure and affronted by what she considered Anne's ingratitude, begged leave—early in 1708—to resign and pass on her appointments to her daughters, Anne went so far as to write to John:

I have had a great mind to speak to you this week, but when I have met with an opportunity I have found such a tenderness coming upon me on the thought of the subject I was to speak of, that I choose rather to trouble you this way with my complaints than any other. You know I have often had the misfortune of falling under the Duchess of Marlborough's displeasure, and now, after several reconciliations, she is again relapsed into her cold unkind way, and by a letter she wrote to me on Monday, I find she has taken a resolution not to come to me when I am alone, and fancies nobody will take notice of the change. She may impose upon some poor simple people, but how can she imagine she can on any that have a grain of sense? Can she think that the Duchess of Somerset and my Lady Fitzharding, who are two of the most observing, prying ladies in England, won't find out that she never comes near me nor looks on me as she used to do, that the tattling voice will not in a little time make us the jest of the town? Some people will blame her, others me, and a great many both. What a disagreeable noise she will be the occasion of making in the world besides, God knows, of what ill consequences it may be, therefore for God Almighty's sake, for the Duchess of Marlborough's, your own, and my poor sake, endeavor all you can to persuade Mrs. Freeman out of this strange unreasonable resolution. I have not as yet ventured to make any answer to her letter, nor dare not, for till this violent humor be over all I can say, though never so reasonable, will but inflame her more. . . .

Whatever she may do I hope you will never forsake Mrs. Morley who, though she can never say enough to express her true sense of the sincere friendship you have shown to her on all occasions, nor how much she values it, yet to her last moment will continue as she is now with all truth and faithfulness your humble servant.

But Anne's feelings had visibly, had indeed pointedly, changed. Sarah herself could write, in November 1707, to a friend: "Tis plain you live in the country by your writing to me to ask a favor of the Queen, to whom I never have the honor to speak of anything but what concerns my own offices"—not that Sarah did not still, by letter, harangue the Queen, or endlessly hold forth concerning Abigail. "After all this," Sarah winds up one effusion,

Your Majesty says "This fine lady is the very reverse of what I take her to be." To which I can only answer that she is the very reverse of what I once took her to be, and I don't at all doubt but when her master Harley has tutored her a little longer—if I do not die very soon—Your Majesty and I shall come to agree in our opinion of her.

Though the door might not have slammed shut on Sarah, already by Christmas of 1707 it admitted a freezing blast. Sarah went to see the Queen during the holidays; "and before I went in," she remarks,

I learnt from the page that Mrs. Masham was just then sent for. The moment I saw her Majesty, I plainly perceived she was very uneasy. She stood all the while I was with her, and looked as coldly upon me as if her intention was that I should no longer doubt of my loss of her affections. Upon observing what reception I had, I said I was very sorry I had happened to come so unseasonably. I was making my curtsey to go away, when the Queen, with a great deal of disorder in her face and without speaking one word, took me by the hand. And when thereupon I stooped to kiss hers, she took me up with a very cold embrace and then without one kind word let me go.

Sarah could partly attribute such a reception to her having recently sprinkled her defense of the Whigs with some "indiscreet expressions" concerning Prince George; indeed, on the Queen's complaining of them to Godolphin, the Duchess had been persuaded to write an apology. But after Anne's cold treatment of her at Christmas, Sarah seized her pen to expostulate—in view of such an icy embrace, could Mrs. Morley wonder at Mrs. Freeman's reproaches? Mrs. Freeman's make-up was "plain and sincere" and for years Mrs. Morley had liked it that way, and "if Mrs. Morley has any remains of the tenderness she once professed for her faithful Freeman,

> I would beg she might be treated one of these two ways, either with the openness and confidence of a friend . . . or else in that manner that is necessary for the post she is in. . . . And if she pleases to choose which of these ways . . . she likes to have Mrs. Freeman live in, she promises to follow any rule that is laid down that is possible and . . . to show that Mrs. Morley never had a more faithful servant.

The Queen in due course answered and "very much softened what had passed" so that Sarah might appear again at Court with what ease she could muster. The business of Abigail, however, was in train of becoming public knowledge; indeed, the Whigs vociferously pamphleteered it to the nation:

> *Wheneas Q---- A--- of great renown*
> *Great Britain's scepter swayed,*
> *Besides the Church, she dearly loved*
> *A dirty Chamber-maid.*

The breach at Court was now, in fact, to become an open one. And it was not to be confined to the Court alone. Politically the Queen and Harley stood ready to break with the Marlborough-Godolphin forces; though John might seem to Anne both desirable and indispensable, Godolphin seemed neither. Scenting the drift of things, the two men— who had long remonstrated over Harley's secret influence on the Queen, and were more and more aware of his "false and treacherous" behavior—now had a "brief, tense" audience of Anne and announced that if he were retained, they must resign. The Queen, her whole weight thrown toward

Harley, took no heed, but rather summoned a Council for February 9, 1707/8, from which Godolphin and John stayed away. "Mr. Harley," reports Sarah, "would have proceeded to business without them," only for the Duke of Somerset to ask what use it could be if neither the commander-in-chief nor the Lord Treasurer was present? The Queen, in a very angry mood, then had no choice but to adjourn the meeting.

And very soon after, she did dismiss Harley—and St. John with him. But to Sarah this clearly seemed done "with his own consent and by his own advice." It was, in any case, only a surface victory for John and Godolphin, for so long as Abigail could freely admit Harley into the Queen's presence, his influence would in no wise diminish—a Cabinet position was as nothing compared to a closet *entente*.[5] All the same, Sarah felt there might still be hope for regaining a measure of influence over Anne. For when—just before Harley's dismissal—John was once again in a mood to resign, and Sarah (with, as she puts it, tears in her eyes) told Anne that she must go from Court if John did, Anne declared she could not endure the thought of Sarah's leaving her. And Anne then promised, what presumably Sarah exacted of her, that should Sarah ever go from Court, the vacated offices would pass to her daughters. This verbal promise Sarah contrived to have also in writing, and no sooner did she have it than she set about resigning all over again, and was again importuned to stay on. Outwardly, much of the time, she even remained on something of the old footing—five or six nights in a row she might come to Court and be civilly received. But, as Vanbrugh wrote to Lord Man-

[5] Thus one day Harley was handed a secret message by a gardener, in which Anne appealed to him for help. He thereupon began creating a group of moderate Tories from which a Government could be formed.

chester: "The Queen's fondness for the other lady is not
to be expressed"; and almost always Sarah's taking leave of
Anne signalized the other lady's coming in to her.

Whatever Abigail's deficiencies in liveliness and charm—
and they would seem to have surpassed Anne's own—she
and the Queen were for as many reasons drawn together as
Sarah and the Queen were pulled apart. Abigail displayed—
what with a sovereign is the better gift—as much talent for
listening as Sarah did for speech. She reveled in petty gossip
as much as Sarah wrangled over affairs of state. She was as
much the Church's champion as Sarah was its critic, and as
High Church as Anne herself. Further, there was Anne's
growing hope that her young brother in France might
somehow, on grounds that nowhere menaced the Church of
England, succeed her. To talk of this hope with Sarah would
have been impossible—Sarah would have expertly summa-
rized James II's behavior toward the Church as proof of
how his son would behave, whereas Abigail sympathized,
not with Anne's personal feelings alone, but equally with
her political hopes. Between Anne and Abigail there existed, finally, the intimate inequality that welds queen and
waiting woman—the almost menial duties, the being always
within call, the being privy to the human necessities of
someone who would seem above human need. Abigail had
helped the Queen on those nights when Prince George was
gasping with asthma; now she was Anne's close companion
on the many occasions when George was "drunk, asleep or
ill." She could inspire in Anne an affection that was all the
greater because it was so untaxing. And increasingly she
was of vital importance as concierge for Harley.

IX

DURING these years of palace turmoil John had been
much away from Court, engaged in a strenuous and
lengthening war. Blenheim had proved such a psychological
tonic, as well as a triumph of arms, as to raise hopes in England of other great victories and even an early peace. But
instead of hastening action, Blenheim retarded it. To begin
with, the resentful Prince of Baden, given no share in the
"glorious victory," manipulated his subsequent command
against the French on a do-nothing basis. Much more cru-
cially, England's allies were so much heartened by Blenheim as to have small appetite for new aggressions. Now,
as earlier, John's great desire was to invade France by way
of the Moselle rather than fight past all the fortresses of the
Low Countries. And indeed, during the autumn of 1704, he
had caught the French off guard and unresistant at Trèves,
made them quickly capitulate at Trarbach, and gained the
right bases for a spring offensive. But with the coming of
spring, John found that the Dutch had crawled back into
their shell of caution and were loathe to emerge; while the
Germans and Austrians, who had also promised aid, refused to supply it. And with Louis XIV strengthening his
Moselle defenses and, a little later, starting action in the
Low Countries, John had to abandon his Moselle scheme
for good and all, had indeed to come flying to the Netherlands to defend the Dutch. Thereafter he had to make a
frontal attack on France, though a backward Moselle entry
was far easier; he had also to make head against the French
barriers set up at the outbreak of war, the Lines of Brabant.
Even this the Dutch generals would have prevented, but
John "perfectly bubbled them into it . . . as you would

manage children." The Dutch troops need only follow him "if he succeeded," only expedite retreat "if he miscarried." Actually he broke through the lines at Elixem, and with the loss of a handful of men achieved a victory worth 3,000 prisoners. He might easily have pressed on to take Louvain as well, but the Dutch either managed to dissuade him or left him too uncertain of their help, and "the enemy were permitted . . . to save Brussels and Flanders for another year."

The Dutch had again reduced the war to slow motion: now cautious in their planning, now jealous of John, they would turn down suggestions one day, pass up opportunities the next. John, at length, with that wisdom he not just possessed but so often applied, abandoned thoughts of the present to insure his hopes for the future, and with grave irony urged the Dutch to work out plans for the Allied army. "I beg you will believe," he informed Heinsius, "that I will with all cheerfulness endeavor to make everything succeed that shall be proposed to me." Actually, not only England but much of Holland sided with him, enough that the States General saw to it that for the 1706 campaign he should have pliant Dutchmen to work with and a free hand in determining policy.

For 1706, a Marlborough who felt hamstrung working with the Dutch and happy campaigning with Prince Eugene proposed leading an army to Italy, where Eugene now fought. He even gained Holland's consent so long as he should take no Dutch troops off home soil. But when Louis of Baden was badly menaced on the Rhine, the Dutch took fright, and Italy had to be abandoned. John was back again in Flanders, but now to his delight the French themselves came calling. Marshal Villeroi, who through Dutch timidity had last year been denied doing battle with John, now spoke of him with contempt, ascribing Blenheim to luck. He was willing, indeed, eager to engage the victor of Blenheim, and advanced eastward with some 60,000 men; John, with the same number, moved westward to meet him. Early on the morning of May 23, John's subordinate Cadogan espied through the mist French troops moving before him and, when the mist cleared, saw the entire French army on the march. Villeroi, occupying high table land in Brabant, assumed that the battle would be joined the next day, but Marlborough, with his habit of meeting the enemy a day earlier than they reckoned, went into action at once. Purposing to break Villeroi's right on the open ground between Taviers and Ramillies, he began by throwing his whole army against Villeroi's left. Falling into the trap, Villeroi vigorously strengthened his left, whereupon John recalled Lord Orkney from his feint attack [1] and—sheltering Orkney's troops from enemy view—moved them, with others, to Villeroi's right. Then the real battle of Ramillies began: Dutch Overkirk first won the town of Taviers, eliminating fourteen French squadrons at one stroke; next Marlborough, leading a massive charge in person (and at one point unhorsed), fell upon the French right and utterly broke it. There was a final great advance of Marlborough's whole line, so shattering as to cause a twelve-mile-by-night French retreat—and Dutch pursuit—to Meldert. John, bruised and weary, reached Meldert after twenty-eight hours in the saddle; after three hours of rest, the pursuit began again, advancing from the capture of men to the capture of cities, and at length to full-scale conquest. Louvain, Brussels, Malines, Ghent, Bruges, Oudenarde, Antwerp all surren-

---

[1] Orkney, who was not in on the trick, was so certain the attack was genuine that it took ten aides-de-camp in succession, and then Cadogan himself, to make him desist.

6 *

dered; within two weeks of Ramillies, virtually all Flanders and Brabant had fallen to the Allies. It was a stupendous victory—the Allies, John said, had at trifling cost achieved in four days what they might have felt lucky to do in four years, and with John commanding the last part of the campaign weary, shaken, and wracked by one of his raging headaches.

The Ramillies campaign, which extended to the capture of Ostend, ended with the coming of heavy rains in October. It proved so great a triumph as almost to give rise to disaster: with the Spanish Netherlands once again in Allied hands, the Alliance all but broke up over who should govern them. The Emperor laid claim to them and wanted John for governor at £60,000 a year. John told the Dutch he would govern only if they approved, and the Dutch, who wanted the Netherlands for themselves, disapproved violently. The Emperor now grew furious at the Dutch; the Spanish Netherlanders loathed them. Very shrewdly, Louis XIV chose this moment to offer Holland a separate peace. On all sides dissension arose, on all sides a show of flagrant self-interest—with Marlborough, as everyone's friend, in time incurring everyone's animosity. In addition, Sweden now became a problem, with France wooing the extraordinary young Charles XII, who, before he was twenty-one, had smashed the forces of the three countries that had sought to parcel his kingdom. John, in the spring of 1707, had to go woo Charles away from the French.

The campaign John planned for 1707 did not center in himself: with the Netherlands reconquered, with conditions grown more favorable in Spain, with Eugene having great successes in Italy, John hoped that a harsh blow in the Mediterranean would send France reeling; and he projected, under Eugene, an invasion of Provence that should culminate in the capture of Toulon. But there now ensued setbacks in Spain and along the Rhine; the Austrians went after Naples in advance of Toulon; the Dutch deputies hobbled Marlborough as he was poised to strike; there were week-long rains; and far from achieving anything of note in 1707, the Allies just managed, through Marlborough's efforts, not to disintegrate.

Activity in the following spring began on the French side, with Louis XIV trying to set down the Pretender in Scotland—a move John quickly foiled. Later in the spring John put Eugene at the head of a Moselle army, purposing that they two jointly compel action upon the French. The French themselves, with a large Flanders army, started an advance and, helped by the always obliging Dutch, recaptured Bruges and Ghent. John, at this point ill with fever, and not knowing how far the French would advance or the Dutch co-operate, abandoned anxiety for action. With the main French army under Vendôme some miles southeast of Oudenarde and a French detachment sent to besiege Oudenarde itself, John—by moving his men thirty miles in thirty-two hours—arrived, after his fashion, a day sooner than he was expected. He next superbly strengthened his position by putting his forces between the French army and the French frontier. Vendôme, incredulous at John's preliminary moves, now discovered there was nothing he could do but fight, and the fighting went murderously against him. What prevented outright disaster was the onset of darkness: [2] with two hours more of daylight, said John, he would have ended the war.

---

[2] Even so, refugee Huguenots fighting with the Allies called into the dark *"A moi, Picardie,"* *"A moi, Roussillon,"* to collect great numbers of French prisoners.

The Queen acknowledged the victory in a letter to the Duke:

> Windsor, July 6, 1708
>
> I want words to express the joy I have that you are well after your glorious success, for which, next to God Almighty, my thanks are due to you. And indeed I can never say enough for all the great and faithful services you have ever done me. But be so just as to believe I am as truly sensible of them as a grateful heart can be. . . . If you were here, I am sure you would not think me so much in the wrong in some things as I fear you do now.

Hard by the victory of Oudenarde came a small crisis not altogether unconnected with it. The brave conduct, during the battle, of the Electoral Prince of Hanover—the future George II—was greatly bruited and much applauded throughout Protestant England:

> *Full firmly he stood,*
> *As became his high Blood,*
> *Which runs in his veins so blew;*
> *For this Gallant Young Man*
> *Being a-Kin to* QUEEN ANNE
> *Did as (were she a Man) she would do.*

And the Whigs now, so inflated with power as to be in a mood to flaunt it and bring the unfriendly Queen to heel, made a move much like that of the Tories three years earlier. They proposed that the Prince pay England a visit and be applauded in person.

The Queen's reaction, when she got wind of the proposal, was her usual unyielding one. Hers was an opposition passionately, pathologically deep-seated, of an almost mystical intensity that no outsider, even with the clearer vision of posterity, can fully account for. It was no doubt a little that the presence of a successor must be a reminder that she herself must die, and wrenching proof that her children had all died before her. It was a little also because the future George I long ago came to England, presumably to make his suit; saw Anne, said nothing, and went away again. It was a little that the presence in England of a future sovereign might well establish a kind of rival Court. But it would seem that most of all the presence of Hanoverians would emphasize the absence of the Pretender. On this head Anne realized, a little guiltily, that her faith was her fortune; that she reigned where, in a strict Stuart view, her brother should be reigning; and now, by the Act of Settlement, he would not reign even at her death. An ailing woman's fears, a young girl's wounded vanity, a mother's pangs, a sister's guilt, a sovereign's pride of place—all these, tangled together, had somehow cankered into an obsession. It had become, indeed, such a King George's head with Anne that she told a dumfounded Jacobite leader she hoped he would "not concur in the design . . . for bringing over the Prince of Hanover."

When Anne heard, first, a rumor that Marlborough approved of the Prince's coming, and then that the matter of his coming was public knowledge, she wrote asking about it of John so as to forestall the need, on her part,

> of refusing him leave to come, if he should ask it, or forbidding him to come, if he should attempt it: for one of these two things I must do. . . . I cannot bear to have any successors here, though but for a week.

John, as it happened, did not favor the visit and, as he wrote to Sarah, would not lend his support to the Whigs:

You judge very right of the Queen, that nothing will go so near her heart as that of the invitation. I think the project very dangerous.

And so violent, indeed, was Anne's opposition to it that the matter was not further pressed and came to nothing.

In other ways, however, during this summer after Oudenarde, John spoke out plain enough to the Queen concerning the Whigs she hated:

For God's sake, madam, consider that whatever may be said to amuse or delude you, it is utterly impossible for you ever to have more than a part of the Tories

and he begged her to follow

the advice of my Lord Treasurer, who has been so long faithful to you, for any other advisers do but lead you into a labyrinth, to play their game at your expense.

The Queen, in reply, insisted that there was "nobody but you and Lord Treasurer that I do advise with," at the same time reproaching him for the thought that she was "being influenced by Mr. Harley through a relation of his." John saw, all the same, how decisively influenced she was, and wrote to Sarah that

we must expect this next winter all the disagreeableness imaginable; for the Tories have got the heart and entire possession of the Queen, which they will be able to maintain as long as Mrs. Masham has credit.

Yet then, as always, he must deprecate hurting "Mrs. Morley, whom I can't but love, and endeavor to serve, as long as I have life."

His Duchess, however, was at her old ways with the Queen, though no longer in the least on the old footing.

How changed things were became clear on the day of
thanksgiving for Oudenarde at St. Paul's—a day of the Marlboroughs' glory. For the occasion, moreover, it was the
Duchess of Marlborough's duty, as Mistress of the Robes,
to choose and lay out at St. James's the jewels that the
Queen should wear. But as she rode with the Queen toward
St. Paul's, she noticed that Anne was not wearing them;
was, it is usually reported, not wearing jewels at all. She
felt sure that Abigail had intervened, and felt that, beyond
being flouted by Anne's favorite, she and John were being
publicly humiliated by Anne's conspicuous, pointed un-
dress.

Just what went on between the two women inside the
coach—however many descriptions have been attempted, or
conversations adduced—no one knows; there may very well
have been no conversation at all. At the top of the steps to
St. Paul's, however, the Queen addressed—or answered—the
Duchess with some agitation ("It is not true. It is not true,"
one questionable version has it), only for the Duchess to bid
the Queen keep still. Those about the two "gaped and
stared" as Queen and Duchess passed into the Cathedral to
render thanks to God.

What conversation, if any, passed between Anne and
Sarah in the coach as they returned, no one knows either.
Sarah had afterwards the feeling that possibly something
had gone a little amiss, and when she presently wrote to
Anne it was in a tone that perhaps echoed the tone she had
used in person:

> I cannot help sending your Majesty a letter [i.e., of
> John's] to show how exactly Lord Marlborough agrees
> with me in my opinion, that he has now no interest
> with you: though when I said so in church on Thurs-

day, you were pleased to say it was untrue. And yet I think he will be surprised to hear that when I had taken so much pains to put your jewels in a way that I thought you would like, Mrs. Masham could make you refuse to wear them in so unkind a manner, because that was a power she had not thought fit to exercise before. I will make no reflections upon it; only that I must needs observe that your Majesty chose a very wrong day to mortify me, when you were just going to return thanks for a victory obtained by Lord Marlborough.

The Queen's answer was regally curt:

After the commands you gave me in the church, on the thanksgiving, of not answering you, I should not have troubled you with these lines, but to return the Duke of Marlborough's letter safe into your hands, and for the same reason do not say anything to that, nor to yours which enclosed it.

Sarah wrote again:

I should not trouble your Majesty with any answer to your last short letter, but to explain what you seem to mistake in what I said at church. I desired you not to answer me there for fear of being overheard: and this you interpret as if I had desired you not to answer at all. . . . The word *command*, which you use at the beginning of your letter, is very unfitly supposed to come from me. For though I have always writ to you as a friend, and lived with you as such for so many years with all the truth and honesty and zeal for your service that was possible, yet I shall never forget that I am your subject, nor cease to be a faithful one.

Anne, in reply, was this time less curt, but not really more cordial. She would "touch upon two things"—first, the Duke's belief, which Sarah had relayed, that he had not "much credit" with Anne:

> I have all my life given demonstration to the world that he has a great deal of credit.

And second:

> to beg you would not mention that person any more who you are pleased to call the object of my favor, for whatever character the malicious world may give her, I do assure you it will never have any weight with me.

Sarah herself must only advance Abigail's cause with the Queen by sneering at her one minute as "a woman that I took out of garret," the next as someone "I took from a broom." Almost certainly the breach between Anne and Sarah was past mending; but Sarah, in any case, had not the slightest notion how to mend it. John himself had written to her:

> I am sure that the interest of Mrs. Masham is so settled with the Queen that . . . by endeavoring to hurt, we do good offices to her.

What perhaps harmed Sarah most with the Queen was not anything she said, but her utter inability to keep silent. How could she ever be successfully abusive when over and over, and on and on, and more and more violently, she pelted the Queen with her abuse? If one great blunder was to forget that Anne was royal, and could not only have the last word but might even dispense with having it, an even worse blunder was to forget that Anne was human. Few subjects in history can have been accorded the privilege of addressing their sovereigns in such tones of freedom on such terms of equality. Few persons in history, on the other hand, can have been so given to harangue; and all the more because her harangues displeased the Queen when delivered in person, Sarah compulsively repeated each and every one on paper. And now Sarah's alarums and exhortations must disturb as well as offend the Queen, for Prince George, this summer, was dying.

Anne had been nursing him, in fact, when the news of Oudenarde was brought to her at Windsor in July. All through the summer he lay in a little house there—a little house that was thought to make it easy for Harley, by way of Abigail, to see the Queen. But Abigail, together with the Queen, was in attendance on Prince George; and during days that were hot, and weeks when the asthmatic, dropsical Prince was being badgered politically,[3] Sarah—far from helping, like Abigail, to nurse him—was hectoring his wife, or whooping up the Whigs, or creating scenes at St. Paul's. With her intellectual contempt for Anne, Sarah could never read Anne's mind. (It was in truth exceedingly hard to read, for Anne was a magnificent dissembler.) But knowing how ill Prince George was, Sarah could scarcely not read Anne's emotions. And knowing how the Whigs were at the sick man's throat, Sarah could hardly not grasp that the sick man's wife must find the Whigs more than ever abhorrent. Sarah was harassing an already harassed woman; and though not all her motives were mean, and some were on her own part wifely, and others from a political standpoint wise, history must judge her actions this summer more severely than, as it happens, did even Anne herself.

Sarah, to be sure, could scarcely know—since the doc-

---

[3] The Whigs wanted Lord Pembroke to replace the Prince as head of the Admiralty.

tors did not themselves—how close to death the Prince (having moved in vain from Bath to Epsom to Tunbridge Wells) had come. But when she learned the truth—just two days, in fact, before George died—she wrote as follows to his wife:

Though the last time I had the honor to wait upon your Majesty your usage of me was such as was scarce possible for me to imagine, or for anybody to believe, yet I cannot hear of so great a misfortune and affliction to you as the condition in which the Prince is without coming to pay my duty, in inquiring after your health; and to see if in any particular whatsoever, my service can either be agreeable or useful to you. . . .

On the heels of this communication, the Duchess, after an all-night drive, reached Kensington Palace, where she was received "very coolly, and like a stranger" by the Queen. She came back again, however, the next day and went—with no one daring to stop her as she passed through the hushed, crowded rooms—directly to Anne. She noted that Abigail was also in the palace, and could hardly not know that it was Abigail Anne wanted there. Sarah, nonetheless, was present when Prince George died. When she tried to console the Queen, Anne, clapping her hands together in grief, took no notice. With more success Sarah, fulfilling her official duties, next directed Anne's movements. To expedite the funeral arrangements, she wanted the Queen to go from rustic, out-of-the-way Kensington Palace to St. James's. When Anne resisted, Sarah at once concluded it was from wanting to be near Abigail; it never occurred to her that it might be from wanting to be near the Prince. Nevertheless, Anne finally consented, though stipulating that she first be left alone for a while. She gave Sarah her watch, with instructions not to come for her till such-and-such an hour, while asking Sarah to send Abigail to her before she should leave for St. James's.

Sarah did no such thing. She explained, when she herself came for the Queen, that sending Abigail—while so many people of greater importance were ignored—would cause talk. Anne, she remarked, could fetch Abigail to St. James's as soon as she pleased. Thus the Queen went on Sarah's arm to Sarah's coach—but not without whispering a message to Abigail's sister Mary, who helped her on with her hood, or without turning to smile at Abigail as she passed through the palace. "I carried her," wrote Sarah,

> very privately through my lodgings to her green closet and gave her a cup of broth. Afterwards she ate a very good dinner. At night I found her at table again, where she had been eating, and Mrs. Masham close by her. Mrs. Masham went out of the room as soon as I came in, not in the humble manner she had sometimes affected, as bedchamber woman, but with an air of insolence and anger.

Later Sarah noted how Anne, in the days following, spent long hours in Prince George's closet—because Abigail could smuggle there such people as the Queen wished to see. Anne herself left just one memorandum—written the night of his death—concerned with Prince George's dying; but in terms of her emotions it seems—spite of any good dinners she ate —sufficient:

> St. James's, October 28, 1708
> I scratched twice at dear Mrs. Freeman's door, as soon as Lord Treasurer went from me, in hopes to have spoke one more word to him before he was gone; but

nobody hearing me, I wrote this, not caring to send what I had to say by word of mouth; which was, to desire him, that when he sends his orders to Kensington, he would give directions there may be a great many yeomen of the guards [*sic*] to carry the prince's dear body, that it may not be let fall, the great stairs being very steep and slippery.

Anne's feeling somehow transpires here—and she is very grand as well. Sarah's only comment is "I believe she fancied she loved him, but her nature was very hard." Thereafter, said Sarah, "I attended upon the Queen

with all the care that was possible to please her, and never named Mrs. Masham to her. She would make me sit down, as she had done formerly, and make some little show of kindness at night when I took my leave, but she would never speak to me freely of anything.

Prince George's death coincided with further gains in power for the Whigs—Somers, just before it, was admitted to the Government, while Pembroke succeeded George as Lord High Admiral. With every new gain, the Whigs sought further ones: what they sought now, indeed, was absolute domination. Matters had reached the stage where John and Godolphin were looked askance at, not least by John's Junto son-in-law, and where Sarah was in no position to be useful and of no disposition to be friendly. In fact, in their awareness that Sarah could no longer help them with the Queen, Sunderland and Halifax seemed ready to make advances to Abigail. Such behavior might, as John wrote to Sarah, seem like madness—for even if Sunderland would have Abigail, why should Abigail have him?—but it exemplified the prevailing Whig morality; and Sarah felt equally alienated and angry.

To John abroad in the early summer of 1709 it for a time seemed possible to do without Whig support of the war, if only because the war must so soon be over. After such long, bloody years of fighting, certainly England wished it to be; and so, certainly, after such losses in men and money, did France. But when, following long, greedy wrangles, the Allies finally arrived among themselves at peace terms, they were such as even a shattered Louis XIV could not accept. For Louis was required, not simply to surrender all the Spanish dominions to Austria, but to drive, with his own troops, his own grandson off the Spanish throne. And he must do so within two months on pain of having war resumed, this time with all the French fortresses in Flanders no longer in French hands. "If I must wage war," said Louis, "I had rather fight my enemies than my children." One, at least, of his enemies—Marlborough—agreed with him, as his children did, and his people. Informed of the Allies' terms for peace, the tottering French somehow mustered the strength to rally round their King for war. And now, when the war continued, it was the English who most violently opposed it. For Louis, England knew, had agreed to banish the Pretender, to demolish the Dunkirk fortress, to acknowledge the Protestant succession, and to grant the Dutch a protective barrier. What more could England ask; why, any longer, must England fight? And the bulk of the English began to center their resentment in their great symbol of fighting. They muttered that John was prolonging the war out of self-interest, and what they muttered, the war-bled country gentlemen and out-of-office Tory politicians proclaimed in full voice.

Matters grew worse when John, in the face of the collapsed peace terms and in the teeth of the charges against him, waged in September his bloodiest victory—what was conceivably, indeed, the eighteenth century's bloodiest battle. John never lost a battle, but Malplaquet was won at sickening cost. The victors' losses, 25,000 men, greatly exceeded those of the vanquished, and the impact of loss was still felt in England long after the flush of victory had faded. John's own scribble of the news to Sarah carried with it neither pride nor excitement, only physical weariness and the admission of a "very bloody battle." Only the Whigs, and they only for party reasons, extolled Malplaquet, and though there was the usual thanksgiving service, all too many had no thanks to offer. France, to be sure, could hardly now sustain another such onslaught—John himself, on the day of the victory, wrote that "It is . . . in our power to have what peace we please." All the same, there was no end of war, no end even in sight. Accordingly, there was a great ground swell of angry mutters, all this—with Tory prompting and orchestrating—leveled more and more at John. Nor, whatever his weariness of war or eagerness to be in England, did John's subsequent behavior do anything to stem it.

With Sarah on such terms with the Queen as not to receive one word of congratulation while Malplaquet was still thought a great victory, she had come to see the need—if she was to boast any relations with Anne at all—of spending a good deal of time in London. Toward this end, already a year before Malplaquet, she had set about building a house in town. She began by having Godolphin remind the Queen that she, in happier days, had promised Sarah land near St. James's. The Queen did not demur, and granted Sarah, for £2,000, land for fifty years. Sarah, who had never wanted Vanbrugh for Blenheim, for Marlborough House chose Wren. She herself, in May of 1709, laid the foundation stone; but the original inscription, ANNO PACI-

FICO, had later—in deference to the truth, as well as with misgivings about the Latin—to be altered. In an architectural view, however, the Latin inscription was then well enough: though Sarah clamored to have the house go up in a hurry, she got on for a while with its almost octogenarian architect. Wren had tiles and bricks, hangings and mirrors, brought over from Holland, and the future royal dwelling—which only yesterday housed George V's Queen Mary—began to take shape. Sarah could not avoid various small contretemps. Thus, the inhabitants of "those little houses" near by were "so impertinent" as to refuse to let her pull parts of their houses down. And, in laying her foundations, she managed to uproot a young oak tree that Charles II had planted, and so to bring down on her head the shocked or simulated wrath of Jacobites and Tories:

> Be cautious, madam, how you thus provoke
> This sturdy plant, the second royal oak;
> For should you fell it or remove it hence
> When dead it may revenge the vile offence
> And build a scaffold in another place
> That may e'er long prove fatal to Your Grace.

And so far from "reasonable," in Sarah's eyes, were the contracts, and so "exorbitant" indeed the rates, that in time Sir Christopher—who because of his age was obviously being "imposed upon"—had to be dismissed.

Alienated from the Queen, execrated by the Tories, disregarded by the Whigs, Sarah now found herself on increasingly shaky ground. The situation, moreover, was one in which she was sinned against as well as sinning, or perhaps in which she sinned all the more for being so sinned against. Abigail's influence and power were as great now with the Queen as perhaps even Sarah's had ever been, which meant, among other things, that what power and prerogatives Sarah still possessed were being constantly challenged, or ignored, or dislodged. Minor offices it had always been Sarah's right to fill now went not to her candidates, but to Abigail's. In like manner, salaries were altered and favors interposed, and there was such friction about Sarah's apartments in Kensington Palace that, to be quit of them, she urged a friend to "make use of anything and everything that is called mine at Kensington." And nothing, she soon found out, could be called hers there: Abigail had appropriated the apartments, and Anne refused to be truthful about it. This replacement of one favorite by another, if at times a reverberant drama on which hung the fortunes of party and conceivably even of England, was yet in its day-by-day transactions a haggling, disreputable comedy. For, over this trifle or that, Anne would let Abigail have her way at the expense of Sarah's traditional rights, and Sarah, some small perquisite usurped or privilege rescinded, would explode upon the Queen her richly documented, minutely itemized anger. She would assault Anne with speeches and pelt her with screeds, and Abigail's pleasure in wresting some small victory can have been nothing to her delight at Sarah's thunderclaps of fury and rage.

And yet there was something less purely comic about it all than might appear. There was something ugly—that is, something quite professionally false and sinuous—about Abigail. The ugliness may well spring from the circumstances of her rise—the meachy, creep-mouse impression that, in all her indigent obscurity, she first conveyed. But there can be no doubt whatever that, with time, Abigail became a more and more practiced, and voracious, and base-bargaining intriguer. Once she had caught Anne's eye, Abigail showed Sarah no gratitude, as afterwards she showed her no courtesy. Doubtless Abigail's great triumph in her role partly stemmed from her seeming so miscast for it: she displaced the leading lady through the very fact that she seemed enormously lucky to have been hired as a walk-on. But her strategy too was always to *act* the walk-on, to remember her station in life, never to claim the limelight or show her hand. Just so, her station in life insensibly altered, and she had displaced at length a duchess to dominate a queen.

How Sarah handled or mishandled Abigail, though not without consequences, was not in the end really important —since Sarah's own fall from power, and Abigail's rise to it, largely rest on how Sarah mishandled the Queen. Still, when Sarah first learned of Abigail's changed status, she behaved quite well if only because she could not grasp how spectacularly changed it was. Once she learned the truth, she could not execrate Abigail enough, and indeed became obsessed with her. Nor, given Sarah's specific make-up—or, for that matter, human nature generally—is it hard to understand why. Abigail had visited upon her not only a rankling succession of defeats, but also, in the way she inflicted them, a jagged succession of shocks. Every kind of emotion now seethed in an excessively emotional woman: Sarah was bitterly balked of power, infuriated by how she was balked, in a boiling rage over who had balked her; more, there was her ruined relationship with Anne and, where politics obtruded, Abigail's ruinous relationship with Harley. Owing to Abigail, Sarah had lost all control, and with that loss of control perished any possible chance to come to an accord with the Queen.[4]

John was always wise enough to see the danger in Sarah's

---

[4] As Kathleen Campbell adds, all kinds of people were busily egging Sarah on—with real or pretended sympathy, with tales and abuse of the Queen.

constant recriminations to Anne: "It has always been my observation in disputes," he wrote in August of 1709, "especially in that of kindness and friendship, that all reproaches, though ever so reasonable, do serve no other end but the making the breach wider." It was certainly so here, but Sarah was not to be stopped. She even made a reluctant John write to Anne in her behalf. Anne's answer showed how very much past mending her feelings were. "It is impossible to help saying," she wrote to John in October of 1709,

> . . . that I believe nobody were ever used by a friend as I have been by her ever since I came to the Crown. I desire nothing but that she will leave off teasing and tormenting me [5] and behave herself with the decency she ought both to her friend and Queen, and this I hope you will make her do.

And in a letter of Anne's, soon after, to Sarah herself one hears the actual death rattle of what had been:

> It is impossible for you to recover my former kindness, but I shall behave myself to you as the Duke of Marlborough's wife and my Groom of the Stole.

Sarah herself has told of her way of rebutting so royal a pronouncement, which was conceivably Mrs. Freeman's masterpiece in this line:

> Upon the receipt of this letter I immediately set myself to draw up a long narrative of a series of faithful services for about twenty-six years past. And . . . I added

[5] And the Queen she was "teasing and tormenting" was just then, we are told, "under a severe fit of gout; ill-dressed, blotted in her countenance, and surrounded with plaisters, cataplaisma and dirty-like rags." In any estimate of Anne, her constant ill-health and physical suffering must be reckoned in.

to my narrative the directions given by the author of
The Whole Duty of Man with relation to friendship;
the directions in the Common Prayer Book with regard
to reconciliation.

X

I N the same letter to John in which Anne would have his
Duchess cease tormenting her, she had written: "I saw
very plainly your uneasiness at my refusing the mark of favor you desired." Exactly what mark this alludes to is not
certain, but it may be one that John had been uncharacter-
istically rash in seeking and that, in terms of the future,
Anne's refusal did not lay to rest. What, at about this time,
he had asked of her was to be made commander-in-chief
for life.

The motive for his request was, pretty incontrovertibly,
not so much a desire for more power as a fear of less. The
changing state of politics at home—with Harley's star, to
which Anne had hitched her wagon, in the ascendant; the
changed sense of public feeling at home, after even a Malplaquet had failed to bring peace, had bred in John a gnaw-
ing sense of insecurity. It was not necessarily inconsistent
that a man who was sick to death of his job should ask it
now for life, since only by feeling wholly sure of it could it
be endurable at all. Indeed, that he should ask it for life in
such a fashion as he did reveals how disserviceably his judgment was at the mercy of his ambitions. For he made the request after it grew obvious that asking was unwise, after
both the Lord Chancellor Cowper and John's man of business James Craggs had searched in vain for precedents.

Even Monk, whom John thought Charles II had made Captain General for life, was only made it, like everyone else, "during pleasure." And obviously there would be something very irregular, something indeed revolutionary, in a sovereign's surrendering so large a prerogative and a soldier's acquiring such unlimited power. But John now made direct application to the Queen, who consulted in turn various men of standing outside the Government, men whom Harley might have suggested to her, men particularly outraged by the idea. The Duke of Argyll, a soldier who resented a military superior of any kind. told Anne not to "be in pain," that whenever she commanded he would "seize the Duke at the head of his troops, and bring him away either dead or alive."

Imprudent for once in what he sought, John comported himself badly on being refused it. He wrote angrily to the Queen, accusing her of having been guided by Abigail, only for Anne to reply: "You wrong her most extremely . . . she knows nothing about it." Anne added in the same letter: "It is not to be wondered at you should be so incensed against poor Masham since the Duchess of Marlborough is so." And from fatigue as well as resentment, John had told Anne that at the end of the war he would quit the job he had just solicited for life. "I am sorry," said Anne, "for the resolution you have taken of quitting my service when the War is ended but I hope . . . you will be prevailed with to alter it."

Whatever the practical advantages of giving John his wish—increased prestige with his allies and enemies, additional stature in pressing on toward peace—the request was very plainly ill-founded, ill-timed, and, on its becoming known, ill-consequenced. It laid John open to charges of swollen ambition and to imputations of attempted dictatorship. All too many people were still alive who remembered Cromwell and the regime of Cromwell. Many remembered, too, how greatly Charles II feared the military power of Monk. But it was not only through analogies that Marlborough was injured: a war-weary nation had come to resent its principal warrior.

The situation between the Marlboroughs and Mrs. Masham now, too—in January of 1710—grew greatly inflamed. A crack regiment having become vacant, the Queen wrote to John desiring it be given to Abigail's brother, Colonel Hill. The implications were obvious. It did not merely betoken Abigail's favor with the Queen; it was quite plainly a maneuver to insult the Duke. Nor was it an insult only to the Duke, in whom as Captain General rested the power of appointments; it was equally an insult to every colonel who was Jack Hill's senior in service or superior in ability. It was like publishing, like indeed proclaiming, John's loss of credit with the Queen, and it must induce a measurable loss of confidence among the Allies.

John refused to make the appointment; and, hearing of his refusal and his determination not to give way, the Whigs promised him full support. So fortified, he had an audience of the Queen at which he pointed out not just the impropriety of appointing an officer with such feeble claims, but the unwiseness of risking disaffection in the army and the unfairness of Anne's treatment of himself. So far from yielding, a cold and hostile Anne at no point even softened: "You will do well," she said in terminating the audience, "to advise with your friends."

Reading the situation in its true light, John was prepared to pass from an official refusal to a personal ultimatum: Mrs. Masham must go, or he would. And indeed—as he intimated to the Whigs—did Abigail not go, presently they themselves must. John abruptly left London for Windsor, not attending a council of ministers that he himself had convoked, but this time, unlike two years earlier, no one among the Whigs made an issue of his absence, and the meeting ran its course. Despite their promise, the Whigs had failed to back him up.

Meanwhile, at Windsor, John wrote the Queen his ultimatum, concluding flatly with: "I hope that your Majesty will either dismiss Mrs. Masham or myself." But Godolphin, to whom John sent the letter, and most of the Whigs to whom Godolphin showed it, were so concerned with averting a rupture that they recommended a compromise. Somers went to plead Marlborough's case, and extol his services, to the Queen, who reserved judgment. Godolphin wavered. Sunderland, John's most vehement supporter, erred in the opposite direction, proposing to demand Abigail's dismissal of Parliament. And though actually both John and Sarah disapproved of their son-in-law's wild project, rumor had them both espousing it. The rumor, however, so agitated Anne that she sent for Somers to affirm her kindly feelings for the Duke and her hopes of demonstrating them when he came to town.

He refused the Whig pleas that he come; but did so far give way as to cut out of his letter to Anne the "either dismiss Mrs. Masham or myself." The letter now ended with mention of his being mortifyingly exposed to "the malice of a bedchamber woman." The Queen, who even before the letter reached her had abandoned the idea of Jack Hill's appointment, now feared that John, by continuing aloof at Windsor, might rouse Parliament, which might in turn open fire on Abigail. John, pending Abigail's dismissal, neither spoke nor moved. But his colleagues were not so wise: they deemed Anne's yielding over Jack Hill a real victory—

she would not soon again flout her commander-in-chief's authority. But they thought that if they pressed further, they might seem to be bullying the Queen and would rally the nation to her support. Moreover, they persuaded John to come back to London, where Anne was all smiles in receiving him. In fact, everyone smiled—John's colleagues for thinking they had triumphed, and Abigail's for knowing they had not. But John himself surmised how little had been gained and how much very likely had been forfeited. Pretty clearly, they had forfeited their last chance to dislodge Mrs. Masham, their one chance to remain in power.

In the next few months the Whigs proceeded to win an even more trifling battle on their way to losing the war. John in relation to Jack Hill was a conquering hero compared with Godolphin in relation to Dr. Sacheverell. This famous high-flying parson, seeking "martyrdom without peril," had preached a sermon advocating an extreme of non-resistance which implied that the 1688 Revolution— which the Whigs considered their very own—was illegal. He had in addition alluded to Godolphin (who much resented it) as Volpone. To avenge such treason embossed with slander, the Whigs felt the need of impeaching Sacheverell and asserting their strength. All they proved, however, was their lack of any.

Sacheverell's trial matters less for guilt than for gingerbread: Wren remodeled Westminster Hall, but even so, what with younger lords demanding eight seats apiece and the place jammed to the roof, the *bon ton* could not all get in. Colley Cibber complained that the trial was ruining the legitimate theater, and that lie-abed great ladies were up at dawn to be in on the show. But to many influential moderates—Shrewsbury, Somerset, Argyll—Sacheverell's at-

tempt to subvert the Constitution counted far less than their
own determination to dislodge the Junto, and though votes
enough were marshaled to find Sacheverell guilty, he was
given the lightest possible punishment—to do no preaching
for three years—and indeed his journey to a new living in
Shropshire was every step of the way a triumph. The Tories
rightly looked on all this as a moral victory, rightly looked
ahead from all this to a material one. For though the Whigs
might still control both Houses, the country itself—roused
now against Dissenters as once against Papists, and clamor-
ing more than ever now for peace—had grown violently
anti-Whig in feeling.

Anne, conscious of that feeling and very sympathetic toward it, took summary action. During the Parliamentary re-
cess in the spring of 1710, she dissolved the Ministry. If
audacious, her action was in every sense permissible: it was
still legitimate—as after the Walpole era it would never be
again—for the Crown to dismiss a Ministry commanding a
majority in Parliament. Indeed, the conception of a King's
or Queen's Ministry that should stand above politics was
then, and in certain quarters for a long while after, regarded
as a great ideal. (Actually it had been the arrangement under which John and Godolphin themselves had first governed.) The Queen, moreover—and such of her advisers as
Harley and Shrewsbury—intended no bold move, no mass
dismissal. A mass dismissal, what with John still of value and
Godolphin not quite sucked dry, was precisely what they
deprecated. Ministers, during the coming months, were not
only to be ousted one by one, but at each man's going, those
who remained were to be elaborately reassured. Nor was
this, at the moment, pure dissembling: Anne and her advisers, beyond definitely wanting to be rid of the Junto, were
not quite sure how far else it would be wise to go; of at

7

just what point, in curtailing Whig power, they might be bound in Tory chains.

In this spring, when there tottered a Ministry that would be quite destroyed by summer, there took place the most historic of all meetings between Anne and Sarah. Relations between the two were now quite beyond repair. Relations had actually, indeed, been broken off: Anne had made plain that she never wished to see Sarah again, and Sarah, to whom John had made it doubly plain, accepted the edict. But such acceptance was precisely what Sarah, in her rebellious heart and retorting mind, could never accept. In February, to be sure, she had got John to ask Anne that, whenever possible, she be allowed to stay in the country, and that, as soon as peace was made, she might surrender her offices to two of her daughters. Anne had cheerfully agreed to the first request, but said no more to the second than that she hoped the Duchess would continue in her service. Pressed later on the subject, Anne first disavowed any recollection of it, then desired to be "troubled" with it no further.

This was but one of many rebuffs that Sarah chafed under, and perhaps was one of many that she made remarks about in public. Her disrespectful language concerning the Queen came—doubtless much embroidered—to the Queen's knowledge, and the Queen's displeasure came back in time to Sarah. There was so much babble and buzz about it all that Sarah demanded an audience of Anne to defend herself against her detractors and denounce their gossip as lies. Anne, desiring that Sarah put what she had to say in writing —"which shall be answered without delay"—did everything possible to avoid an interview. Each of three several hours that the Duchess suggested, the Queen found impracticable; a fourth that Anne finally named she canceled on the plea of going to Kensington. But Sarah thereupon went after her there, sent in a page to beg the Queen to receive her, and sat waiting, as she put it, "like a Scotch lady with a petition, instead of a trusted and lifelong confidant." She sat waiting for a very considerable time, assuming—no doubt correctly —that the Queen was closeted with Abigail over whether to receive her. The afternoon had deepened into late evening when she was told at last to go in.

As Sarah entered, the Queen looked up to say that she had been just on the point of writing to her. Sarah protested that she had not come to be restored to favor, but only to vindicate herself of false charges, which she now began to reel off. "Whatever you have to say," Anne interrupted, "you may put it in writing." The Duchess again sought to clear herself. "Whatever you have to say," the Queen said again, "you may put it in writing." Sarah now asked to be vindicated of "some particular calumnies with which I have been loaded." The Queen so far relented as to listen with her face turned the other way; when Sarah quoted calumnies she was as incapable of uttering as of "killing her own children," the Queen answered that "without doubt there were many lies told." Sarah now begged know of Anne what, exactly, had given offense; but Anne fell back on a stipulation in Sarah's written request for an interview, that she only listen to the Duchess and need not answer her. "You desired no answer," said the Queen, "and you shall have none." When Anne now got up and moved toward the door, Sarah followed, expostulating. "You desired no answer," she was reminded, "and you shall have none." At this the overwrought and now weeping Duchess began making hysterical inquiries whether, throughout long years, she had ever played Anne false; making hysterical innuendoes that, had she but dissembled, she might have retained

Anne's favor. When the Queen appeared to be listening, Sarah rushed forward—or back—to the question of just what rankled in Anne's mind, and once more Anne replied: "You desired no answer, and you shall have none." As Sarah again launched forth, the same words came again from the Queen. Then "I could not conquer myself," Sarah confessed, "but said the most disrespectful thing I ever spoke to the Queen in my life: 'I am confident your Majesty will suffer for such an instance of inhumanity.'" "That will be to myself," answered the Queen, and went out of the room. Then Sarah went out too, the opposite way, and "I sat me down," she recorded, "in the long gallery to wipe my eyes before I came within sight of anybody," gaining sufficient control of herself, it was observed, to leave the palace "like a fury." A few days afterwards Anne wrote to Sarah, desiring the return of "all my strange scrawls," a request that Sarah ignored.

The most historic of their encounters was also their last; they never met again. And now Anne—just a week later, while John was at The Hague and Godolphin racing his horses—began that reconstituting of her Ministry which meant the end of the Whigs. She first got the Whig Marquis of Kent to give up being Lord Chamberlain on condition of becoming a duke, and bestowed the place on Shrewsbury. Shrewsbury was of worldly temper and moderate views, was indeed a kind of Whig, but he was not of the Whig politicos. He had been chosen and doubtless wooed and won by Harley; and his appointment, as John wrote, was the first hole in the dike. Very significantly, as Godolphin informed Anne, she had made the appointment without informing him or John of her intention. But despite Godolphin's protest and the Whig Ministry's dislike of Shrewsbury's joining it, there was no hint of real opposition.

Shrewsbury stayed, and, Shrewsbury staying, it was plain that other Whigs would go.

The "Proud Duke" of Somerset—like Shrewsbury, a sort of grandee independent—was now wooed and won [1] by Harley, and was chiefly responsible for the dismissal in June of Sunderland. In dismissing him, Anne offered him a pension of £3,000 a year; but he answered, with a probity that equaled his priggishness: "If I cannot have the honor of serving the country, I will not plunder it." His going caused noisy protestations from his fellow members of the Junto and other leading Whigs, but they were soon paying congratulatory calls on his Tory successor, Lord Dartmouth, whose appointment the Whigs had in fact agreed to. The sole action they took was to beg John not to resign the army because his son-in-law had been pitched out of the Cabinet.

John did not resign, nor Godolphin either. Instead, early in August, the Queen pitched out Godolphin too—in Trevelyan's words, "as a squire would discharge a cheating bailiff." On August 7, Godolphin, expressing—while in audience with the Queen—his difficulties over her loss of confidence in him, asked: "Is it the will of Your Majesty that I should go on?" Unhesitatingly she answered "Yes," only to dismiss him by letter that very night. The Ministry that bore, and still bears, his name, that had seen France humbled, England and Scotland joined, and Anne raised up to glory, came to an end without so much as a personal interview between Queen and First Minister. A certain Mr. Smith in some versions of what happened, a mere liveryman

---

[1] On his own terms. Somerset parleyed with "all the clandestine pomp of conspiracy," insisting that he come to Harley's house in a sedan chair with drawn curtains, which was to pass "unexamined" through the hall door.

in others, brought Godolphin the Queen's command to break his White Staff of office.

Harley was made Chancellor of the Exchequer at once, though not Lord Treasurer till the following spring. The Whigs who still remained, whatever their hopes of hanging on in conjunction with the emerging Harleyites, were one by one to be replaced by Tories. The wise, honorable Lord Chancellor Cowper,[2] the one Whig Queen Anne really liked, the man, too, whom Harley desired to keep in office—he might sway others toward the moderation Harley wished for—was the one Whig who refused to stay: he knew the Tories would force him out as soon as any powerful Tory coveted his place. In September, after five times refusing to let him resign, Anne could refuse no more, and the last Whig was gone from the Ministry. Now that it was entirely reconstituted, there followed a dissolution of Parliament and a new election. It appears to have been an exceptionally drunken[3] one, but in their cups or not, the voters could only create a Tory triumph. Nor were the Whigs, however shabbily or surreptitiously this one or that might be dished, entitled to rule any longer. Effectively though they had waged a war, they could not—now it was urgent—make a peace. Swift now could write to Stella: "The Queen passed by us with all Tories about her; not one Whig . . . and I have seen her without one Tory."

It was at just about this time that Swift entered the period of his greatest living fame and began exerting his extraordinary influence on public affairs. He had been coming for

[2] Of him Sarah wrote: "My Lord Cowper was the only Whig that behaved himself like a gentleman to me. He owned me when I was under a hurdle."

[3] "I am always drunk for a week," said one man of elections in general; indeed, he would not dream of voting for anyone who did not make him so.

years from Ireland to London to seek the remission of first
fruits of livings; he had moved in high Whig circles and
made friends of Addison and Steele; but in respect of the
Church he got nothing from Whig ministers, nor for himself
the Irish bishopric he coveted and thought he was put down
for. Harley and St. John, on their coming now to power,
better understood his worth as well as his nature. Both men,
as it happens, genuinely cared about knowing him, genuinely enjoyed dining and talking with him; while Swift
himself could have asked no higher wages than to fellow-
ship with such grandees. They won his heart, and with it his
genius: resenting the treatment he had been shown by the
Whigs (" Rot 'em for ungrateful dogs; I will make them
repent their usage"), he aligned himself vengefully with
the Tories, and in November of 1710 began writing his
scorching attacks in *The Examiner*. Nothing, in ferocity,
exceeded the attacks on John: [4] beyond being called hide-
ously grasping and avaricious and a would-be dictator, he
was portrayed as thinking himself the victim of the basest
British ingratitude. On this last head Swift executed one of
his most inspired strokes, drawing up a balance sheet of
what Rome expended—complete with sacrificial bull, laurel
crown, triumphal arch, and triumphal chariot—on a conquering general, all of which came to £994 11s. 10d.; and of
how much Britain—what with Woodstock, Blenheim, jewels, pictures, grants, and offices—had spent on Marlborough,
which came to £540,000. Was this "ingratitude"? [5]

Besides being excoriated in the press, John now, in one
small way after another, was insulted by Queen and Min-

[4] As in mendaciousness nothing surpassed Swift's making Sarah Godolphin's mistress.
[5] The Whigs in rebuttal wonderfully increased the damage by asserting that John had captured twenty-seven towns (worth £300,000 each,
or £8,100,000 in all), which left Britain £7,560,000 in debt to the Duke.

istry. Chiefly to incense Marlborough, the Duke of Argyll
was gazetted General of Infantry in the British army. Next,
when Lord Scarbrough proposed in the Lords that the
Duke be thanked for his victories, Argyll protested the motion, which Scarbrough, after further opposition, withdrew.
And when three of John's officers drank their commander's
health—and confusion to the new Government—they were,
for an almost nightly offense in the army, and with no hearing or trial, straightway cashiered.

A month later, in January 1711, came a far sharper blow:
Sarah was dismissed from all her Court employments. This
formal severance of all relations between Sarah and Anne
had been preceded and was attended by great and diverse
alarums. The Queen, who by now felt compulsively hostile
toward the Duchess and ached to be rid of every sign and
reminder of her, had been deterred only out of her need of
the Duke, her fear that were Sarah dismissed John would
resign. Sarah, aware of this one thread of safety, and fearing
it would be snapped as soon as John came victorious home
to England, now schemed on her own against being dismissed. She threatened to publish all Anne's early letters to
her, with their damaging or embarrassing comments and
confidences about William and Mary and other great public
figures. (This pretty maneuver was probably meant as no
more than a threat, since Sarah published nothing after her
dismissal.) Meantime, while St. John was calling Sarah "a
fury" and "a plague," *The Examiner* virtually branded her
a thief: she was accused of pocketing, from her various offices, some £20,000 a year. On Sarah's bringing this to the
notice of the Queen, Anne proffered her celebrated vindication: "Everybody knows," she remarked, "that cheating
is not the Duchess of Marlborough's crime."

At the beginning of 1711, John returned from the Conti-

nent, a man past sixty now, who showed the double strain
of hard military service abroad and of his wife's and his own
lowered credit at home. Of this last, it was important that
he have accurate knowledge. He was concerned for Sarah's
position not only as a deeply devoted husband, but as a
contestant in a political struggle and a commander who
must preserve his prestige throughout Europe. And Sarah
seems to have been sufficiently concerned for John to write
Anne a letter of extraordinary—of, for her, nothing less
than abject—humility. To keep her employments and thus
save "my Lord M—— from the greatest mortification he is
capable of, and avoid the greatest mischief in consequence
of it, to your Majesty and my country," she was ready "to
promise anything" Anne thought reasonable, and to do
nothing that might give Anne "the least . . . uneasiness."

On January 17, John had an audience of the Queen and
tendered her his wife's letter. At first Anne would not read
it, then did so with great reluctance, at last remarking: "I
cannot change my resolution." In a desperate hope that
Anne yet would, the Duke fell on his knees before her and,
putting his pride from him and his charm and persuasive-
ness to the touch, entreated that Sarah be retained. But
Anne, who surpassed in loathing what even John might
boast of art, refused: her honor demanded the Duchess go.
The Gold Key must in fact be brought to her within three
days. The Duke now begged that his wife be given ten; the
Queen in answer required the key in two. Till she had it,
she said, she would discuss no other business.

He went home to tell Sarah that they had lost. She in
turn—as some say, flinging the key to the floor—had him
convey it to the Queen that very night. Doubtless one reason why Sarah had wanted to keep her places was that Abigail should not get them; and Abigail, now, was made

7*

Keeper of the Privy Purse, but not Groom of the Stole, which went to the Duchess of Somerset, the heiress of the last of the Percy earls of Northumberland and "the best bred as well as the best born lady in England." The Rangership of Windsor Park, having been bestowed for life, Sarah was able to keep.

Anne, in dismissing Sarah in the face of John's husbandly and humiliating supplications, could not but know that she risked forcing him to resign. Perhaps, in her neurotic need to close her accounts with Sarah, she was beyond considering the price; perhaps, even more neurotically, she was willing to pay it. Or perhaps, in such a welter of perhapses, she suspected, surmised, had some obscure sixth sense that he would not resign. In any case, he did not. Not now—when he fell on his knees, aging, ailing, dismastered, out-of-favor—any more than in victorious if vexatious earlier days, would John resign. Not now, when his wife was being meanly stripped of office and after Godolphin had been insultingly pushed out of it—not now and not, as it happened, ever would the Duke of Marlborough resign. Why didn't he? The question clamors the louder from John's so constantly threatening that he might, so forcibly insisting that he would.

In actual fact, despite all the provocations John suffered and the threats and protests he made, there were yet many more valid reasons for choosing to remain than for deciding to retire. To be sure, a wholly rational and philosophic man of thought might make out an irrefutable case for retirement, might argue that John had achieved prodigious fame and amassed a princely fortune, had served his country as few men ever could—and against vast odds and in the face of stupendous obstacles. In the course of beating the French he had had—even in the best days—to shout down opposition at home; had had to plead with his allies abroad, had had indeed to trick them: winning victories was child's play compared with being given permission to win them. Now the minister who had been his right arm in England was gone, a hostile sovereign reigned, a hateful party governed, and in torment from headaches and earaches he must yet go on with the war—open to criticism, sure of complaint, whatever he might do. Whatever fresh laurels he still might win (the man of thought would argue) were as nothing to the obstructions and indignities he must face, to the mental strife and the bodily damage and the capital danger.

But whatever his meditations upon war and the waging of war, John was as little as possible a man of thought; was, in as full, fruitful a sense as history can boast, a man of action. War was his trade, and quick, fateful decisions his talent. The philosophic argument, however irrefutable, was wholly irrelevant. It was predicated of what Marlborough had done and not of what Marlborough was like, it rested on his achievement instead of his nature. It might well bear out every claim of reason, but it equally ignored every craving of temperament. It left wholly out of account what John was, what he might imagine he was, and what he desired to be.

To resign might, for example, be wise and sensible, might even be dignified, but it would certainly not be noble or magnanimous. Far nobler, certainly, to persist in the face of hardship, to set duty above happiness. Even nobler still to save England and Europe while enduring slaps and insults ill-suited to a bungling general, let alone an inspired one. All this John could honestly believe his duty, at whatever cost. But if there was truth in all this, the more rooted truth lay elsewhere. And the more rooted truth was itself

a tangle of impulses, a merging of needs—it was half volition and half vocation, half what made John great and half
what proved him human. The Duke of Marlborough would
not resign because, in the deepest sense, he loved his job; because, also, he had come to know, and need, and not be able
to dispense with power. In terms of the professional soldier,
there always persisted in John the creative excitement of
planning campaigns and fighting battles. One man's Sistine
Chapel is another man's Blenheim; it is as—shall we say
simple?—as that. As I have said elsewhere of Marlborough,
there is a valid sense in which those who conquer by the
sword shall perish by putting up the sword. Here, moreover, desire was in league with duty: at a time of crisis, to
withhold one's services and see things botched is not simply
unprofessional—it is unpatriotic. John's professional conscience, furthermore, was a very tender one. He looked
after his men as scrupulously as if he loved them—perhaps
even more, for love shows feeling sooner than thought. He
constantly—to be near his men—exposed himself to enemy
fire. He not merely left nothing to chance; he left as little
as possible to others. He ran the show, and the most famous
of all tributes to his mode of action, Addison's

Rides in the whirlwind and directs the storm,

can be applied to less momentous occasions on less dramatic terms. Retiring, he might have felt and said:
"Othello's occupation's gone." Continuing as a warrior, he
could say—however soaked with blood the war: *"Dieu me
pardonnera, c'est mon métier."*

But bound up with the professional's creative pleasure
there was clearly the commander's sense—and need—of
power. And of more than military power, for whether directly, or by means of Godolphin, or of Sarah, or of Anne,

John, in order to run the war, had needed to rule the nation. But military power stood foremost, and however patriotically motived, one who endlessly bewails the burdens of a commander-in-chief does not, from patriotism or prudence alone, ask—most imprudently—to be appointed commander-in-chief for life. Less relevant here than any "desire" on John's part for power was his deeply ingrained habituation to it. We are sufficiently aware that power corrupts, rather less so that the need for power conditions. And doubtless the wish to hold on to it will increase in proportion as it becomes threatened: resigning now, John might appear forced out where earlier he would have obviously withdrawn. And, whatever his position at home, so long as he retained his command he could hold his head high abroad. Swift's and other men's libels might stab John "to the heart"; yet he hung on, he had still the stomach to endure. I do not think the need for power diminishes what he was: it simply confirms what he was not. Sir Winston and some of John's other champions protest too much—not only more than is permitted, but more than is required. The Duke was no scoundrel, but though he had preeminently the patience of one, still less was he a saint.

There were perhaps two other factors involved in John's never resigning. The first concerns the temper—one might almost call it the technique—of the age, which had men loudly protesting everything—their love, their loyalty, their duty, which made men depreciate what they conspired for, disparage what they coveted. Thus, even where quite privately conveyed, John's words of protest are conventional enough. Nor is the matter one of words alone. The struggle, during that age, for power was constant and arduous and ugly, and John, though more grandly, was not much differently circumstanced than most of his contemporaries.

The buffetings, even the betrayals, must have come to seem like part of the game, and the rewards (as he had particular reason to know) might make them worth bearing. Surely just giving up his huge income as commander-in-chief would have made John unhappy.[1]

There was, finally, Sarah. He cared for her passionately; no other woman, once he married, ever faintly mattered; she generally enjoyed his confidences; she always pleaded his cause; theirs was "the most famous love match in England." Nothing told of John is better remembered than that, coming home from the wars, he would possess Sarah without stopping to take off his boots. But one must admit all the same that she was a difficult and, in these years of her fall from favor and her change of life, an often intolerable woman. Again and again, to be sure, John professed how above all else he yearned to live quietly apart with her. But if one not just constantly protests one's weariness of war, but endlessly professes a desire for wife and home, and still does not exchange the one for the other, something beyond the claims of artistry and ambition, something not military at all, must enter in too. As a warrior, Edward Thomas said of John: "he was under nobody, not even the Duchess." Counterpoised against John's sense of power on the battlefield was very likely a presentiment of a losing struggle for power in the home. All too frequently as it was—in the matter of the Queen, of the Whigs, of Abigail, of Sunderland as a prospective son-in-law, of Sunderland as a prospective Secretary of State—wherever his wife pressed or nagged or upbraided him, "his submission to her was a proverb." In his love John was instinctively wise as well as ardent, and by living much away from Sarah he helped preserve that love to the end.

[1] John also, knowing how sick Anne was, may have wanted control of the Army in any Succession wrangle should she die.

XI

HENCE, in the spring, John went back to the Continent in the service of the Allies. Though, unknown to him, peace negotiations with France were about to begin, and though he was no longer a kind of Minister, but "General only," his position was made tolerable enough. Anne, in February, had written to the States General, praising John's ability and asserting her support. But all too soon there were disappointments. St. John commandeered five of his British battalions to send to Quebec; Eugene, a month after joining John in the Low Countries, was ordered with all his men to the Rhine; and John, besides losing the one colleague he valued and trusted, had now no such army as the French had under Villars. Nowhere—not in Vienna or in London or at The Hague—could he find ways to bolster his strength, and the hideous headaches, which produced sick stomach as well, became constant. An air of dejection and even despondency hung over him and all he did; and his army—and Villars too—saw in him a commander shorn of all brilliance and composure.

But though truly enough out of sorts, John was yet making military capital of it. In that summer's campaigning he outfoxed Villars early and late. Thus, for one example, wanting the key French river fort of Arleux demolished so that he could cross the stream, but realizing that if he captured Arleux and demolished it himself he would reveal his plans, John first captured and fortified it, then left it poorly defended, so that Villars won it back and demolished it in high glee. His ruse succeeding, Marlborough went about looking chagrined, became indeed ostentatiously peevish. Next he let it leak out that despite inferior forces he would attack Villars, and was even observed reconnoitering the enemy lines. The French were jubilant, John's own men aghast. They thought, wrote Captain Parker, that affronts and ill usage "might have turned his brain, and made him desperate." "The sun set," writes Sir Winston, "upon two hundred thousand men who expected to be at each other's throats at daybreak." But tattoo no sooner beat than orders ran through Marlborough's camp to strike all tents immediately; and in half an hour or less the entire army began marching eastward in the moonlight. It was the occasion for that charming and celebrated command, "The Duke desires that the infantry will step out." All night they moved on, in a sixteen-hour march during which many men dropped in exhaustion and others died of it; but those who kept going traversed thirty-five miles and were in position to besiege Bouchain, which surrendered a month later. The successful feint, the spectacular march by moonlight, the passing the French lines without the loss of a single man in battle have been acclaimed the most brilliant of all Marlborough's strategic strokes. Certainly John himself looked on this campaign, the last he ever waged, with a particular pride. Indeed, the tapestries for Blenheim Palace, whose weaving he supervised, celebrate Bouchain above Ramillies and Blenheim. And with Bouchain, incidentally, John won the only victory of the year.

He was to have no part in ending the war whose outcome he had predestined. In fact, the Bouchain campaign was merely to serve as an added bargaining-point in the peace negotiations. Bouchain is a tapestry triumph only: John was soon to be as bereft of power as Sarah. She meanwhile, though banished the Court and stripped of office, had neither slunk away nor fallen into a decline. In the political sphere she did what few things she could to rally the routed Whigs, and at the next election of the Bank of England she sufficiently intrigued—which may mean bribed —to get her chosen Whigs elected. She had moved into Marlborough House and had set up as hostess there, with considerable though seldom favorable publicity. It is not easy to ascertain how popular she was, or what friends she had, or who even among the Whigs came to see her.[1] For she was shunned now for worse reasons than being dropped by the Queen, though—with her rages and rancors—for much the same reasons as the Queen's in dropping her. Before John set forth on his final campaign, a Whig ball had been planned at Marlborough House on the night of the Queen's birthday, but when John discovered that it was being looked upon as a kind of spite party, or as "vying with the Court," he had it canceled. Sarah, all the same, invited several ladies to come that night to "a dancing"; but the reaction was still so unfavorable that word now went out "that there would be no dancing"—though word now went out too that the Duchess still would be glad to see anyone who might care to come. Who came is not told.

After John set out for the Continent, Sarah left London for St. Albans, where, wrote one contemporary, she "kept open house" and where, wrote another, she "knew when to lay aside all state and ceremony." But as was also remarked, though one of her entertainments was "very fine and noble" and might earlier have had great *réclame*, it now came to nothing. Now too there was a last rub with Anne, in some ways the least creditable of any. While sending in a statement of her accounts, Sarah claimed for the past nine years the annual pension of £2,000 that Anne had offered in 1702 and that Sarah had then refused. Indeed, Sarah actually now took it upon herself to deduct £18,000 from the

[1] Tories on the lookout noted only Cowper.

accounts themselves. The Queen, who was never mean-minded about money, let it pass.

There was also the vexatious business of Blenheim Palace. It had been building a good many years now, but was very far from built. The irritations had mounted. There was always the fundamental quarrel between Sarah and her architect: where she wanted, as soon and sensibly as possible, a home, Vanbrugh—with time and cost no matter—desired more, even, than a princely habitation. This conflict in aim between the two was aggravated by an equal unyielding-ness of manner, for Vanbrugh had an artist's obstinacy to match Her Grace's highhandedness. Sarah incessantly meddled, so much so that Godolphin wrote of it to the Duke; she fretted and grumbled, too, over the expense, though the Government was footing the bill. Already some time back, it is true, money had begun running short, and as time went on, tempers grew shorter. Though Vanbrugh might haunt Blenheim "like a ghost from the time the workmen leave off at six o'clock, till 'tis quite dark . . . studying how to make [it] the cheapest as well as (if possible) the best house in Europe," Sarah could only suspect that Vanbrugh dallied out of self-interest and procrastinated from malice.

In the midst of all this, there arose the problem of the ruined Manor of Woodstock: Vanbrugh found that Rosamund's Bower might be retained—and lend romantic appeal to Blenheim—for much less money than it could be demolished. But Sarah, who grudged having to spend any money at all, and thought Vanbrugh's real reason was his wanting to live in the Manor House himself, objected loudly. Indeed, she got Godolphin—than whom there was scarcely a worse aesthetic judge in all England—to come look at the ruin and decree that it must go.

She not only gained her point; she became more convinced that at all points Vanbrugh was extravagant, dilatory, mendacious—sending "false" drawings, suggesting that something would cost "only" another £100, insisting (when the Duke wasn't in England to bear him out) that certain gardens and courts had not been part of the original estimate. And then, forsooth, he could one day write: "I believe when the whole is done, both the Queen, yourself, and everybody (except your personal enemies) will easier forgive me laying out fifty thousand pounds too much, than if I had laid out a hundred thousand too little"—this at a time when the Queen had turned against the Duchess and doubtless regretted she had authorized any expense at all! Sarah, indeed, fussy over every delay, fumed and haggled over every penny.

When, on Godolphin's dismissal from office, work was halted at Blenheim, Vanbrugh sought at least to shield from frosts and winds what work had already been done. Going there two months later and finding that Sarah had written the contractors "to put a stop at once to all sorts of work," Vanbrugh insisted—both for the sake of the workmen, who could not summarily be laid off, and for the sake of Blenheim, which could be disastrously damaged—that some work still go forward. At length the contractors were forced to show Vanbrugh a postscript in Sarah's letter forbidding them to pay any attention to anything he might say or do. Vanbrugh could only appeal from the Duchess to the Duke, who upheld him. And for once, indeed, Sarah wrote to Vanbrugh, not only freely admitting she had been in the wrong, but acknowledging herself to be substantially in his debt. She would not have been Sarah had she not interjected a touch of reproof—in this case that each should forgive the other!—but there is about her here, as on other occasions, a kind of harridan honesty and directness. She had nothing less than a genius for misreading facts, but she perhaps never deliberately misinterpreted them.

And indeed the whole Blenheim situation was confused just now, and Sarah's relation to it—with the Queen, this January, dismissing her her posts at Court—rather undefined. Yet during January work at Blenheim was resumed, some £7,000 due on a warrant of Godolphin's being honored, with Harley (now Earl of Oxford) inquiring how much more would be needed to complete the job. Vanbrugh, who had already spent £200,000, thought he could finish work on the house and grounds for £87,000 more. Harley, who had been led to believe the cost would be far greater, received Vanbrugh's statement very amiably, promising him £20,000 at once, and more thereafter. (Sarah felt—correctly, it would seem—that Harley had arranged for the £20,000 as one way to keep John from resigning.)

Whether the Queen would consent to spend the further sums required seemed, at the moment, very doubtful. Not only was Sarah in Anne's deepest and most settled disfavor generally, but when, not long before, she had been asked by the Queen to vacate her rooms at St. James's—the message was not happily worded, and reeked of Abigail—Sarah had proceeded to take with her, in departing, the very brass locks off the doors. The Queen, overweight and gouty though she was, had gone to look at the vengefully vacated apartments, and was so furious over the Duchess's behavior that she vowed not to go on with John's house with Sarah dismantling hers, and refused to sign Harley's warrant for the £20,000. The mingy farce of the doorknobs threatened briefly to put a tragic halt to Blenheim, but Harley—aware among other things that to abandon the palace might create too much sympathy for its intended occupants—eventually got the Queen to sign. So, for a time, the building proceeded.

But work was to be halted again by an event of great magnitude, which saw out the year that Sarah's downfall had ushered in. In the autumn, John had come back victorious from the wars to an England already far advanced in peace-making. The peace negotiations had been conducted with the greatest secrecy, the Duke being no part of the secret, but one of those rather it was to be most urgently kept from. So far as the desire for peace went, not just the Tories but England generally craved it, and in one good form or another might have had it for some years past. As for John, become now the great symbol of warmongering, the Government stood ready to denounce him the moment it should have no further need of him. For a long while he had been not at all acceptable to the Queen and the Ministry; he had only been indispensable. They might allow, to be sure, that at one time he had more or less saved Europe, but that went back years, after all, to 1704 or so, and here it was—or would be tomorrow—1712. So, under date of December 31, with the Queen in attendance, it was inscribed on the books of the Council:

> Being informed that an information against the Duke of Marlborough was laid before the House of Commons by the commissioners of the public accounts, Her Majesty thought fit to dismiss him from all his employments, that the matter might undergo impartial investigation.

But before asking whither this carried the Marlborough fortunes, we must turn back to what led up to it. We must touch again on that turbulent stealth which half characterizes the age. The Whig manner of waging war had been politically as nothing compared with the present Tory manner of negotiating peace. The first feelers and overtures, begun in the summer of 1710, were as unofficial as they were clandestine. Gaultier, a French priest in London who was acting as a French agent, had gone to France on behalf of Harley, Shrewsbury, and Lord Jersey, to open very private and very secret negotiations. Nothing was committed to paper, but Gaultier at length brought back a proposal of Louis XIV's which was really the broad outline of the Peace. This the Queen laid before the Cabinet, and it was at this Cabinet meeting that St. John, who is usually credited with the whole negotiation but in truth knew nothing of it for some nine months, first got wind of the matter. Thereafter, he controlled it completely. Anne subsequently, on St. John's advice, sent Matthew Prior, whose diplomacy was as neat as his verses, with Gaultier to Paris to negotiate further, and there were further negotiations still in England. Many ticklish matters had to be ironed out: the Pretender could not stay in France; the French Bourbons could not stay in Spain. But the most astonishing thing in all this, and the thing that most astonished the French, was that Harley and St. John were quite prepared to ditch their Allies and negotiate a peace on their own. It was just this, of course, that had occasioned so much secrecy, with no ally but Holland aware of the negotiations, and with Marlborough kept in ignorance till the French-English preliminaries had been signed.[2]

When the peace terms became known, there was enraged indignation from the Allies; and over the peace terms, at

[2] Actually the whole story gradually leaked out: John himself knew all about it many weeks before it was made public.

this juncture, the disaffected Nottingham Tories, in union with the Whigs, had a very real chance to defeat the Ministry. The Ministry knew it was in trouble, and the Queen was in a panic over how to proceed. The Ministry went to work, however: it got Swift to write down the Whigs; it coerced the Queen into a famous action; and it set about discrediting Marlborough. A very Tory House-of-Commons Commission of Accounts, investigating the Godolphin Ministry's "thirty-five millions unaccounted for," brought up the matter of John's receiving a commission, "for his own use," on all army bread contracts and a percentage from the pay of foreign troops. John, once the matter became public, wrote to the Commissioners pointing out that the bread money had, since "before the Revolution," been an acknowledged perquisite of the commander-in-chief, and that he had applied every penny of it to the secret service. As for the 2½ per cent of foreign soldiers' pay, that, beyond going into the secret service, bore the Queen's warrant. We shall revert to the ethical aspect of the perquisites later; here it is only necessary to discuss the political angle. Obviously, if John—who disapproved of the peace terms—was going to use his influence to block the Ministry's peace, the Ministry would in turn seek to blacken the Duke's good name. As an obstacle in their path he must plainly be removed.

The Ministry were themselves hard pressed. There might be strong support in the Commons, but in the Lords it was touch and go, and it was shilly-shally and shift with the Queen. Things came to a head when, as the Lords were moving thanks for the Queen's Speech, Nottingham offered an amendment disruptive of the Ministry's peace terms "that no peace could be safe or honorable to Great Britain, or Europe, if Spain and the West Indies were allotted to any branch of the house of Bourbon." John supported this amendment, and upon division the Ministry, rather than winning as they had supposed by 10, were defeated by 12.

Harley, writing of this unlooked-for overturn, set it down to John's placing himself at the head of the Whigs and such others as "promised to screen him from the discoveries" of the Commissioners of Accounts. And the repudiated Ministry was indeed in danger of falling, only that the Commons rejected the Nottingham amendment the same day that the Lords sustained it, and a sadly wavering Queen at last mustered the courage to sustain her Government. "Poh! poh! it will be all right," an unperturbed Harley told an agitated Swift. And Harley helped make it right by straightway proceeding ruthlessly against John. On the very night of the division, a letter went off to inform the Dutch that John was to be deprived of his command. The actual doing required a little time, for Harley had to rouse the Queen to act. His purposes required, indeed, that she act twice: not only dismiss John, but create twelve peers to make sure the peace proposals would pass the Lords. The Queen raised no objection to the peerages, but in the matter of dismissing Marlborough, though no less willing, she was somewhat more hesitant. After all, there might *be* no Peace, and might yet be more campaigns. To get past this fear, the Ministry had to breed in Anne a fear of a different kind: the feeling that, with John at their head, the Whigs might somehow capture the Government—nay, the country—and set up an atheist republic, with Marlborough a second Cromwell and herself a second Charles. Charles's granddaughter was by no means swayed by that single danger alone, but it seems to have proved a useful clincher. On December 30, Marlborough

appeared at Court, where there were no Whigs to befriend
him, and was completely shunned. The next day took place
the Cabinet meeting that records the Queen's dismissal of
him, and that night she dismissed him personally by letter.
Its contents perished when John, in one of his rare rages,
threw the letter on the fire.

The next day, New Year's Day 1712, the *Gazette* announced both John's dismissal (Ormonde succeeding him)
and the creation of the twelve peers,[3] one of them Abigail
Masham's husband. It took great persuasion to make Anne
ennoble Mr. Masham: she did not approve of making Abigail into a "great lady." As a peeress, the Queen felt, Abigail
would take offense at such duties as having to lie on the
floor. But of all that was said of these events in a buzzing,
tattling England, nothing perhaps signifies so much as
what Louis XIV remarked in France: "The affair of dis-
placing the Duke of Marlborough will do all for us we
desire." As for the charges by which the Duke was displaced, though they were patently a political maneuver,
they leave an ethical residue that needs to be analyzed. On
the score of the $2\frac{1}{2}$ per cent (totaling more than £280,000)
from the pay of foreign troops, this—as the Duke could
show, and as we have said—was an established custom, one
authorized indeed by the Queen, and the money, beyond
being expended on the secret service, was so used in lieu of
any official secret-service grant. Since John had followed
traditional practice while nowhere indulging in personal
gain, there can be no relevant moral indictment.

---

[3] The whole thing led to much town gossip and Parliamentary josh-
ing. When the twelve peers took their seats, Wharton rose and inquired
whether they would vote by their foreman. Interestingly enough, the
revolutionary Tory maneuver of creating peers to put through legisla-
tion became in after days a Liberal club for beating the Tories into sub-
jection.

The matter of the £63,000 that during nine years John received from bread contracts is not on quite the same footing. Here also John's defense was that he had used the money for secret intelligence. But even so, this hardly justifies the manner by which he obtained it: "Sir Solomon Medina," wrote Swift, "paid him £6,000 a year to have the employment of providing bread for the army"—which even in 1712 could justly, however vindictively, be called a bribe. Nor is there quite such good reason to feel sure that John diverted all the money, or even most of it, into secret-service channels; it is quite possible that he feathered his own already very downy nest. His relative vindication is that what today would surely be termed corruption in his own day passed muster: it had been done by his predecessors for a generation; everyone presumably took for granted that it was being done; indeed, John's principal accuser, St. John, had just (in the matter of the Quebec expedition) done it himself; and it was to be done again by John's immediate successor, the Duke of Ormonde. Even so, the ethics of it must have been recognized as dubious: Sarah, in a fairly analogous situation, came to condemn—and abandon—the long-established sale of places at Court.

But a Ministry whose life depended on achieving peace would have somehow contrived to indict anyone who constituted a threat to the peace terms. And indeed, unless Marlborough were discredited, the peace terms must be. Many, even, of those who favored the Peace, and one, even, who had virulently denounced the Duke were appalled by his dismissal. Swift had to confess that "we have had constant success in arms while he commanded," and to concede that "the Queen and Lord Treasurer mortally hate the Duke of Marlborough, and to that he owes his fall," and could only conclude: "I do not love to see personal resentment mix with public affairs." [4]

Hardly had John been dismissed when Prince Eugene arrived in London. He came—as it happened, in vain—to try to improve Austria's strained relations with the Queen and to stave off action that would nullify the Grand Alliance. Harley and St. John were by no means happy to have such a friend—and advocate—of Marlborough's in England, and had tried to keep him from coming. His visit proved the sensation of the season. So many distinguished callers poured into his house as to crack the anteroom floors; at the Opera, where he went with John, he was twice huzza'd by a rabble addicted to booing; and at the Earl of Portland's great dinner, no servants waited at table—their places were all bespoke by gentlemen. Eugene appeared everywhere with John to accentuate his regard for him, and as the Prince would do nothing to discredit the Duke, the Prince must himself be discredited. Rumors were actually started that the two men were in a plot whereby Eugene would set fire to London, after which John would make off with the Queen. But nothing more sinister ensued than that Anne summoned Eugene and presented him with a diamond-encrusted sword, and that Eugene exchanged some furtive, and quite fruitless, visits with the incorrigibly devious Harley. Earlier, at a dinner, Harley had toasted the Prince as the greatest general of the age. "If that is so," Eugene answered, "I owe it to your lordship." Indeed, the Prince's retorts in defense of his friend are the only lasting memorial of his visit. On another occasion when Eugene

[4] The Whigs rallied round John and, searching for a parallel to his fate, brought forth the name of Belisarius. When Sarah asked Bishop Burnet to enlarge on the allusion, and he spoke of Justinian's mistreatment of his general, she then asked what had been the cause. The Bishop is said to have answered: "Because he had a brimstone of a wife."

was shown a libel declaring that Marlborough had been "once fortunate," he replied that there could be no higher praise, seeing that he had been always successful.

Meanwhile the peculation charges were being made ready for debate in the Commons. The Ministry were aware of the difficulties involved, not simply because of Marlborough's popularity with the masses, but because of the nature of his defense and the prestige of some of his defenders: the Paymaster of the Forces, for example, had made known that he would support the Duke. Despite loud cries of impeachment—which was as far as the Commons could go; they could not punish a peer—there was every desire for some kind of deal. The Government, concerned less for an outright conviction than for hearings that should achieve all the damage of one, were prepared to soften their censure in proportion as Marlborough would weaken his defense. But John would not accept a kind of pardon in exchange for pleading a kind of guilt. He rather thought at first of appearing and speaking in his own behalf, but, being dissuaded, prepared a detailed and sufficiently cogent answer to the charges, which was not at once made public. As for the actual proceedings in the Commons, the Duke was censured, by a big vote, on both charges. Here the matter was allowed to rest. There was no impeachment, and no attempt at one, and had there been, it might have proved embarrassing—what with the very Ministers who had just got John censured authorizing Ormonde to accept the same commissions that John had been censured for.

In June, John performed his final public action during the Queen's lifetime: he protested, most unavailingly, the terms brought forward in Parliament for a separate peace between Great Britain and France. Thereafter, though

hardly on the long-sought-for terms, he could live privately
with Sarah. He and Sarah spent this summer of 1712 at
St. Albans, where they observed the anniversary of Blenheim with a great Whig feast, and where the Duke set up
on the bowling-green the superb tent he had so long campaigned in: it drew large crowds at a charge (not too unfairly derided in the Tory press) of 6d. per person. But
despite friendly neighbors, and solicitous visitors, and
sixpenny sightseers, the summer somehow drooped and
flagged. Among the house guests, indeed, had been someone mortally ailing, whom Sarah tended and nursed, and
whose death in September ended the truest and warmest
friendship of John and Sarah's life. Godolphin died, with
his last breath importuning Sarah never to "forsake" the
young Robert Walpole. He was buried in the Abbey, but
not before his body had lain for three weeks in the Jeru-
salem Chamber till enough Whig Knights of the Garter—
what with the recalcitrance of Tory ones—could be assembled to bear the pall. He died poor, and "what he left
at his death," as Sarah wrote, "showed that he had been,
indeed, the nation's treasurer and not his own."

It was during the weeks that followed that John decided
to leave England, and late in November he set out with the
smallest of retinues for Dover. Fifty thousand pounds preceded him to The Hague, to enable them to live if, as Sarah
wrote, "the Stuart line were restored." She, it was decided,
should follow him a little later: there was much to arrange.
He himself, after waiting a week for favorable winds,
crossed—an ordinary citizen, in an ordinary packet boat—
to Ostend.

Why he went has never been altogether satisfactorily
explained; reasons are equally many for his choosing to go
or being asked to leave. The theory, however, that Harley

did not want him in England for fear of his influence there, and got him out through such threats as exposing his correspondence with the Pretender, scarcely seems to fit. It is true that at this time Harley met John—as Harley preferred to meet anyone at almost any time—in secret, and furtively conveyed to him a passport from the Queen; and motives, even documented motives, are not wanting. But at most Harley's wish was brother to John's own thought: John himself, for going, had good reasons and to spare. At home he was officially in disgrace; abroad he still was looked upon with honor. With an English election coming up next year, he might well become a target for obloquy; and certainly, so long as he supported the Whigs, he must be impugned by Anne and the Tories. Further, on the peculation charges against him he might—the more if he stayed in England— be found liable for as much as £250,000; he might be forced to meet some of the expenses of Blenheim; conceivably, he might even be in a certain peril—on lesser charges Walpole had recently been sent to the Tower. The nub, in any case, is why he should want to stay. Even on the one palpable and indisputable English tribute to his genius, even on Blenheim Palace, a restraining hand was now laid: the Queen, during the summer, had stopped work there.

Once out of the country, John found an immense change: on his landing at Ostend there were salvos and salutes; at Antwerp there were the honors accorded to kings; everywhere there were crowds and attentions, and in Flanders the fashionable remark of the moment was "Better be born in Lapland than in England." It had been intended that Sarah should follow John to the Continent inside a few weeks; but she did not leave England till the beginning of February. John's letters in the interval reveal his loneliness and make plain that he had expected her

sooner: it may be that, with business and domestic matters
to settle, she was really prevented from coming. But it is
clear that only her feelings for John induced her to come
at all. That she did agree to leave England, or that he had
had to beg her to, argues as much as anything how much
John wanted—or needed—to go. Preferring, as she put it,
an English cottage to a palace abroad—to be sure, she had
never lived in a cottage—she had not been out of the country since going to Holland in 1679 in the suite of the Duchess of York. She left, now, with some ceremony, giving
several friends diamond rings "worth," said Swift, "two
hundred pounds apiece." There was also a certain joy
among her enemies. Swift thought the Queen's speech
opening Parliament that year should have begun: "In order
to my quiet and that of my subjects, I have thought fit to
send the Duchess of M. after the Duke."

Crossing from Dover to Ostend, Sarah finally joined John
at Maestricht, whence soon after they made their way into
Germany. She was an attentive traveler, and though not the
harsh critic she had been in England, was still on occasion
sufficiently critical. Thus she remarks that she could conceive no possible reason for atheism "if the Priests . . . did
not act in the manner that they do in these parts"—systematically extorting money from the poor. She was in fact decidedly anti-Catholic, noticing "in one Church . . . 27
jolly-face priests" with nothing to do; and remarking elsewhere—of the religious processions—that there was a "folly
for almost every day in the year." But most of her spleen
was at the expense of the England she had quitted; of what
she noted on the Continent she was usually admiring:

'Tother day we were walking upon the road, and a
gentleman and his lady went by us in their chariot who

we had never seen before, and after passing us with the usual civilities, in half a quarter of an hour or less they bethought themselves and turned back, came out of their coach to us, and desired that we would go into their garden, which was very near that place, and which they think, I believe, a fine thing, desiring us to accept of a key. This is only a little taste of the civility of people abroad, and I could not help thinking that we might have walked in England as far as our feet would have carried us before anybody that we had never seen before would have lighted out of their coach to have entertained us. . . .

All the same, she had neither forgotten England nor despaired of returning to it. In London, Marlborough House was being decorated and "I am very desirous," Sarah wrote, "of having it finished." Indeed, whatever the "civility of people" abroad, Sarah longed increasingly for the scenes of home, and she was anything but philosophical about being "forced to live the rest of my life in these durty Countrys." "Living abroad," again, "makes one very indifferent whether one's life be long or short"; and it was all the worse for someone speaking "nothing but English." At Frankfurt, where they spent two months, they saw Prince Eugene, as well as two Electors who came expressly to salute the Duke. So far from home, she insisted she was not at all disturbed "that a thousand lies are set about of me"; whoever, she wrote, read such screeds as The Examiner "would write the screeds if they could," and consequently do not "add to one's enemies." Letters from England told Sarah how the Jacobite Lady Masham and the Hanoverian Duchess of Somerset battled for favor with the Queen, and how intense was the scheming to bring in—when the ailing

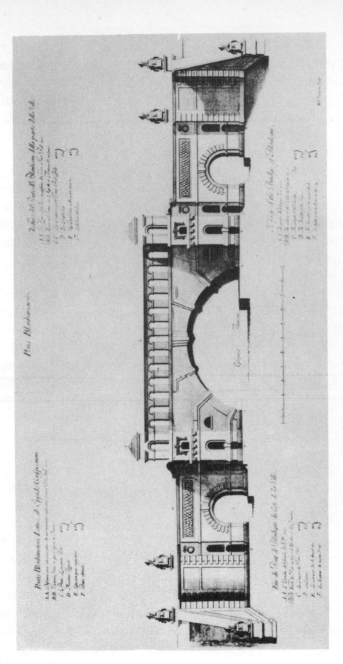

Blenheim Bridge

Blenheim

Queen should die—the Pretender. In letters back, Sarah haggles over tradesmen's bills from England—the paneling of a coach "lined with green"; or has to confess that, dismal as England is, it is the only place where one can safely invest one's money; or reminds her man of business that, if she survives all the horrors and calamities she foresees, he has promised her one of his cottages. Or she offers to buy his wife some lace, adding—Sarah-like—"I will take as much care to serve her . . . as I did the Queen, whom I had the honor to save a hundred thousand pounds in nine years, which I can prove to anybody."

From Frankfurt—"the best town one can be in abroad," despite its "intolerable" stoves—the Marlboroughs proceeded to Antwerp. "Like sick people," wrote the restless Duchess, "I am glad of any change." While they were at Antwerp, in March of 1714, came news of the death from smallpox of their daughter Elizabeth, the Countess of Bridgewater. The news—"the greatest blow . . . since . . . the death of Lord Blandford"—made John drop his head on the mantelpiece and lose consciousness. "The loss of my poor dear child," wrote Sarah, "is indeed very terrible to me," but "one ought to remember the other blessings which are yet left," and the poor girl herself "is happier . . . than in such a world as this." In March, too, the Queen fell seriously ill. The fierce, fomenting drama of the Succession—in which John, for being an exile, was not less in his way an actor—was at its highest pitch of stealthiness and suspense. John still played a kind of double role—was still making polite obeisances to the Pretender, doubtless just in case he should succeed, which the Pretender prettily acknowledged, doubtless on the remote chance that John still might prove of use. But this did not even constitute a speaking part for John; it was merely a studied bit of pantomime, a series of hat-doffings and genuflections and bows. The Duke's real allegiance, the Duke's remaining energies, were all for Hanover.

Indeed, as early as December 1713, John had had military orders from the Electress of what to do should the Queen die, and it was to be nearer the center of things that John went from Frankfurt to Antwerp. Though not so bold as to join a rather conspiratorial Whig group then organizing, by the late spring of 1714 he had decided—which was all in all much bolder—to return home. In June he sent word to the Elector of Hanover (the Electress Sophia had just died) that he thought "being in England" would prove more useful than "continuing abroad."

His actual motives for going back remain quite as unprobed as those for coming away, for though the Queen was sick, she had been so often sick there was no assurance whatever she would die, hence that the Tory Ministry—however shaky—would fall. Perhaps a good enough reason is that he yearned for home; a much more certain one is that Sarah did. Her feelings are so vigorously conveyed in her letters to outsiders that they must have been incessantly rammed home in her conversation with John. To be in England again, she confessed on the eve of returning, she would "even submit to Popery." By mid-July all was fixed for the journey to Ostend; once there—Sarah hated being for long on the sea—they must await a fair wind to Dover. They were still at Ostend, "in a very clean house," on July 30; they did not reach Dover, in fact, till August 1, and there they learned that Queen Anne had died earlier that day.

TAILPIECE
TO THE REIGN OF
QUEEN ANNE

WITH Queen Anne's death had ended an era in every way the antithesis of the Queen herself. There had seldom been a more stolid woman or more impatient age; a duller woman or an age more brilliant. During the twelve years she reigned, England was restored to its old Elizabethan stature, subduing France, reconstituting Europe, winning substantial new territories in America, and becoming—what would prove its real passport to future greatness—absolute mistress of the seas. At home, Pope had begun writing its poetry and Swift and Defoe its prose; Vanbrugh, along with Farquhar, was still its playwright, as he was its architect with Hawksmoor and Wren. Newton as much dominated the world of thought as Marlborough the world of action. Those twelve years gave form, where they did not give birth, to the daily newspaper and the periodical essay, the coffeehouse and the penny post. For writers they proved an almost unexampled era in politics and worldly affairs—Steele became an M.P., Prior an ambassador; Addison, already an Under-Secretary, was on the road to becoming a Secretary of State; while in political journalism Defoe became a kind of spy and Swift a kind of scorpion. Perhaps no other sovereign can lay claim to a reign so short and yet so splendid, and possibly no one who has ever reigned at all has been popularly accounted such a figurehead and survived as such a dullard. For two centuries "Queen Anne is dead" became a contemptuous cliché for the stalest and flattest of news, yet "Queen Anne is dead" was to prove, as an actual statement, a gate swinging shut on history.

Socially she had been stodgy enough, and intellectually contemptible, and personally all too often sullen and stubborn and petty. But conceivably, for all that, she had been wiser than any of the flashing geniuses who haunt and heighten her age, had been, too, a steady-conscienced tortoise among a hundred swift unprincipled hares. She was the last monarch who at all succeeded in lawfully governing England (George III maneuvered and bribed and in due course failed), and she became this as much by virtue of what power she exacted as what power was freely acknowledged. She became this despite how bullyingly she could be worked on by Sarah or how wheedlingly by Abigail, and in the face also of dealing with some of the most notable, most knowledgeable, and most unethical politicians in English history. Politically her reign was even more devious and disturbed than it was resplendent. "I wonder," once wrote Shrewsbury from retirement in Italy, "that a man can be found in England who has bread, that will be concerned in public business." And without a somewhat fuller sense of that England and its methods and morality we may not really understand what was least admirable in the Duke of Marlborough or most individual in the Duchess.

One distinguishing quality of Anne's reign was its Englishness—her succeeding, as Lord Stanhope long ago noted, a very Dutch king and being succeeded in turn by a very German one. There are none of boorish William's Dutch male favorites or of boorish George's German mistresses to reckon with; nor a sovereign who felt more at home in Holland or only at home in Hanover. Yet Court life under Anne was no more glamorous than it had been or would come to be. It lacked, as we know, all formal elegance; it shunned all casual gaiety. Where the Queen proved "worldly," it was after the fashion of her humblest subjects: card parties, the races, gossip, and drink. When she "entertained," it was as a duty-driven hostess who longed for nothing so much as to be rid of her guests. Lord Chesterfield called her "a prude" who "discouraged . . . the most pardonable vices of courts" and whose Drawing Rooms suggested not Court but church. George I at least "loved pleasures," even if "not delicate in the choice of them."

Yet however dreary the atmosphere of the Court, it was always the focal point of Anne's reign; and those who fled or flouted or antagonized it did so—as they one by one found out—at their peril. Anne might be the dullest woman in England, but she was immeasurably the most important human being. If Anne, moreover, was very nearly as middle-class as Victoria, she was infinitely more powerful. Victoria might detest a Gladstone, but there was nothing she could do about him except rail and fume. Not just those she loathed, but those too she had long esteemed, Anne as it suited her dispensed with.

Thus, equally for high-minded statesmen as for self-seeking politicians, it was essential to seek her favor, which does something to explain, if not justify, the treacherous, two-faced methods of the reign. A Marlborough may have been by nature silky, or a Harley devious, but no one so constantly fed and fostered such master traits as Anne, who was of them all, from her unique position, the most dangerous dissembler. Those who by nature were more forthright could only, in the struggle for survival, flatter or pretend.

As it happens, despite all the attention she craved and deceit she inspired, Anne in the final reckoning much less hindered than helped. She could be maddeningly obstinate, could come to decisions for the most personal reasons. She tended to judge statesmen by how much they loved the Church, or had disliked William, or led virtuous lives. Deep down in her, small slights permanently rankled and were often—long afterwards—avenged. But, for all her quite glaring limitations as a woman, she was in her own way a scarcely less than magnificent queen. She had, sometimes in a ridiculous form, sometimes to a ruinous degree, a sense of duty; but that, in such a personage during such a age, had its tremendous worth. Again and again it led Anne to make sound decisions and even dangerously brave ones. However vitiated, in after days, might be the famous Bolingbrokian— which in origin was more truly Harley's—idea of a patriot king, Anne—for all her favoring the Tories and prejudice against the Whigs—was oftener than not a true patriot queen. She could rise with the occasion above party or herself; and, for a woman who could not reason, could even be rather eloquently cogent on the subject:

All I desire is, my liberty in encouraging and employing all those that concur faithfully in my service, whether they are called Whigs or Tories. . . . Why,

for God's sake, must I, who have no interest, no end,
no thought, but for the good of my country, be made
so miserable, as to be brought into the power of one set
of men?

And though Sarah first, and Abigail afterwards, were in-
struments at times for influencing her politically, far oftener they were simply the props and stays of her sickly,
lonely private life. In the end, few of her crucial policies or
decisions were at the expense of her desires or beliefs. Her
very limitations had value. At least in an England almost
plagued with brilliance, and swollen with ambition, Anne's
blinkered, stolid sense of duty proved at times a brake, a
deterrent, a corrective; even, in a sense, an example. She
could on occasion channel the brilliance of those about her,
as she could neutralize its ill effects, and though without her
the England of her reign would have had equal—and perhaps superior—glitter, it is not so certain that it would have
shown a comparable achievement.

For blazing talent in Anne's England stood at the mercy
of raging ambition. Even worse, what was unscrupulous
about it went hand in hand with what was fanatical. And in
such an atmosphere there could exist less and less sense (or
even semblance) of fair play. Venomous pamphleteering
was rife, and was harshly punished by the party in power,
the printer being imprisoned when the author could not be
traced. And yet it was not the personal venom or outright
vituperation that seemed most hateful, or even the hired
ruffianly press. These things were relatively out in the open
and could be returned in kind; these things smacked of
exaggeration even to a credulous, or a partisan, public. Far
baser was the constant treachery and double-dealing. Those
who most extravagantly praised John to his face most tire-

lessly plotted his overthrow. Those who were loudest for
Hanover were likeliest to connive with St. Germains. But
even self-seeking is at times no match for self-righteousness,
and it was those who believed fanatically in the divine right
of kings or the divine rightness of Whigs or Tories, it was
often those who were above place or beyond bribery who
threw decency farthest to the winds and spat out the worst
abuse. Whoever thought differently from them was not
just called traitor or murderer, but also debaucher or slut.

There were other men, of course—high-souled like Cowper, upright if narrow like Nottingham, politically honest,
personally loyal. Such men might never partake of power,
or would suddenly be shorn of it, but going with this group
or that, as they saw their duty, they acted as an offset or
safeguard to the rapacious and the ruthless. And in the end,
all the filth of politics under Anne is yet secondary to the
stress: great issues and great objectives alike hung in the air
and heated the blood. In the clash between Whigs and Tories, the future was fighting the past, which is by no means
to suggest that good was in the same sense jousting with
evil. The Tories might, for the last time in England, be making religion a central issue of politics, but if there was henceforth to be less organized bigotry, there would, under the
Whig drillmasters, be much better organized corruption.
More modern the world was certainly becoming, but not
everywhere was the millennium unarguably closer.

If Anne's reign is filled with political grime, it abounds
equally in social and artistic glitter. This, as we know, was
certainly not owing to the Court; nor was it very much
more, perhaps, because of any widespread or even highborn sheen or gloss. For great ladies and grand seigneurs, for
masked balls and lustrous entertainments after the manner

of France or fiction, we shall look mostly in vain. The English in modern times have seldom imparted enchantment to rank: their patricians, in large part, prefer to be shy, or rustic, or pathological. And it must always be remembered how much the great Augustan patricians lived outside the capital. London's town houses were never a patch on Paris's, but England's great country estates were becoming unsurpassed throughout Europe—the English, it has been said, did from pleasure "what banishment alone would force on the French." Anne's, all the same, was singularly an age when society patronized intellect, when talent consorted with wealth, when men of diverse distinction mingled in coffee-houses, just before the give-and-take of London's coffee-houses petrified forever into its walled-town life of clubs. Whatever Sarah's treatment of him, a Vanbrugh lived on easy social terms with most of his patrician clients; a Swift's sharp tongue was as pleasing to Harley and St. John as his pen was useful. Alexander Pope, who was barely twenty-five at Anne's death, was already being sought out, and before he was thirty would be regularly making the grand tour of country houses: "After some attendance on my Lord Burlington," he would write,

> I have been at the Duke of Shrewsbury's, Duke of Argyle's, Lady Rochester's, Lord Percival's, Mr. Stonor's, Lord Winchelsea's, Sir Godfrey Kneller's . . . and Duchess Hamilton's

—and not simply to dinner, but for visits of "some days." The same Duke of Shrewsbury might refuse, to be sure—during the preliminaries to the Peace of Utrecht—to serve as co-ambassador to France with a mere unpedigreed writer like Prior, but Prior himself, writing from Paris, need not "milord" Bolingbroke in his letters: they were Harry and

8*

Matt to each other. And what counts most is that a Prior could serve as an ambassador, that a Kit-Kat Club among the Whigs, or a Scriblerus among the Tories, could be a dazzling blend of what in time would seem so far apart as a White's and an Athenaeum.

And if so brief an era has seldom boasted such a roll-call of names among the arts, what a race of artists in their way, and of wits and actors and connoisseurs, were the men of rank themselves. To which group indeed shall a Boling-broke be assigned? He was patrician, man-about-town, and rake; yet where during the age was there a more accomplished statesman? In terms of oratory, at the head of all vanished things he wished could be recovered, Mr. Pitt put a speech of Bolingbroke's. In terms of prose, Matthew Arnold judged him, a century and a half later, a master. In terms of magnetism, Bolingbroke guided Pope, influenced Voltaire, became a model for the young Disraeli. And yet it is not the Bolingbrokes, the obvious geniuses in public life, whose more private performances are most impressive, but rather a whole body of men, no less bookish than rakish, as good judges of country houses as of horseflesh, of wit as of wine, who could as easily hold a table with their talk as Parliament with their oratory, and whose effortless round-the-clock feats involved mind as well as body, and hard work no less than deep play.

As for women under Anne, nothing could be more misleading than to judge their position by Sarah's. For Sarah to achieve so cardinal a place, she had to be more than the Queen's favorite and the Captain General's wife—she had to be passionately concerned with public life and of a commandingly assertive nature. Much as her personality differed from most other women's of her time, more still did her penetration into the world of men, for except as Abigail and, much less, the Duchess of Somerset had some place in the nation's counsels, we can pretty much dismiss women from politics. Indeed, where sexual intrigue does not enter in, we can pretty much dismiss them from the larger social world of men. It is not at all that they were reduced to a form of harem life or restricted to such staid enjoyments as left nothing very much to enjoy. There were amusements and frivolities enough, only women had to find them chiefly among themselves. The men of the age found their chief enjoyments away from home, in coffeehouses and gambling and women of the town, in riding or sport, in reading or conspiracy; nor must it be forgotten that Parliament, in those days, often sat till very late at night or that, during almost all of Anne's reign, England was at war and English men were helping to fight it.

Left so frequently to themselves, Augustan society women had a chief adversary in ennui. It was but the earliest dawn of improved education—women were well-off to be proficient in "the Needle, Dancing and the French tongue," and were sooner taught shellwork, mosswork, and embroidering with wire than anything so downright as geography or spelling. Their spelling is notorious—e.g., *yousles* for *useless*. Not many of them, clearly, would have had the qualifications, even given the desire, to become *salonnières*. And the early-eighteenth-century woman of fashion took pains to conceal learning when she had it. Of Lady Hervey—the "beautiful Molly Lepel"—Chesterfield wrote: "She understands Latin perfectly well, though she wisely conceals it"; and Lady Mary Wortley Montagu was to insist that her granddaughter should hide her knowledge as she would hide being crooked or lame. It was too soon, even, for English ladies to dispense fashionable charity: when Sarah was up betimes bombarding the Queen or conferring with Lord Treasurer, most of London's well-born women were lying lazily abed, their hair adroitly disheveled, their nightgowns thrown enticingly off their shoulders, a lapdog on the coverlet, visitors—gossiping and laughing—ranged round the room. Later in the day—after a late-forenoon "nuncheon," or as we should say, snack—such ladies might call for their sedan chairs [1] or trip about town on incredibly high heels, to shop or drink tea or play cards—for both sexes, a historic age of gambling was under way. Few ladies read much, and what they read was usually lewd and long-winded trash. But if ill-educated, they were often not unquick—the most harebrained gadabout might have a turn for phrase or infuse wit into her malice. Talk was lively and talk was coarse: Sarah herself could swear like a trooper.

And as they were pleasure-loving, and often foul-mouthed, and all too often bored, society women were not an ounce less cynical. "Caress the favorites," Lady Mary was to counsel a little later, "avoid the unfortunate, and trust nobody." If it would be difficult to fabricate more appalling advice, it would perhaps have been no easier—in the *grand monde* of those years—to provide any that would prove more useful. The great world, which had seen James II whisked off his throne, seen his royal daughters at loggerheads, seen James abandoned for William, William betrayed for James, Anne shunned and Anne courted, John triumphant and John abased, Sarah raised high and Sarah flung aside—could such a world fail to show wariness and distrust? The great world was not the only world, but it was the only one Sarah knew, and as Anne's reign worked to its extraordinary close and Harley, the master trimmer,

---

[1] A very great convenience. One lady went by sedan chair all the way from London to Bath.

fell from power and the master of treachery, Bolingbroke, strove to gain it, the great world flared with ominous, angry, vividly lethal color.

For, with the disease-racked Queen almost on her last legs, the question of her successor had grown tense. In most English minds only the Pretender's Catholicism stood between him and the throne. Yet, though told that if Paris had been worth a mass to his great-grandfather, London should be worth a sermon to him, he refused to change his faith or even dissemble it. But many uninformed people still supposed he might; there was considerable sentiment for bringing him in; and with Whig support of Hanover assuring Hanover's good will to the Whigs, Tory statesmen could not but look, however shiftily, toward the Pretender. Moreover, the two chief Tory statesmen, having for some time been at daggers drawn, were now at knife-in-the-back. The brilliant, headlong, insanely ambitious St. John had never willingly been Harley's official subordinate, and had by now successfully conducted under his own hand the negotiations concluded at Utrecht. St. John had also come to resent Harley on personal grounds. Harley had been stabbed by an assassin and become the nation's darling; had received, as St. John had not, the Garter; had been made an earl where St. John became only a viscount.

In such a mood, the new Viscount Bolingbroke had set about bribing the Queen's favorite in order to gain the Queen's favor. The new Earl of Oxford now resented in turn the new Viscount's machinations, while himself abetting them through his laxness, through being "scarce sober once a week" and drunk and muddled even before the Queen. Though Bolingbroke's profligacy [2] must always

---

[2] He had, among other things, run naked through the park and lived with "the most expensive demirep in the kingdom"; and when he be-

offend Anne's prudishness, he managed—by dancing attendance on her, and advising her after her own heart, and showing concern for her health—to gain considerably in favor. He continued also to ensure Lady Masham's support. All that was lacking was any semblance of political support. The moderate Tories were solidly for Harley and Hanover, and when Bolingbroke sought backing from the Whigs, who, though out of power, were on the rise again, they glacially refused him any. "Bolingbroke, that great schemer, had no scheme ready": he could but connive by candlelight with French agents in the name of English Jacobites and extremists; and how many, and how powerful, were they? Then a scheme did occur to him: to push through Parliament so vindictive a law against Dissenters as might make the Whigs fulminate and even rebel, wherefore he would bring in a French army to crush the rebellion, and with it the Pretender. But the Whigs would not indulge such a vicious daydream, and though, with Abigail's help, Bolingbroke got Anne—in a terrible scene that hastened her death—to dismiss Harley, he now grasped the helm with no course to steer. His Jacobite scheme was premature; mild Tories everywhere turned him down; Whigs everywhere were in pursuit. The dying Queen, moreover, refused him the White Staff of office she had snatched a few days earlier from Harley. At a Council gathered round her deathbed, he had to assent that it go to Shrewsbury. Two days later the Queen was dead; without a hint of opposition George I was proclaimed King at St. James's, and the most brilliant and unprincipled of his new subjects plummeted from power, never to rise again.

---

came Secretary of State, a madam crowed: "Five thousand a year, my girls, and all for us!"

PART THREE

OLD MARLBOROUGH

XII

THE MARLBOROUGHS returned to England in triumph: at Dover, where they landed, there was a salute of guns, and cheering crowds; at Chatham their way was strewn with flowers; at Rochester they were met by a delegation on horseback; and as at last, in their glass coach, they came over London Bridge, they were salvoed, it was remarked, as though the Duke had won another Blenheim. The London they came home to was stanchly Hanoverian: though the new King was still—as he would be for some days more—at Hanover, the nation he had no great wish to rule, and none whatever to live in, peacefully and pliantly awaited his coming. To govern in the interval, twenty-five regents had been appointed, who, it was said, appeared to a Bolingbroke at bay like twenty-five sovereigns. Bolingbroke was still nominally Secretary of State but with his power—and his party—shattered, and the King was to fling him brutally out of office even before arriving in England. A ruined Harley, finding a continuing solace in drink, found greater solace—like Volpone toward Mosca—in Bolingbroke's greater ruin. He also proved himself far manlier in adversity: Bolingbroke fled the country, but Oxford stood his ground, faced his impeachment calmly, and went for a long but not painful confinement to the Tower. The dead Queen, as earlier the dying one, be-

came the Court responsibility of the Duchess of Somerset—
Abigail quickly vanished with her husband into the country, almost never to be heard of again.

John had not been named one of the regents, and felt
offended for not being, though the belief that he was out of
the country has been offered in explanation. And it is true
that the very first document George I signed as king created Marlborough once again Captain General. There was,
all the same, some reason for excluding John from the Regency—for one thing, his flirtations with the Pretender; and
conceivably for another, George I's remembering and resenting that John had concealed from him the plans for
Oudenarde. Equally, moreover, with being denied this
show of confidence by the King, John—no Whig at heart—
would later be excluded from the new Whig party's inner
councils. Sarah, on her side—and genuinely, it would seem—
desired the no longer young, physically no longer hale,
mentally no longer agile Duke to keep clear of politics: "I
begged of the Duke of Marlborough upon my knees that
he would never accept of any employment." Beyond her
awareness of his declining powers, she felt that a man with
his past achievements and present fortune "would be of
more use to any court than they could be of to him," and
she herself was determined never to "put it into the power
of any King to use me ill."

But negligible though their influence might be, the Marlboroughs' position was again very assured. "The Duke of
Marlborough's levee," it was reported, "is as much crowded
as ever." The King, as soon as he reached London from
Hanover, received John cordially, remarking: "I hope your
troubles are now all over." And on George I's entering
London it was noted that "the Duke of Marlborough was
more huzza'd . . . than King George, and that the accla-

mation *God Save the Duke of Marlborough!* was more frequently repeated than *God Save the King!*" Ten days after
the King arrived, he went to supper at Marlborough House;
and as a different sort of testimonial, when the celebrated
Dr. Garth soon after received a knighthood, his request was
readily granted that he might take the accolade with the
Duke of Marlborough's sword. And the Duchess of Marlborough, though with no official employment herself, might
be gratified that one of her daughters and two of her sons-
in-law received Court posts, a third son-in-law a regiment.
To be sure, the fourth son-in-law, Sunderland, was fobbed
off with the Lord Lieutenancy of Ireland, though he soon
came back to be Secretary of State.

If Sarah had no official place at Court—where, according
to Lady Mary Montagu, John made "the same figure . . .
he did when he first came into it"—the Court itself was not
one to beckon her. A stolid conversationalist had but given
way to a boor who spoke no English, had long ago banished
his errant wife, and now consorted with two rapacious German mistresses, one of them monstrously fat, the other spec-
trally thin. Whenever possible, George hurried back to
Hanover, and at such times as business detained him in
London, Court life grew not gayer but more grim. With
her own Holywell House, on the other hand, Sarah, when
she got there, would not part "for any I have seen"; and
when she got there she was "more tired than [at] any of
my travels." For the present, she remained generally apart
from things, being not the first to hold cheap what she
could not have. Also, as we shall see, there was the building
of Blenheim to occupy her.

When, in 1715, the Pretender, partly through the influence of Bolingbroke, went to Scotland to lead a rebellion
as claimant of the Crown, John as Captain General had the

task of routing him. Unable to take the field, he remained a sidelines generalissimo, but he was alert enough to replace the too lax Argyll with Cadogan, and distance sufficiently lent discernment to the view for John to predict correctly that the advancing Jacobites would be halted at Preston.

But the Duke of Marlborough's fighting days were forever over, and even his fit days sadly numbered. The year 1715 was an ill-fated one for him and Sarah. In the spring their second daughter, Lady Sunderland, died of pleuritic fever. She had not only been loved and admired by the world at large; alone of the Marlboroughs' daughters she had never quarreled with their mother. Her death deeply affected John, with his always intense feeling for his family, and Sarah, with her need for someone she could love. Lady Sunderland's death was to create, too, a certain alteration in Sarah's way of life, for Lady Sunderland had left her husband a letter having to do with their children:

> Pray get my mother the Duchess of Marlborough to take care of the girls and if I leave any boys too little to go to school; for to be left to servants is very bad for children and a man can't take the care of little children that a woman can. For the love she has for me and the duty I have ever showed her, I hope she will do it and be ever kind to you who was dearer to me than my life.

This letter of his wife's Sunderland sent to Sarah, who, in returning it, wrote as follows:

> May 13, 1716
> I send you enclosed that most precious letter which you sent me yesterday by Mr. Charlton. You will easily believe it has made me drop a great many tears, and you may be very sure that to my life's end I shall ob-

serve very religiously all that my poor dear child desired. I was pleased to find that my own inclinations
had led me to resolve upon doing everything that she
mentions before I knew it was her request, except
taking Lady Anne, which I did not offer, thinking
that . . . she would be better with you than me. . . .
I have resolved to take poor Lady Anne Egerton [her
granddaughter by the Duchess of Bridgewater] who,
I believe, is very ill looked after. She went yesterday to
Ashridge, but I will send for her to St. Albans, as soon
as you will let me have dear Lady Dye [Lady Sunderland's second daughter] and while the weather is hot,
I will keep them two and Lady Harriot [Godolphin],
with a little family of servants to look after them, and
be there as much as I can; but the Duke of Marlborough will be running up and down to several places
this summer, where one can't carry children; and I
don't think his health so good as to trust him by himself. . . . I desire, when it is easy to you, that you will
let me have some little trifle that my dear child used to
wear in her pocket, or any other way; and I desire
Fanchon will look for some little cup that she used to
drink in. I had some of her hair not long since, that I
asked her for; but Fanchon may give me a better lock
at the full length.

The children accordingly came to live with Sarah.

Owing in part, it would seem, to the shock of his daughter's death, John—some six weeks after it—suffered a para-
lytic stroke. Though at first he lost the power of mind and
speech alike, he gradually—under the care of Dr. Garth—
recovered both, and was so far improved by the summer as
to go off and take the waters. Upon Sarah there now fell

not just the worries and duties of a wife, nor the added problems of running a large house containing both small grandchildren and a sick husband, but also the need of administering very extensive business affairs, of being in touch with a variety of agents and lawyers respecting investments and houses and lands. Moreover, in November of 1716 John had a second and severer stroke—from which, rather miraculously, he recovered once again.[1] This time, however, he lost permanently a certain power of speech, and no longer finding it easy to express himself, he spoke less and less outside the family circle. But he still kept up an interest in public affairs—in 1717, indeed, he went and voted for Harley's impeachment, though at the time, Sarah reported, he was "so ill that he could not go fifteen miles without being tired." In the five years remaining to him, though he must now be thought of as a sick and disabled man, there was still much to engage his interest, whether in Parliament or in London generally, or at St. Albans, or the Lodge at Windsor, or in connection with Blenheim. He sometimes played ombre and piquet, though for far more modest stakes than Sarah did. There was his family to occupy him too, particularly now his granddaughters: on at least two occasions they and their friends—who included young soldiers hoping for a glimpse of John—staged private theatricals. There was a *Tamerlane*; and then an *All for Love*, with Sarah deleting

---

[1] It may be of interest to record John's regimen and diet after this stroke. "Besides taking steel wine two or three times a day," the doctor counseled, "to drink as much as he pleases of good French white wine, all red wines being apt to bind too much. But above all to go to bed about ten o'clock and to rise about eight or nine, and if possible to ride on horseback morning and afternoon; to dine at one o'clock . . . and not to eat much fruit whose juices are too cold for the stomach. The Duke must forbear all manner of meat at night, and ought rather to eat broth made of an old cock, bruised to pieces, bones and all, now and then two eggs poached in gravy, or five or six oysters just warmed in their shells."

whatever she thought too risky, and forbidding people to embrace. But even more than among the scaffoldings of Blenheim, Sarah created discord at home, and John's last years were oftener scenes of family strife than of family sentiment.

A year and a half after Lady Sunderland's death, her husband remarried, and in Sarah's view, beneath him. In addition she objected—on behalf of her grandchildren—to the financial settlements he made, and straightway spoke her mind. Sunderland, always Sarah's match at acerbity, and more gifted at public speaking, spoke back; and when, a year or so later, he became Secretary of State, he and Sarah no longer were speaking at all.

Sarah fell out, far more discreditably, with John's long-time stanch comrade-in-arms, Cadogan, charging him with misusing the £50,000 that John, on the eve of going into exile, had put into his hands. Cadogan, it seems, had reinvested the money at a much higher rate of interest, only for the capital to shrink considerably over the years. Sarah contended, how correctly there is no way of knowing, that Cadogan had himself pocketed the difference in interest. In any case, with the compliance of the now all too compliant Duke, she sued for repayment of the full capital, won the suit, and forced a hard-pressed Cadogan to make restitution.

But amid all the family squabbling and the more public accusations and lawsuits—whether those already noted, or others with such current great office-holders as Townshend, Walpole, and Craggs—the chief wrangles of this period were with Vanbrugh. It is time, indeed, to conclude that loud, unseemly drama—all of whose stormiest scenes are not by the dramatist, but by the lady—even though the conclusion itself, reached through a maze of events and a medley of litigation and insult, still lies many years ahead. After John's disgrace, all work had been stopped at Blenheim, and an indiscreet reference on a too loyal Vanbrugh's part, concerning the "bitter persecution" of the Duke, had got the Duke's architect dismissed from the Office of Works. Indeed, the very architecture of Blenheim was being ridiculed:

> . . . 'Tis very fine
> But where d'ye sleep, or where d'ye dine?
> I find by all you have been telling,
> That 'tis a house but not a dwelling.

But after Anne's death, with the Marlboroughs returning to England and the new King on the throne, the situation altered. The Duke, to requite Vanbrugh's suffering in his behalf, obtained for him George I's first knighthood on English soil, and John had hardly set foot in England before he was discussing plans with his architect for proceeding with Blenheim. If Parliament would not vote to pay off the workmen's claims, John would continue the building at his own expense.

So work at Blenheim was resumed. Though Vanbrugh and Sarah were now on friendly terms, she was soon grumbling over Sir John's management of the workmen (who themselves had taken to grumbling), and she was furious that, far from having torn down the old manor house, Vanbrugh was actually living in it. Even worse, across a little ditch that "anybody could jump," Vanbrugh—having first converted the ditch into a rivulet—was constructing a 390-foot-long bridge "in which," Sarah recorded, "I counted thirty-three rooms"—rooms to sit in, she burst out, "while the coaches are driving over your head." And when she remonstrated, Sir John was so bold as to joke that he would yet "see your Grace fonder" of the bridge than of anything else at Blenheim, and that if he did build a house upon it, Sarah would "go and live in it." She was not at all amused; and perhaps, after some dozen years, to be so concerned with mere fancies, and so very far from finished with the house, was not altogether amusing. "Painters and poets and builders," it was Sarah's opinion, "have very high flights, but they must be kept down."

At the moment, however, Sir John was also serving the Duchess in a different capacity: at her suggestion, he was acting as matchmaker between her granddaughter, Lady Harriet Godolphin, and his young friend and concurrent employer, the soon-to-be Duke of Newcastle. He had gone at the business as offhandedly as he could, from time to time contriving praise of Lady Harriet while sipping claret with the noble *parti*. The young man, though chiefly concerned for breeding and character, had certain reservations about the young lady's physical charms: he wished that her "bodily perfections" equaled "her mind and understanding." Sir John, though he could not declare her beautiful, felt she would have what is called a "good countenance," and insisted that "in two years' time no woman . . . would be better liked." And Newcastle himself was much stirred by the thought "of having a posterity descend from the Duke of Marlborough," though, after consulting with Whig advisers—for this was more than a personal or even a social matter, it was a great party alliance—he called for a dowry of £40,000. When Vanbrugh relayed this condition to Sarah, "I never heard of such a fortune," she exploded. "Lady Harriet is not a Citizen, nor a Monster." Perhaps, she declared, this was the young man's way of saying No to the match; for her part Sarah would think no more of it.

But, time passing, the Duke of Newcastle—out of an ever

greater resolution to marry—himself inquired about Lady
Harriet of Vanbrugh, who inquired after her of her grandmother and, being now not Sarah's but Newcastle's envoy,
acclaimed the young Duke "the best match in England."
Sarah was once again warm for the match, though just
now—what with Vanbrugh taking it upon himself to plant
fruit trees at Blenheim—very cool toward the matchmaker.
And, meeting at Bath another friend of the Duke of Newcastle's, Mr. Peter Walter, she unburdened herself to him
of the matter, with the thought that he might carry it further for her. When she next saw Vanbrugh—at Blenheim,
where he was now perpetrating new walks and new walls!—
she was more out of sorts with him than ever. She said not a
word of Lady Harriet, while Vanbrugh, thinking nothing
could be said till he saw Newcastle again, asked not a word
of her, either. But Newcastle, immediately on seeing Vanbrugh, asked impatiently about the Duchess, and Sir John's
surprise at being asked was nothing to Newcastle's at not
being answered. He could only make mention of Mr. Walter—who was in his house at the very moment—and of
Sarah's employing Mr. Walter to expedite matters.

Vanbrugh passed swiftly from astonishment to anger.
Here he was, at Sarah's request and for her family's advantage, acting the thankless role of matchmaker; and at length
when the match was made, not so much as notified, let alone
thanked. He sat down and wrote Her Grace of Marlborough a simple summary of his endeavors, but, growing more
incensed as he proceeded, wound up with a flourish:

A matchmaker's is a damned trade, and I was never
fond of meddling with other people's affairs. But as in
this, on your own motion, and your own desire, I had
taken a good deal of hearty pains to serve you, and I

think with a good deal of hearty success, I cannot but wonder (though not be sorry), you should not think it right to continue your commands upon
    Your obedient humble servant

J. VANBRUGH

Sarah answered in her prettiest tones, arguing that she could see no harm, on meeting a great friend of Newcastle's,[2] in soliciting his interest, and adding that "if any third person will say that I have done anything wrong . . . I shall be very . . . ready to ask your pardon." But her real answer was to fire at Vanbrugh, by way of a building contractor, a broadside of "twenty or thirty" sheets of paper trumpeting all his crimes over the years and charging him with putting the Duke of Marlborough to such expense as might "deprive his grandchildren of the provision he inclined to make for them." As the catalogue of wrongdoings mounted, as the accumulation of indictments unrolled, Vanbrugh understood that it was not as matchmaker only that Sarah wanted him removed: as so often she had had the blood, now finally she wanted the very body and bones of the architect of Blenheim.

So much Vanbrugh could not endure; and indeed he wrote to Sarah as someone taxed beyond all endurance:

These papers, madam, are so full of far-fetched, labored accusations, mistaken facts, wrong inferences, groundless jealousies and strained constructions, that I should put a very great affront upon your understanding if I supposed it possible you could mean anything

---

[2] Actually, though a "celebrated personage," Peter Walter was a professional matchmaker and moneylender, Pope's

> *What's property, dear Swift? You see it alter*
> *From me to you, from you to Peter Walter.*

in earnest by them, but to put a stop to my troubling
you any more. You have your end, madam, for I will
never trouble you more, unless the Duke of Marlborough recovers so far as to shelter me from such intolerable treatment.

Thus Vanbrugh ended all working connection with Blenheim Palace, and Sarah might have in the matter a clear conscience as well as a satisfied mind, for her architect—in even
writing to whom she was "sorry that I had fouled my fingers"—had not been dismissed, but had stepped down. Yet,
however welcome his resignation, the insolent manner of it
was quite something else, and though Sarah's precise reactions are not on record, they can perhaps be inferred from
the fact that the very next day John had his second stroke.
Vanbrugh, meanwhile, was writing to the Duke of Newcastle of "this abominable woman's proceeding; which shall
not, however, lessen my regard to my Lord Duke, nor good
opinion of his granddaughter, who I do not think has one
grain of this wicked woman's temper in her; [3] if it did, I
wouldn't advise you to take her, though with the allay of a
million." And Vanbrugh continued to do all he could, even
to waiting on the girl's own father, to further the marriage.
And in time, despite Sarah's having to "be left to her own
throws," the marriage indeed came off. It was in a sense
another victory for the Duchess, for the dowry bestowed
was £22,000 rather than £40,000, and, the loser in his demands, Newcastle came off no better in his desires, for the
marriage, being childless, provided no posterity descending
from the Duke of Marlborough.

Though Vanbrugh came no more to Blenheim—when an

[3] It has been pointed out that Lady Harriet's other grandmother,
Godolphin's wife and the Margaret Blagge memorialized at book length
by John Evelyn, was as great a saint as Sarah was a shrew.

ailing John was moved to wonder why, Sarah explained that he had thrown up the job—his involvement in it was not wholly finished. Litigation more than kept pace with construction: in 1718, workmen sued the Duke for some £8,000 on unpaid work from Queen Anne's time, and Vanbrugh, having—under a warrant from Godolphin—signed the contracts for John, his name was conjoined to the Duke's. The Duke, claiming the indebtedness was Queen Anne's, fought, and in 1721 lost, the case in the Courts; then unsuccessfully appealed it—his own family voting against him—in the Lords. Sarah, who was actually running the show,[4] now sought to make Vanbrugh—who felt Blenheim owed *him* some £2,000—responsible; but, it being made clear in the warrant that Vanbrugh was acting as the Duke's agent, the Courts refused her judgment. Balked of the law, she had recourse to that other instrument of her displeasure, the pen—writing and printing up an attack on Vanbrugh in which he was accused of not being sufficiently vigilant about contracts and of snaring the pivotal warrant out of Godolphin by trickery. John, she maintained, had not even been aware that the warrant existed, and though he must pay the £8,000, still "the infamy of it must be upon another, who was perhaps the only architect in the world capable of building such a house, and the only friend in the world capable of contriving to lay the debt upon one to whom he was so highly obliged." During the same period, though with less turbulence of spirit, Vanbrugh—who in all this never blamed, or ceased to feel kindly toward, the Duke—was composing a *Justification* of his own, and making such rejoinders as that Sarah, for all her complaints

---

[4] Sarah had a point in insisting that it was "quite new to make any man pay for a building to compliment himself." But of her activities generally, "I wonder," said Vanbrugh, "her family don't agree to lock her up."

about the Blenheim contracts, had paid far higher prices in building Marlborough House. As for the warrant Godolphin was tricked into and John had never heard of:

> Will any one believe, that in so many quiet, fireside, evening conferences, as happened between these two great lords and her Grace, the manner and method of receiving in, and laying out, these hundreds of thousands of pounds should never be part of the amusement? Sure there's some great forgetfulness in this matter.

Sarah was not through: next, Vanbrugh learned, she had started a case in Court "against everybody that was ever concerned in the building of Blenheim down to the poorest workman." But while this hung fire, the Duke—who for the past three years had happily spent much time at Woodstock—was to die. The palace was still far from complete, but the Duke in his will carefully arranged for its completion. Taking note of that will, with its disposal of a vast estate of over £2,000,000, Vanbrugh for the first time spoke meanly of John: "And yet this man would neither pay his workmen their bills nor his architect his salary." And he went on to speak scathingly of Sarah: "But the Duke had given his widow (may a Scotch ensign get her) £10,000 a year to spoil Blenheim her own way; £12,000 a year to keep herself clean and go to law." [5]

Go to law she surely did, but Sarah, as Vanbrugh had noted, was "though a—worse thing, not a fool": she had Hawksmoor—the architect nearest Vanbrugh in feeling and talent—finish Blenheim in strict accordance with Van-

---

[5] And when, before John's death, there was talk of his resigning as Captain General, Vanbrugh remarked that doubtless Sarah would "haggle for a pension to support the poor old officer and his wife."

brugh's designs. In time all sorts of other famous men of the
century, Burlingtonians among them, would set off Vanbrugh's baroque—Kent, Chambers, Capability Brown; and
in wood-carving, painting, and sculpture, Gibbons, Thorn-
hill, and Rysbrack. A home after Sarah's inclinations it
might not become, though Robert Adam was to insist that
Vanbrugh understood better than Inigo Jones or Wren
"the art of living among the great." Something so dramatic
could scarcely seem domestic; nor could anything with so
massed a grandeur impart a classical grace. The corner
pavilions, to go no further, are like proclamations in stone—
whether of Marlborough's victories, or of his authority, or
of his wealth. No doubt such baroque has the drawback of
seeming flamboyant, but then, much that is classical will
have a contrary fault, and seem frigid.

Blenheim cost £300,000 in all, the nation paying four
fifths, the Marlboroughs the remainder. And to take leave
of its litigations, of Sarah demanding reimbursement of
Vanbrugh and Vanbrugh seeking arrears of Sarah, matters
seesawed and dragged along until 1725. "Since being forced
into Chancery," Vanbrugh wrote to Jacob Tonson,

> by that B. B. B. B. old B. the Duchess of Marlbh . . .
> I have prevailed with Sr. Rob. Walpole to help me, in
> a scheme I proposed to him, by which I have got my
> money in spite of the hussy's teeth, and that out of
> a sum she expected to receive into her hands and of
> which she resolved I should never have a farthing.

He had, in other words, got Walpole, who by now was
Prime Minister, to deduct at source—from the £30,000
that the State owed Blenheim—the £1,663 claimed by its
architect. He thus won a kind of final victory, but he did
so within six months of his taking leave of life and after he

had not only taken all professional leave of Blenheim, but had actually been locked out of it.

In the summer of this same year, 1725, Lord Carlisle of Castle Howard, being "better in point of gout than usual," had a desire to go look at Blenheim and take the architect of both palaces with him. Sir John was understandably eager to see once more, and in its present form, the lordliest of his projects; less understandably he lacked a certain instinct about going where he must so plainly be unwelcome, as he lacked astuteness in supposing he would ever be let in. "We stayed two nights at Woodstock," he wrote to Tonson. "There was an order to the servants, under her Grace's own hand, not to let me enter Blenheim, and lest that should not mortify me enough, she having somehow learned that my wife was of the company"—had debarred Lady Vanbrugh also.[6] Moreover, Sarah wrote Lord Carlisle a long, violent explanation for keeping out this man whose "bones ought to have been broke." And Sarah's vigilant gardener wrote to her, among other things, that Vanbrugh had been observed going on his own to Old Woodstock, where he peered "over the wall to see the water."

Examined retrospectively across the centuries, the Blenheim battle is as many-sided as it was harshly fought. Everyone, whether in emotion or in logic or in law, had a case of a kind: the unpaid workmen very obviously, the harassed architect very obtrusively, and John and Sarah too—not just because what the nation had proposed as a form of homage had become a source of vexation, but also because there was a measure of real wastefulness and perhaps of dishonesty involved in the outlays. Much the strongest

[6] Actually Vanbrugh was *e pluribus unus*. "The Duchess," remarks a contemporary letter, "has given out a list of persons who may not see the house"—among them two of her daughters.

Sir John Vanbrugh

Holywell House, St. Albans

cause of dissension was politics and slow time, and gentler souls than the Duchess might have grown exasperated from the very sight of the endlessly finishing yet never finished palace, of that "wild, unmerciful house" she had never wanted from the outset. But even if we allow, with one of her biographers, that in later years Sarah fought "every inch of the way not so much . . . from avarice as from pride and anger"—and had challenged prices even when others were paying the bill—we have the same biographer's admission that Sarah "fought over every carload of stone, every bushel of lime, every yard of iron railing, every foot of wainscot" and that, for the information of her lawyer, she filled sixty-nine sheets of foolscap enumerating "every letter from the workmen, contractors and surveyors, every voucher, every discrepancy, every detail." Indeed, Sarah's friend Lady Lechmere once cautioned Her Grace against catching cold from always dashing out-of-doors at Blenheim to find out what the workmen were doing. And yet, having disliked the conception, opposed the plans, impeded the building, hectored the builders, and expelled the architect, Sarah herself, after John's death, and in less time and for less money than John had stipulated, brought the vast pile to completion while in no smallest way detracting from it.

XIII

WITH other dissensions, too, these embattled years of Blenheim and Vanbrugh were full enough. Sarah had seen most of her Queen-Anne adversaries sufficiently ruined, and was once more, herself, a personage. Had it

9

been possible, she would perhaps once more—in spite of her deprecations and denials—have also become a power, and she doubtless felt that this new regime should show proper recognition to one of England's stanchest Whigs. But the Whigs who ruled under George I proved hardly more satisfactory than the Tories under Anne. Sir Robert Walpole lost favor with Sarah almost as soon as he acquired power; she did not like Lord Townshend any better; and by the time her former son-in-law, Sunderland, briefly became Prime Minister and ousted the other two, she was on bad terms with him for remarrying. The best she could do was stay much of the time in London—and make John stay there also, as a kind of ineffectual rallying-point for malcontent and out-of-favor Whigs. And Sarah soon enough managed to be on hardly better terms with the Court than with the Cabinet, though the circumstances here were different. At family quarrels, the Hanoverians might have won admiration from Sarah herself. There was, for one example, the future George II, who hated his father only a trifle less than he came to hate his son. And in these early years of his father's reign he had set up a kind of anti-Court party and a kind of rival court. Sarah—whether from preferring him (or at any rate his extraordinary wife) to George I, or from a need to play with fire, or from feeling that with her special tact she could succeed with Montagues and Capulets alike—began visiting the Prince and Princess of Wales. This was noticed: "The Duchess of Marlborough having been without permission to see the Princess with some other ladies," His Majesty made known that whoever should visit the Princess would not be received by the King. But though, somewhat later on, the Marlboroughs had once more the entree with the King, they were still paying court to the Prince and his wife. Indeed, wrote Sarah, the Duke of Marlborough and I had such a reception as would fill more than this paper to repeat. . . . All the attendants . . . were so civil that I thought myself in a new world. There was very good music [1] though her Royal Highness, I saw, thought I liked the noise of the box and dice, and contrived it so as to make me play on when she left us.

And Sarah confesses to "play ill" at cards and to lose considerably, but will play notwithstanding, "as I have nobody, or but few, to take care of when I am dead."

In time, however—and on more vulnerable ground than friendship with the heir apparent—Sarah really fell foul of the King. Indeed, a rather wild charge arose. She could easily enough, by her mouth or her meddling, have ignited other men's malice, and she herself admitted that, in her opposing the South Sea speculations, she "talked to all the Parliament men that I knew," although "I did not say one word . . . that was the least offensive." Still, Sarah confessed, "my lord Cadogan (who can never forgive me for defeating his design of cheating the Duke of Marlborough of £50,000 . . .) took this handle . . . to go to my lord Sunderland and my lord Stanhope and told them millions of falsities that I had said of them." This, it appears, put Sunderland "into such a violent passion that he sent immediately to speak with the Duke of Marlborough." The ensuing conversation so "harassed the poor Duke . . . that he came home half dead"—as well he might have done, for Sunderland had announced that Sarah "was in a plot to bring in the Pretender." During the 1715 uprising, it was charged, she "had remitted a great sum of money for that service," and "the King could prove it." It is much to be

[1] Music was the one cultural interest of the first Georges.

doubted that the King could have done any such thing;
1715 was least of all a time when Sarah would have been a
traitorous malcontent. The rumor pretty certainly arose
from political or personal malice,[2] or from the habit of the
age to implicate almost everyone, sooner or later, in conspiracy. Sarah herself, on hearing Sunderland's wild tale
from John's white lips, haughtily poopoohed it and, in explanation, had all too many enemies whom she could pin
it on. She first chose Mr. Secretary Craggs as her maligner,
but was later disposed to favor Sunderland himself. Still,
hearing that John too was named in the plot, she could not
wholly disregard it. She thought she would attend a Drawing Room at Court to see how things went, and she saw
very clearly, being everywhere snubbed. But lest she had
somehow judged wrong, she went to Court a second time,
and was thoroughly snubbed once more. Thereupon she
seized her pen and set about refuting the "absurd and incredible" accusations against her, had her remarks trans-
lated into French (she knew no French, and the King no
English), went and put them into the hands of the King's
ugly old mistress the Duchess of Kendal, and though she
would not stay for an answer, an answer in time arrived,
curt as kingliness and boorishness could make it:

St. James's Dec. 17, 1720
Whatever I may have been told upon your account, I
think I have shown on all occasions, the value I have
for the services of the Duke, your husband; and I am
always disposed to judge of him and you by the behavior of each of you in regard to my service. Upon

----

[2] And was doubtless repeated from malice; Vanbrugh wrote, a good
while after: "[The Duchess of Marlborough] is now looked upon as a
thorough professed Jacobite, and her having furnished money to the
Pretender not denied by her family." One could almost say of that age
that where there was smoke there was ire.

which, I pray God, my Lady Marlborough, to preserve you in all happiness.

GEORGE R.

A week later she wrote with increased vigor to the Duchess of Kendal, but in reply was merely referred to His Majesty's previous communication. Thus, having done everything she could in the service of truth and reason, and been
not the instigator but the victim of conspiracy, she very
pointedly joined the anti-Court circle of the Prince and
Princess of Wales, who very effusively welcomed her into it.

If indeed—as may be doubted—all this noise over Sarah
and the Pretender had its origin in the hysteria of the South
Sea Bubble, Sarah, where the Bubble itself was concerned,
had been for once—and very exceptionally—in the right.
The narrative of this national craze for getting rich quick,
of this rabid faith in fiscal miracles, has been often and di-
dactically enough told. It but crowned an age, of course, of
innumerable lotteries (one, indeed, had been used to pay off
Queen Anne's debts), of inordinate gambling (though gambling yet more inordinate was still to come); it but charac-
terized an age when men were ready, eager, determined,
frantic, to invest in anything. They poured out money for
perpetual-motion machines, for companies that would make
salt water fresh, for revolutionizing "the Art of War" with
square cannon balls and bullets, even for "an undertaking
which shall in due time be revealed." Few better examples
than the South Sea Bubble exist of man's greed, or man's
folly, or man's credulousness; yet Sarah—and her enemy
Walpole—were among the few people to see, when the
stock was roaring up to over a thousand per cent of par,
that it must catastrophically explode and plummet. " 'Tis
not possible, by all the arts and tricks upon earth," Sarah

wrote, "long to carry £400,000,000 of paper credit with
£15,000,000 of specie." And against everyone's, including
the Duke's, entreaties and advice, the Duchess was one of
the very few who disposed of their holdings before the promoters had sold out. Amid widespread financial ruin, she
could boast £100,000 profit. Only Walpole, who had
warned the country against the Bubble, made more: it was
out of the economic upheaval of the South Sea disaster that
Walpole achieved—and for almost a generation maintained
—his political ascendancy.[3]

Those years were busy ones, what with a plethora of such
other matters as instructing the mayor of St. Albans how to
win an election, or conducting all John's business affairs, or
watching over John's health; and in this last she was as
fierce and tigerish from devotion as so often elsewhere from
hostility. Her care, coupled with John's own extraordinary
calm, did bring pleasure to his years of decline, though
Sarah's quarrels with her daughters brought to those years,
and to John's very deathbed, distress as well. John had the
great—and necessary—ability to let fall away whatever had
been and gone, though doubtless, now, a certain falling
away of the man himself must be reckoned in. However
that might be, during his last years he wrote nothing, and
would seem to have said nothing, in respect of either the
achievements or the ambiguities of his career. The one remark about himself that has been preserved (and it comes
too pat) has him turning with a sigh from an intent study of
Kneller's portrait of him, saying: "That was once a man."

The end was to come, following another stroke, at Windsor Lodge in June of 1722, quietly, or comatosely, enough

[3] Craggs and Sunderland had indeed been among the promoters, and
were indeed involved in the "scandals and widespread ruin" that ensued.
Sarah was loud in wanting them brought to trial, but just then both of
them "with mysterious suddenness and unanimity" died.

at the last for the Duke, but in an atmosphere of rage and hate. Not only did the frantic Duchess swear at the local doctor—who could do nothing—and want to pursue him and pull off his wig, but she was on bitterly bad terms with her two surviving daughters, Lady Godolphin and the Duchess of Montagu. As her stormy relations with her family constitute the major theme of Sarah's widowed life, we can for the moment pass over the roots of conflict, the long itemization of discord, restricting ourselves to the more than sufficient scene—it is Sarah herself who recounts it—wherewith John's life moved toward its close:

The afternoon before her father died, when I had no hopes of his recovery, I was mightily surprised and troubled at what I did not expect, that the Duchess of Montagu and my lady Godolphin were without. . . . I am sure it is impossible for any tongue to express what I felt at that time; but I believe anybody that ever loved one another so tenderly as I did the Duke of Marlborough may have some feeling of what it was to have one's children come in, in those last hours, who I knew did not come to comfort me but like enemies that would report to others whatever I did in a wrong way. However at the time I thought my soul was tearing from my body and that I could not say many things before them, yet I would not refuse them to come in, for fear I should repent of it. Upon which I desired Mrs. Kingdom to go to them and tell them that I did not know what disorder it might give their father to go to him now, but I desired they would judge themselves and do as they liked, but I begged of them that they would not stay long in the room because I could not come in while they were there, being in so much affliction. Mrs. Kingdom delivered this message and she told me that the Duchess of Montagu answered that she did not understand her but that if she meant that they were not to see their mother they were very well used to that.

They stayed a great while and not being able to be out of the room longer from him I went in though they were there, and kneeled down by him. They rose up when I came in and made curtseys but did not speak to me and after some time I called for prayers. When they were over I asked the Duke of Marlborough if he heard them well and he answered *Yes, and he had joined in them.*

After that he took several things and when it was almost dark, these ladies being all the time present, I said I believed he would be easier in his bed, the couch being too narrow, and asked if he liked to go to bed. He said Yes, so we carried him upon the couch into his own room.

Later the two daughters went into the drawing-room, where they waited until four o'clock in the morning. "When they went to London," Sarah wrote indignantly, "they and their creatures reported to everybody that I had turned them out of my house, and that I had ordered that nobody should give them anything to eat or to drink . . . and that they heard [Sarah and Mrs. Kingdom] talk a great deal and laugh as they sat in the next room . . . and that after such . . . behavior . . . they would never any more take any notice of me."

John died the next morning at dawn at the age of seventy-two. He had been, perhaps, the greatest gentleman of his age; even one who disliked him spoke of "his perfect manners and his gentleness"; while the greatest gentleman of the next age, Chesterfield, said that "his manner was irresistible" and that he "possessed the graces in the highest degree." Only Wellington can challenge Marlborough's claim to be the greatest military genius in all English history. A great *man*, if the word implies something more than achievement, something rooted in character and inwardly large, he was not. He could not pass beyond dignity to nobility.

Whatever the want of decency that preceded his death, every sign of funeral pomp and martial splendor followed it. Sarah refused the State's offer to bury him, and bore the expense herself, and the whole occasion was extraordinarily grand. For weeks the embalmed body lay in magnificent state at Marlborough House, and on the 9th of August there was a great funeral, with military bands coming first, and then heralds and cannon, and then John's body beneath a canopy of plumes; while behind, as the cortege proceeded from Marlborough House to the Abbey, walked eight Gartered dukes and all manner of lords and generals and statesmen; then a succession of coaches, with the King in one and the Prince of Wales in another.[4] At length, in Henry VII's chapel, "Thus it has pleased Almighty God," Garter King of Arms proclaimed, "to take out of this transitory world, into His mercy, the most high, mighty, and noble prince, John, Duke of Marlborough.

When it was all over, Sarah retired into Windsor Lodge, where she could be, as she wished to be, alone, and where she declined a visit from a friend—in a few instances, she confessed, she had had to see people, "but I had been much

[4] Sarah discovered and made known, however, that she had been defrauded: "There were in the procession only seventeen trumpeters, and yet there are twenty-four in the bill"; "ffeathers [sic] for the horses" were charged for twice, and two chaplains were charged for who were not seen in the procession.

9 *

more easy if I had seen nobody." But soon enough she was called forth from retirement, first by the usual family matters attendant upon a consequential death, and thereafter by the usual Marlborough family quarrels. The Duke had left, as has been said, a very great fortune of more than £2,000,-000. Sarah, by his will, received £25,000 a year in addition to what she possessed already, such as the London, Windsor, and St. Albans houses; Blenheim came to her by Act of Parliament. She had an income of not less than £40,000 a year, and was possibly, as Sir Winston remarks, "the richest woman alive in any country."

There was some trouble over the will—what with the size of the estate and the nature of the beneficiaries, how should there not be?—even though Sarah had taken great care to have it signed publicly in the presence of distinguished witnesses, and had then chronicled the signing and stowed the document away for reference. The principal complainant was the inheritor of the title, Sarah's eldest daughter, Henrietta, Lady Godolphin.[5] Not deeming herself sufficiently well remembered, Henrietta accused her mother of authoring her father's will and induced Sarah's sons-in-law to take her side. And indeed Henrietta may have received less than she had reason to expect, or than John had at one time planned to leave her; though the answer there would lie in her own behavior (whatever the provocations) toward Sarah. For whenever mother and daughters quarreled, John tended to take Sarah's part or to believe her story. As for the new Duchess's manner, when writing to her mother, even before her father had been buried, she subscribed herself "Marlborough."

    [5] A decree that John's title might descend to his daughters—now his son was dead—was one of the marks of esteem shown to him after Ramillies.

Necessarily the relations between Sarah's daughters and their mother were agitated and harsh, for the bad blood between them was on both sides Sarah's own: harshness, haughtiness, unfilialness were part of her daughters' inheritance. It was unfortunate that Sarah's dutiful, sweet-tempered daughters should have been the two who died young, but the wonder in the end is that there should have been any good daughters at all. For Sarah's era and rank conspired very much with Sarah's character to make for quite unmotherly—and wholly unfilial—conduct. Where rearing children was concerned, Sarah seems to have been in no way touched by the new precepts of Locke, but to have felt that they should play wholly submissive roles and exhibit wholly unquestioning obedience. Life at Court made for a certain bleak ceremoniousness even in the nursery; it made even more—particularly if one had duties about the Court, or served a princess—for neglect. Nor, whatever her natural affections, can we imagine that Sarah—like so many neglectful great ladies—would particularly indulge her children during the snatched moments she was with them. It was rather John who knew how to play with them, who when Sarah was away could report: "They are so fond of me, that when I am at home they will be always with me, kissing and hugging me. . . . Miss is pulling me by the arm, that she may write to her dear mamma." With Sarah, all her life, whatever the relationship, there was the compulsion to correct, to edify, to instruct; all her life, too, edification and instruction and correction took the form of nagging; and if Sarah's Queen was never spared her disquisitions, surely her children would not be. And quite as much as she was in all seasons a teacher, she was at all hours a taskmaster, exacting respect, enforcing submission. Again, when in due course she married her daughters off, it was—

the Godolphin alliance partly excepted—with social and even political considerations foremost. Of her four girls, one was eighteen when she married, two were seventeen, and a fourth was fifteen, and if they were chiefly married for worldly reasons, it is not strange that some of them should emerge as worldly people. What might be thought strange, though this is to be too logical, is that Sarah, having married for love, saw no reason why her children should do the same.

Her relations were worst, and presumably from furthest back, with her youngest daughter, the future Duchess of Montagu. The great beauty of a family of beauties, she seems to have become an elegant great lady, sufficiently matching Sarah in arrogance as to get on very badly with her, and so surpassing her at length in rudeness as not to let down her glass to greet Sarah from a sedan chair, or, for that matter, to greet her in public. Sarah herself has told how, as early as John's illness in 1716, she was resolved "to bear whatever [the Duchess of Montagu] would do rather than hinder" her from visiting the sickbed; yet the Duchess and Lady Godolphin alike "never came to see their father . . . but at hours when company was there, going up toward him without taking any notice of me, as if they had a pleasure in showing everybody that they insulted me."

And such sickbed occasions aside, the daughters never set foot in the house at all. Very late in John's life, the Duchess of Montagu writes to him to say: "I was very sorry not to be at home when you came" and to urge him to say when he would like to come again and whom he might care to meet there, adding that her brother-in-law Godolphin is "a very good whisk player" and that her sister "can play." John returned thanks, but "I observe," he wrote, "that you take no manner of notice of your mother: and certainly

. . . you can't imagine that any company can be agreeable to me who have not a right behavior to her." This led his daughter to set forth grievances against her mother. "I am not only concerned but surprised," John wrote back,

at your manner of expressing yourself about her, when you tell me she will own to me she has done things that were never done by another mother, kind or un-kind. . . . Upon showing your letter to your mother and enquiring of her what you mean with regard to that very harsh expression "that she had done what no Mother did" I can't find that you had any reason for your complaint, but she had a great deal.

It is a pity that both the daughter's accusations and the mother's defense are not recorded, though where her duch-ess daughters were concerned, it was oftener Sarah who accused. So abusive, indeed, did she find her daughters gen-erally, that she could only indite one more of those Justifica-tions of herself which must have done something to allevi-ate the pangs of a malign, erring, and ungrateful world:

I am sure [she writes to a friend] you cannot but have heard all the vile things that have been reported of me, which has forced me . . . to vindicate myself to those that I value most, and as I have had reason to think you always my friend, I desire the favor of you to read this long paper. . . . I have endeavored to hide my misfor-tunes from the world, but now there is hardly a possi-bility of a reconcilement between me and my children, from the very injurious aspersions which they have publicly thrown upon me, I neither can nor I think ought to suffer any longer under it; and if I had not taken so much pains to conceal their faults . . . I be-lieve it had not been possible for them to prevail so much as they have done. . . . Having bore what I have done for so many years, rather than hurt my children, I hope nobody will blame me now for what I do, which I am forced to by them to prevent my being pointed at wherever I go.

And to her long-employed man of business, after he had read the "paper," she wrote: "I must own when I was collecting the whole together . . . I thought as you did that it was incredible and sounded like . . . *Robinson Crusoe*."

Sarah's loves and hates among her grandchildren, their loyalties and derelictions and deaths, the game of prizes and the game of forfeits that their relations with her became, belong to a later stage of her twenty-two-year widowhood. More immediate upon it, a little indecorously in fact, were the two offers of marriage which soon came to her. The first, conveyed just six months after John's funeral, was from an old family friend, the Earl of Coningsby, who wrote to the sixty-two-year-old Sarah like a scared smitten schoolboy, adding as a postscript to his proposal: "There is no such cattle or sheep as your Grace desires, to be had till July next." Sarah's reply, though concerned for his feelings, was unfavorable. The second proposal, proffered immediately upon the failure of the first, was of a grander—and in one respect, a very gratifying—sort. It came from the "Proud" Duke of Somerset, from him who had been a sort of make-weight in the reign of Anne. "His pride of birth," it was said, "amounted almost to . . . mental derangement," and his dukedom was, indeed, second only to that of the Duke of Norfolk, who bore the disqualifications of a Catholic. When Somerset went a journey, roads were cleared of all prying eyes and plebeian faces; his own children were not permitted to sit down in his presence, and one who did so (while believing him asleep) forfeited £20,000 of her inheritance. His second—and merely well-born—wife happening one day to tap him playfully with her fan, "Madam," said the Duke, "my first wife was a Percy, and *she* never dared take such a liberty."

It was his first wife who, along with Abigail, had shared special favor with Queen Anne after Sarah's downfall, and to be asked to succeed Somerset's last Duchess, whom she had hated, may have been what most gratified Sarah in the proposal from the Duke. All the same, his proposal was a genuine tribute, and though she could not accept it, it must be declined with more than ordinary thanks. Sarah was equal to the occasion: she found language not just suited to a high ducal treaty of courtship, but worthy of the most sumptuously trashy historical romance: "If I were young and handsome as I was," the famous answer runs, "instead of old and faded as I am, and you could lay the empire of the world at my feet, you should never have the heart and hand that once belonged to John, Duke of Marlborough." [6]

Later, at the Duke of Somerset's request, Sarah found for him a less exacting bride.

[6] These lines have been everywhere much admired, but, however sincerely actuated, surely they are stagy in effect and—considering they are in answer to the compliment of being sought in marriage—decidedly rude in expression. Of this sort, the really fine remark is Sarah's to John himself, possibly while he was confined in the Tower: "Wherever you are, whilst I have life, my soul shall follow you, my ever dear Lord Marl, and wherever I am I should only kill the time wishing for night that I may sleep."

XIV

BUT there was more to Sarah's later life than rejecting haughty dukes and refuting unfilial duchesses: by virtue of who she was or once had been, she was part of a distinguished society. Even Sarah's faults—however reprehensible, however costly—are not to be thought uncommon. It was an age of bitter faction, as of ugly quarrels, and the wellborn were for the most part not well-bred. Although on very different lines, Court life under the first Georges was —like that under Anne—to seethe with dissension, yet be peculiarly dull. The political atmosphere, it is true, was different: one party, the Whig party, was so wholly sovereign as almost to constitute both Government and Opposition; while one man, Sir Robert Walpole, was for some ten years so completely in command as to be the Whig party in person. But though, owing to these two facts, there was from John's death almost until Sarah's no real disruption or overthrow, there was no want of dramatic tensions, of combustible issues, of explosive crises; no lack of squabbling, however unprofitable, or of scheming, though never so feckless. If the Walpole era survives—through other agencies than Sarah Marlborough—as one of England's great eras of peace, Sarah was yet of a populous breed: the disaffected were legion.

What really expired with Anne was government by old-fashioned stealth and cabal or equally old-fashioned royal favor and royal connivance. Anne was the last English monarch ever to annotate an Act of Parliament with *La reine s'avisera;* every monarch since Anne has, however unwillingly, concurred with *Le roi le veult.* Anne's was the last reign before modern Parliamentary government in some

sense took effect, the last in which a Sarah or an Abigail—
or, for that matter, an Anne—could have played just the
role she did.

But what brought England peace yet meant, for many an
Englishman, dissatisfaction and inner tension. Lack of
power also corrupts, and of those out of sympathy with the
Walpole regime, all too many were equally out of office.
Nor, though they had much less power than Anne, were
George I and George II by any means without it: their support of a Ministry could be decisive, their dislike of a place-
hunter fatal. Moreover, their hostility to each other—and
the later and fiercer hostility between George II and his son
—infected the social climate and the political scene, produced a world of rivalry and backbiting and quarrels. We
must not give all the limelight to Sarah's quarrels; never was
there such a fifty years of quarreling—between Whigs and
Tories generally, between Mary and Anne, Bolingbroke
and Harley, Addison and Steele, the Duke of Hamilton and
Lord Mohun, Pultney and Hervey, George I and George II,
George II and Frederick Prince of Wales, Lady Mary and
half her acquaintance, Pope and half of England, Lady
Mary and Pope themselves. The whole period is carpeted
with anecdotes of their anger and scorn; their retorts have
passed into literature, their retaliations changed the movement of history.

Thus, for Sarah's warring spirit embroilment was not
hard to come by. In the matter of quarrels, indeed, the
world was all before her where to choose, and prominence
her guide. For a chief quarry, for a lasting and implacably
stalked foe, she would have nothing less than the Prime
Minister of England, Robert Walpole; and presently, along
with Walpole—for the crime of supporting him—she chose
the Queen. Of her two choices, the one—on the whole be-

neficently—governed the country; the other, with rueful wisdom, ruled the King. It is among the marvels of real life, with its sober facts that would give pause to the boldest fiction, that Sarah should have made Walpole and Queen Caroline her enemies while keeping, to the last, Pope and Lady Mary for her friends. Sarah's hostility to the Prime Minister and the Queen was, to be sure, a political one; yet in Sir Robert might be found Sarah's own massive common sense —except as it was divested of all her vitiating prejudices and willfulness.

The burly Norfolk squire, who created the long Parliamentary week-end that he might have his fill of fox-hunting, and who always read his letters from his gamekeeper in advance of the dispatches and documents of state, was a *novus homo*—in a new age. Sense, sound management, realistic purpose were his arms and armor: the high-held sword, the bravely defended lost cause—for that matter, the field of honor itself—were as much beyond him as personal vindictiveness was beneath him. He was determined, from the day he gained power, to give a war-weary England peace, for only so, he felt, could England prosper. To that end he was not finical about means, or particularly thoughtful of principle, or especially considerate of persons; to that end he put aside all colonial and Continental temptations, overrode all forms of opposition. Before he fell in 1742, he had succeeded superbly—he had given England peace and had made England prosper. This maneuver had its price: few regimes have been so riddled with corruption. The seventy-odd Whig families who almost literally legislated for England also managed systematically to loot it. The very infants among their relations were on the Government payroll, and where nepotism ceased, bribery began. The cynic in Walpole had accepted the maxim that one must govern by either corruption or force, and had chosen corruption. The justification of his policy must be that he used base means to achieve statesmanlike ends.[1] And so far as personally misusing power or amassing wealth was concerned, Walpole—judged by the standards of his time—was moderate in his malpractices, as, in his private relations, he was jovial and likable and bluff, with none of his son Horace's "wellbred ill-nature." Historically his overwhelming fault was the obverse of his commanding merit—along with making England prosper, he made her fall at prosperity's feet. Not corruption, but philistinism, is his principal heritage; not so much a season of thieves as a nation of shopkeepers.

It is a little curious, in view of Walpole's becoming Sarah's most hunted quarry, that, granting a hundred differences of personality and circumstance, he should have been —in material achievement as in moral stature—so often the counterpart of John. He was as vigorous a careerist of peace as was John of war. Like John—however splendid his services—he nowhere transcends his age; he everywhere embodies it. Neither *man* was truly great: both brilliantly executed large jobs and exacted large remuneration; both craved power inordinately, but used it well; both contributed much to Britain and little to humanity; and both, in death, have been oftener disparaged than honored.

At the outset—in the days when she and John were ruling lights and Walpole was a rising one—Sarah had favored so promising a Whig, and Walpole had acknowledged his "infinite" obligations to her. It was at her insistence that he was made Treasurer of the Navy; but even then, she claimed long afterwards, being employed to talk down Abigail's

[1] Peter Quennell has turned up a great defense of Walpole's policy in Burke: "Walpole was an honorable man and a sound Whig. He was not . . . a prodigal and corrupt minister . . . he was far from governing by corruption. He governed by party attachment."

husband and brother to Queen Anne, Walpole secretly pro-
moted Abigail's interest. In this Sarah seems to have been
wholly mistaken; as her other charge, that Walpole on at-
taining power used her with "folly and insolence," may
only mean that he too seldom consulted, or concurred in,
her opinion. It is in any case plain that Sarah was partly
driven into opposition from being denied all equivalent of
office. She who had been the bulwark of Whiggism—and
truly its bludgeoning force—had no place in this tremendous, all-powerful, unending ascendancy of the Whigs.
Doubtless Sir Robert's initial blunder toward her was a failure in diplomacy—his bluff manner, confronted by Sarah,
might quickly turn boorish, as, confronted by Sarah's insistence, his imperviousness might smack of contempt.
Once, definitely, when Walpole laughed at Sarah, she informed him that great men, what with people soliciting their
favor, very seldom heard the truth—and when they did hear
it, judged whoever told it to them mad. Should he, she
added, ever care to hear it, she would have pleasure in telling it to him.

Alienated by his brusqueness and neglect, she could soon
enough set down her hostility to his corrupt use of power,
and even more to his reversal of a State policy ingeminated
by John. To John, as to William of Orange, France was the
great, was indeed the rooted, enemy of England, but to
Walpole, alliance with France was the one real gateway to
peace. Thus Sarah saw Sir Robert—even more in his foreign
than in his domestic aims—carrying Britain to the verge of
ruin. What with personal pique and political outrage, and
the two things merging and mounting and becoming gro-
tesquely misshapen in Sarah's mind, opposition to Walpole
passed over into obsession; he grew from a man of many
faults into a symbol of all evil and, at length, into a portent

of utter calamity. "It is plain," Sarah scrawls at one point, "he has ruined England." "I do really believe," she says at another, "that there never was any instance in any government of so much brutality, ill principles and folly." "Whatever happens," she announces somewhere else, "England can never be what it has been, unless France could have such ministers as Sir Robert and his brother, which is not possible," and is finally moved to declare: " 'Tis thought a fault to wish anybody dead, I hope 'tis none to wish he may be hanged."

Despite her calamity-howling scrawls and armchair fusillades, there were few real blows she could strike against Walpole or the ominous power of France. For one thing, Sir Robert stood firm against an almost comic sequence of Oppositions—in which one clamorous old lady the more would very little matter. For another thing, by now there was something no less familiar than shrill about Sarah's outcries: she was a Cato howling that one Carthage after another—Tories, Papists, Abigail, Harley, Craggs, Walpole, France, George I, George II—must be destroyed, and with rather less the effect of Cato than of the boy who cried Wolf! All the same, she was not without a certain real political influence, partly owing, in an odd way, to this very conviction that the country was going to the dogs. Believing that Walpole's policies must blow up the stock market and abrogate the national debt, Sarah now, with monotonously hysterical regularity, bought land. "From fear of a sponge," she announces, "I have sold my stocks low and bought land dear"—and again: "In the city to bid for Lord Yarmouth's estate . . . because land will be the last thing taken from us." Beginning, indeed, with the year of John's death, and continuing straight on to the year of her own, Sarah acquired "manors, parsonages, rectories, advowsons, messuages, tenements, tithes and hereditaments" to reach a total of thirty estates in ten counties. Such great possessions of land not only brightened her old age with sumptuous prospects of litigation; they also gave her distinct power at the polls, and she was not slow to use it. "I have writ," she confesses, "to all my tenants and people that I have influence over," offering, as she imagined, high-minded advice, but actually telling them how to vote in very plain language. No longer in any sense a Whig, she indeed—as so large a landowner—controlled a fair number of Opposition seats, but a paltry few, all the same, compared with those of the immense Whig landowners supporting Walpole.

There were other ways in which Sarah could make herself felt, and in one, at least, very grandly. On a certain occasion the notes of the Bank of England being heavily discounted while those of Child's Bank remained at par, the Bank of England contrived something of a run on Child's by accumulating vast numbers of their notes and then demanding payment for them all at once. Getting wind of this, Sarah gave Mr. Child an order for £100,000—drawn on the Bank of England.

Sarah's hostility to Queen Caroline—whom Sarah herself described, after her death, as having "great understanding and goodness"—was much owing to the Queen's support of Walpole. And, indeed, on the accession of George II, Caroline's support had proved decisive. It was so generally supposed the new King would dismiss Walpole that at a levee following his accession, as soon as Lady Walpole entered the room all the women present pointedly snubbed her. Then the news leaked out that Walpole had been retained, and when his wife withdrew, the ladies bowed so low before her that she could have "walked across their heads."

The original assumption—that a George II who had been implacably hostile toward his father would have no traffic with his father's Minister—was so logical that Walpole himself had shared it. But though George II, with his heavy German military airs, might huff and puff, and splutter and bellow, and conceive himself an awesome ruler, he was as wrong as in thinking himself a model Englishman. In everything that counted he was governed, with exquisite diplomacy, by Caroline; and Caroline, appreciating Walpole's value, saw to it that he was retained.

Sarah never forgave Caroline this; yet at the level of Court life and high politics—of all that Sarah knew best and prided herself on most—there was hardly another woman in England to compare with her. The daughter of a German margrave, she had absorbed in girlhood a certain intellectual culture; she had made the acquaintance of various eminent men. Rejecting the Emperor of Austria because she refused to turn Catholic, her Protestantism foundered at the same juncture, for by comparing the two religions she lost faith in both. Being married to George II, she might well have lost faith in any religion, for though he profoundly admired her and said at her death that no other woman was worthy of buckling her shoe, so long as she lived he never ceased to browbeat and upset her, or to explode if she kept him waiting, or fume if she took sick, or sneer if she proved wise. She had to be his whipping-boy and his nurse by turns, and, most of all, his confidante in the matter of his mistresses.[2] Whenever the palace favorite palled—and so mechanical were George's rendezvous that, before keeping them, he "frequently walked about his chamber . . . with

---

[2] Of a well-known mistress, George said to Caroline: "You must love the Waldmoden, because she loves me." Caroline had her made Mistress of the Robes.

his watch in his hand"—Caroline would agree that he should dally for a season in Hanover. However unwelcome and exhausting her various roles, they never embittered her; whether from loving the King, or from being able to govern him, or from realizing his own fundamental esteem for her, she was quietly patient, even in the moment of death. George, having long poopoohed her last illness, at length had to face the grim truth and was convulsed with tears. The Queen urged him to remarry. "No, no," he sobbed in French: "no, I shall have mistresses!" "*Mon Dieu*," the Queen replied, "*that* needn't prevent you from marrying!"

Before Caroline became Queen and championed Walpole,[8] Sarah—as we know—favored her and her husband against George I. Now, with family history repeating itself, there grew up around the new Prince of Wales a new Opposition court, and to this one in turn, with its more furious hatreds, Sarah eagerly repaired. She had only just failed, indeed, to become part of the royal-family quarrel itself, and to intensify the quarreling. Wishing at one stroke to elevate her favorite granddaughter, Lady Di Spencer, and to irritate her enemy the Queen, Sarah had presumably contrived to marry Lady Di to the detested Frederick Prince of Wales. There was then no Royal Marriage Act to prevent her; the girl was charming; Frederick and Sarah had a bond in their loathing of the Court; Frederick was heavily in debt, and Sarah stood armed with a £100,000 dowry. The affair had reached the stage where a secret marriage was arranged for at Windsor, but at the last moment Walpole got news of it and stopped its taking place.

It is plain enough that in all these maneuvers a Sarah who

---

[8] It must be confessed that Caroline's support of Walpole was not altogether disinterested: both she and the King were bribed (or rewarded) with large personal incomes.

had once fiercely triumphed in the arena could do little but
foment uproar from the sidelines. If her teeth had not yet all
been drawn, at least her fingerprints had been taken. But
whatever her frustration in so very inferior a role, in a certain sense she must always—short of enjoying completely
uncontested power—have been frustrated. She could not
look at a mantelpiece any more than a Ministry without
finding something to object to or meddle with. Criticism
was her vocation, warfare her only technique, and, like that
other embattled figure of her age, the great Dr. Bentley at
Cambridge, she adored litigation. But if warfare was her
only technique, it was not less her principal excitement: it
was, in perhaps an almost literal sense, the breath of life for
her; and in exerting her violent antipathies and regarding
them as moral crusades, she remained young in spirit and
zestfully ill-tempered. Indeed, as a commentator once wrote
of her, she came to feel "that self-restraint was treason to
sincerity."

Thus, excoriating Walpole not only gave her many lively
moments; it helped win her many superior friends. Possibly Opposition politics makes the strangest bedfellows of
all: it was to reconcile Sarah, for one example, with that erst-
while villain Bolingbroke; it was to bring her into lasting
friendship with Lord Chesterfield. Walpole, more than anyone else, made her later years less lonely. Graciousness had
been no part of her birthright, and no more than she did
anything else did Sarah grow old with grace. But she did
something conceivably better: she did not grow old at all.
Whatever the aches and pains, the gouts and rheumatisms
and scurvies, the medicines and spa waters, the crutches and
wheeled chairs, never once is there an aged beldam's quaver
to her outbursts, a shortness of breath to her laments. There
is the story of her insistence on walking—lame and aging

though she was, and weighted down with velvet robes and a five-foot train—in George II's long, fatiguing Coronation procession. When at one point the procession halted, she seized a drum from a drummer and blithely sat down on it while the crowd first burst out laughing and then cheered.

Though Sarah's friendship with Lord Chesterfield invokes the easy sneer that only such a pattern of the graces could have got along with such a dragon, actually Sarah—like many ill-bred people—was peculiarly observant of good manners, and particularly appreciative of them. And there was much more than opposition to Walpole in Sarah's liking for Chesterfield. It is a thousand pities that his popular fame should rest so squarely on two things. There are, first, the *Letters to His Son*, which shrivel him to a kind of urbane nag, hurling at the oaf he had begotten [4] all the maxims of a Rich Richard's Almanac. And there is, secondly, the pulverizing letter that Dr. Johnson addressed to Chesterfield. With neither correspondent was the Noble Lord remotely at his best, while with his wit, his elegance, his sense of the great world, his veined and marbled wisdom, he would be very much at his best with Sarah. Neither of them, as it happens, had many real friends—he from too much coldness, she from too great heat. She would be amused by a man who could say of a certain marriage that "Nobody's daughter has married Everybody's son." She would have been charmed, had she been alive to hear them, by his so Chesterfieldian last words: "Give Dayrolles a chair." Most of all, she—who prided herself on a rather exorbitant bluntness and distaste for all flattery—must have been quickly

---

[4] It goes beyond irony into the sheerest slapstick that this endlessly instructed son of such a byword for the graces should, at a very grand dinner party given by his father, tuck the tablecloth into his waistcoat from thinking it was his napkin, and on getting up and walking off, pull after him the entire vast and priceless dinner service.

won over by such a master flatterer. Though of one of the wildest breeds of the cat family, she was always cat enough to respond when properly stroked. And Chesterfield never flattered better than by seeking, of Sarah, her favorite granddaughter's hand:

> . . . The person, the merit and the family of Lady Diana Spencer are objects so valuable, that they must necessarily have . . . caused many applications of this nature to Your Grace . . . and though they may be all so much better founded than mine . . . I could never forgive myself if I omitted even the least possibility of being so happy. Your Grace will therefore permit me to throw myself at Lady Diana's feet, and with the utmost respect to offer her the absolute disposal of myself and fortune. I am sensible . . . how small a chance I have of their being accepted since I can only hope for it from an error in both your Grace's judgement and hers. . . .

Though he was not accepted, Sarah never forgot his offer or other instances of Chesterfield's regard, and he will reappear in our story with the reading of the will.

There was much to inspire friendship with Lady Mary also; for if these were the two most quarrelsome great ladies of their time, they were in many ways its most masculine-minded, life-loving, and forthright ones. Lady Mary was twenty-nine years the younger, yet near to middle age when the friendship began; and as someone who had educated and indulged and asserted herself—she was eventually both a duke's daughter and an ambassador's wife—hers was a slightly soured worldliness and a faintly acrid wit. Mr. Wortley (later Wortley Montagu) having failed to win her father's consent, Lady Mary pushed him into an elopement; Mr. Wortley Montagu, as time went on, not sufficiently interesting her, she left him in middle age. Their son proving an unamiable ne'er-do-well, she appraised him as worthless and showed him her back. Meanwhile, she had served humanity by being inoculated in Turkey against smallpox and introducing inoculation into England on her return. She was to serve posterity by writing letters of extraordinary vividness and gusto, and something of their quality, and their glancing acerbity, must also have got into her talk. Her reputation for closefistedness was in no wise inferior to the Marlboroughs'; her reputation, as she grew older, for being dirty was altogether unrivaled. Her famous feud with Pope was put down in certain quarters to her borrowing sheets of his mother and returning them unwashed, and when someone, meeting her at the Opera, told her that her hands were dirty, she is said to have answered: "You should see my feet."

With this woman, whom Fielding—it is true he was her cousin—called "the glory of her own sex and the wonder of ours," Sarah appears to have got on altogether happily. Indeed, she writes to her of wanting "to return your goodness to me in the best manner I can." They were perhaps the better united by their keen appreciation of the shortcomings of everyone else; and Sarah's advanced age would have saved her—face to face, at least—from any signs of Lady Mary's asperity (though Lady Mary, I think, had very good manners). It was to Lady Mary, among others, that Sarah told a now celebrated story that Lady Mary's granddaughter in turn told to the world. There was nothing of Sarah's that John so much loved as her wonderful fair hair; wherefor, to spite him one day when they had quarreled, she cut it off and laid the shorn hair where he was sure to see it. Concerning what she had done, however, nothing was ever said afterwards by either of them, but at John's death she found her hair carefully preserved in a cabinet where he kept his most precious possessions; and at this point of the story Sarah "regularly fell a-crying." Long after her own death Sarah's shortcomings were to be found carefully preserved in Lady Mary's cabinet of recollections. "I think my time better employed in reading," wrote Lady Mary at sixty-eight to her daughter, ". . . than the Duchess of Marlborough's, who passed the latter years of her life in paddling with her will, and contriving schemes of plaguing some, and extracting praise from others, to no purpose; eternally disappointed, and eternally fretting." And it is true that Lady Mary read voraciously, and with considerable understanding, where Sarah read hardly at all; but Lady Mary's own old age was, for all that, not less lonely and a good deal more disheveled.

In later life, too, Sarah got to know the famous Selina Countess of Huntingdon, that gaunt indomitable Methodist who is among those alluded to in Cowper's ghastly line

We boast some rich ones whom the Gospel sways

and who made Wesleyanism—or, at any rate, hearing Wesley preach—the rage at Bath. Bare Deist that Sarah was, she was sufficiently impressed by Lady Huntingdon to ask her to become a kind of Mother Confessor. "Your Ladyship must direct me," Sarah wrote to her,

> . . . I always feel more happy and contented after an hour's conversation with you, than after a whole week's round of amusements. Perhaps my wicked heart may get some good from you in the end.

As Sarah never canted about religion, there must have been some real response.

But of Sarah's latter-day friendships with the famous, none seems more unclouded than that which might be thought most destined to lashing storms. From the late 1730's, when they became acquainted, till 1744, when he died a few months before she did, Sarah and Alexander Pope seem always to have been on genuinely friendly terms. It may have amused such a pair of vilifiers—Pope with his learned mockery and Sarah with her savage wrath—to stay good friends and cheat the town of the gossip it looked forward to, but it is just as possible that they interested and amused each other. Theirs was in any case one of those *ententes* where the wasp lies down with the whirlwind. At the outset, opposition to Walpole [5] would have helped to unite them, but what surely counted more was Sarah's indulgence toward whoever paid her skillful court, and Pope's great courtliness toward whoever skillfully indulged him. They had come to ill-nature and abusiveness by opposite roads: Sarah from an excess of good fortune—beauty, health, possessions, power, a queen's favor, a great man's love; the crippled, pigmy Pope from a dearth of all such blessings. As such, he craved affection and could richly return it; indeed, were he not so notorious for his enmities, he might be remembered for his friendships—for Swift and Bolingbroke, Arbuthnot and Prior, Chesterfield and Gay. Where he and Sarah were quite unlike—he having to excess what she had not at all—was in sensibility. As for his vituperativeness, more even than it was part of his nature, it was integral to

---

[5] But Pope, however politically hostile, immortalized Walpole's personal merit:

> Seen him I have, but in his happier hour
> Of social pleasure, ill-exchanged for power;
> Seen him, uncumbered with the venal tribe,
> Smile without art, and win without a bribe.

his genius: had there not been a goad, it would have been necessary for him to invent one.

Nor was Sarah's cloudless friendship with Pope mainly lived on paper. Pope, it is true, wrote fulsomely to her, but they must have met fairly often. Pope visited Sarah at Marlborough House, at Windsor, at Wimbledon; now he and Chesterfield have dined with her and spent the night, now he and Patty Blount are asked for a visit. Sarah, for her part, is to come to Twickenham: what does she think of bringing Pope in her coach "and supping there, now that moonlight favors your return?" On another occasion, what day will she visit him? On still another, would she not like to have his house when he goes away? Sarah, for her part, showed him just the attentions he loved from great ladies: sent him venison and wine; had him fetched in her coach; asked his advice in preparing her Memoirs. "You have loaded me down with presents," he writes to her. "Your bounty has enabled me to make a great figure at Twickenham these holidays." Clearly, too, the old cripple sought to lavish much greater benefits on the younger one: "First," Pope writes to her,

> I owe you my house and garden at Twickenham, for you would have purchased them for me. . . . Secondly, I owe you a coach and horses, notwithstanding I fought you down to an armchair. And the other day I but named a house in town, and I saw with what attention you listened to it.

"What a girl you are!" he well might write, on another occasion.

She was forbearing, too, in more unexpected ways—as in letting the little semi-invalid fall asleep in the midst of talking to her, so much so that he need not even try to stay awake. "If I awake," Pope writes to her, "you enliven me, if I nod you indulge me." Most significantly of all, they spoke well of each other behind one another's backs. As for bonds between them, Pope had reserved for the man Sarah held in even worse abhorrence than she did Walpole—for the influential Lord Chamberlain, Lord Hervey—the most annihilating abuse in the language:

> . . . *Familiar toad,* ·
> *Half froth, half venom, spits himself abroad.*
>
> . . . .
>
> *Beauty that shocks you, parts that none will trust,*
> *Wit that can creep, and pride that licks the dust.*

And for Sarah's sake Pope had suppressed "in as many copies as he could recall" [6] some lines, alluding to John, that conclude:

> *Now save a People and now save a groat.*

When "that long disease, my life" ended for Pope, Sarah herself had not five months more to live. But only now was to begin the most famous—and, as some would think, the most characteristic—part of their relationship. Whatever her old affection for Pope, Sarah was yet wary enough to inquire of one of his executors—who in turn inquired of Bolingbroke, the legatee of Pope's unpublished MSS.—whether, among them, there were any references to John or herself. In reply Bolingbroke stated that just before his death Pope had got ready a volume that regrettably included "a character of Atossa." "There is no excuse," Bolingbroke adds, "for [Pope's] design of publishing it, after he had re-

---

[6] But, says F. W. Bateson, editor of the definitive text of the poem, "no copies . . . have so far turned up in which the passage is cancelled."

Queen Caroline

Alexander Pope

ceived the favors you and I know." And actually this edition (though already printed up) was never published, but suppressed at birth.

Two years later, however, the verses on the "character of Atossa" did get published (with Bolingbroke's connivance) under the title "The character of a certain great Duchess deceased, by a certain great poet lately deceased," and with a note reading: "It is generally said that the D——ss gave Mr. P £1,000 to suppress them." Gossip immediately identified Atossa as Sarah; gossip next proclaimed that Pope had read Sarah the verses and been bribed (as she supposed) into suppressing them. Thus was created a suitably unhappy ending to a friendship that, by every canon of reason, ought never to have flourished at all. But though, as time went on, the anecdote persisted in even the most cultivated circles, its accuracy came to be questioned in the more scholarly ones. The name of Katharine Duchess of Buckinghamshire began to dispute with Sarah's the title to Atossa: one critic said flatly that the verses were meant for Katharine; another contended that Pope had meant them for Sarah first, but recast them for Katharine afterwards. And presently there develped a pendant to the original anecdote, to the effect that Pope read the Character to both duchesses, telling each it was meant for the other; but that Sarah, at least, was not fooled and said she knew very well whom it was meant for.

Yet it now seems virtually certain that Atossa never *was* meant for Sarah. As Mrs. Campbell, who is admirable on the whole subject, has said, it only required from the outset that people should "examine the Character itself"—for, in terms of Sarah, much of it clearly fails to apply. What it always really required was a likelier candidate: lacking that, enough of it did apply to Sarah, and enough people existed

10

to suppose that all of it must, for no one to look further. Once the Duchess of Buckingham was proposed, however, it was clear whom Pope's slipper really fit. If certain pretty general allusions hit off Sarah—

> *Finds all her life one warfare upon earth*

or

> *Who breaks with her, provokes revenge from hell,*

the more individualizing touches do not fit Sarah at all:

> *From loveless youth to unrespected age*

or

> *To heirs unknown descends the unguarded store,*
> *Or wanders, heaven-directed, to the poor.*

As for the Duchess of Buckingham, she—as the illegitimate daughter of James II—was, like the historical Atossa, a royal offspring; she had quarreled with her husbands, children, friends, and—most pertinently and violently—with Pope; had contested her husband's will, survived all her children, and died before Pope did. He thus, in mentioning her "unknown" heirs, was drawing on well-known facts. I would further suggest that since the title speaks of the D——ss as "deceased" and the poet as "*lately* deceased," chronology itself points to Her Grace of Buckingham. Seldom has tattle that quite fails to hold water been so long and solidly frozen into "truth."

The Duchess of Buckingham, it so happens, is linked with Sarah in a second famous anecdote. When the Duchess's son died, and she requested of Sarah the funeral chariot in which John had been borne to rest, Sarah answered curtly that the car had carried the body of "my Lord of Marlborough," and should certainly carry no other. To this

anecdote also there is a pendant: the Duchess of Buckingham said that Sarah's refusal was no matter, that she had
been assured she could hire a much superior chariot for £5.

In these later years Sarah did not consort only with the
famous, or journey from feud to feud: at times she was
merely rather typical of her sex or her class or her century.
There happily exists, from among Sarah's letters to her
granddaughter Lady Di, an account of a trip she took—fifty
years in advance of Sheridan she might have called it *A
Trip to Scarborough*—which is at once a neat revelation of
Sarah caught in transit and an agreeable contribution to
English social history. If here also she is quite unmistakably
Her Grace of Marlborough, she is at the same time just an
aging, ailing great lady examining the social terrain and taking the waters; here are Scarborough grumbles rather than
Blenheim growls; and, writing immediately of what she sees
(and feels) rather than retrospectively of what she has let
herself imagine, she is more life-sized, if still loud, in her
grousing and irritation.

Family matters as well as her own physical ailments—only
Sarah would simultaneously contract scurvy and gout—
troubled her in the approaching summer of 1732: her grandson by marriage, the twenty-four-year-old Duke of Bedford, having played hob with his family fortune,[7] now further displeased Sarah by becoming dangerously ill. Worst
of all, he determined to go for his health's sake to Lisbon—
and to make his wife go with him. The "poor Duchess of
Bedford," whose "constitution"—Sarah writes to Lady Di—
"is extremely worn," and who dreads such a trip, "now desires," says Sarah

---

[7] By which Sarah's descendants could be twice cursed: for if (as
seemed certain) he died childless, the title and depleted estates would
pass to his brother, who was Lady Di's husband.

my advice but I don't know what to say, only that if
I were in her circumstances I am very sure that I would
not go. I have always persuaded her to submit to everything in the world, and to live in any manner he would
have her in his own house. And this is all I think that
anybody can expect from her.

A little later Sarah adds, with ingenious logic:

As the Duke of Bedford has always lived with her, he
can't possibly have any pleasure in taking her with
him.

In any case, the poor young Duchess

should not hazard her life to go with so great a brute
. . . Whether the law will give him power to force
her away against her will is the question.

"I know nothing of that," winds up grandmama—"but I
will enquire about it."

Having determined, soon after, to make the five-day journey to Scarborough for her own health, Sarah decided to
interview the great brute of a Duke on her way there. What
with their respective ailments, the meeting boded ill, but
"tis not possible," Sarah informed Lady Di afterwards, "for
any man to behave better than the Duke of Bedford did in
all respects." Being at Woburn, the Duke's great country
house, Sarah must needs go on a tour of inspection, and in
conducting her about, the Duke would not even own that
he was ill, though she observed that "when we went into the
Gallery to see the pictures, he sat down very often, which
I conclude proceeded from weakness." And, all in all, "it
was impossible to see him in such a condition without being
touched with some melancholy." Then on she goes toward

Scarborough: "As I came through Northampton I met with one that told me by chance what I thought seemed very odd; that a man just married should choose to go in a chaise with his sister, and his wife ride by herself on horseback." At York "the church is a Gothic building the finest that ever I saw, a vast deal of what they call architecture." At length she reached Scarborough, where she took lodgings and sat down to give Lady Di "some account of this place, which is the worst that ever I saw in England." The place where "they assemble to drink the waters" is in itself so dirty and so difficult and disagreeable that "I resolve to take my waters at home." But

> there was one thing I saw today which is such a curiosity that I must tell you of it. There is a room for the ladies' assembly, which you go up a steep pair of stairs into, on the outside of the house, like a ladder. And in that room there is nothing but hard narrow benches, which is rather a punishment to sit upon than an ease. When the waters begin to operate, there is a room within it, where there is above twenty holes with drawers under them to take out, and all the ladies go in together and see one another round the room, when they are in that agreeable posture, and at the door there's a great heap of leaves which the ladies take in with them. . . . I came home as fast as I could for fear of being forced into that assembly.

As for Scarborough in general: "I believe, upon the whole, the place is worse than Hanover." And though Lord Chesterfield, who is staying at the spa, insists that her house is the envy of the community, "I think it a very bad one, very dirty and so noisy that I am going to lay straw in the street before my house. . . . My Lord Malpas is my next neighbor, but I hope he won't come to me, for I am sure he is a most disagreeable creature." Indeed, "if anything could make this place tolerable," it would be Lord Chesterfield and his sister Lady Gertrude Hotham, "who are both extremely well bred."

By her next letter things are no better: "The place where they drink the water is so horrid, that it is impossible to go to it. . . . There is no company here that one would not choose rather to be dead and dumb than to be with them." (True, Lord Chesterfield and his sister are "both charming," but "one can't see them often enough to recompense me for what I go through.") And on top of everything else: "This is the sixth letter that I have written to you"—without having a word from Lady Di.

Despite such a perfect conspiracy of evils, Sarah must soon report that "I have taken these waters but seven days and the itching that tormented me so much, which was from the scurvy, is almost gone." And though, on the other hand, "I very much fear that I will not recover much strength as to my limbs," she will stay on and simply be patient. Four days later:

> I am as well now as you have seen me a great while, and I do believe these waters have done me some good and will do me more. . . . I don't think of leaving this place till I have got as much benefit from the waters as I can hope to, and I am not so uneasy with the place and meat as I was, but I am sure I will never see it more after I leave it.

Two days later:

> I am very sure I will never see Scarborough more . . . if the waters happen to do me good . . . I will have

them bottled up carefully, putting oil upon the top and
then wax upon the cork . . . they will be very good
to take at any of my own houses, which I will do if I
live. . . .[8]

And now I will tell you how the day passes. The
morning is the best, when I drink my waters, and at
dinner I have a very good stomach. Soon after that a
little room is filled with visitors, most of which I never
saw before, and to avoid having it as dismal as a funeral
. . . I play at quadrille for half a crown a fish.

At night it is less satisfactory:

After I am in bed . . . I am awakened with the bark-
ings and howlings of dogs and hounds . . . kept . . .
for the entertainment of fine gentlemen in this place.

The races at York, near by, she finds do "a great deal of
mischief"; not only do "the horses make great havoc in the
corn," but "all the young women lay out more than they
can spare in hopes to get good husbands, which in general
ends in being debauched." As for my Lord Malpas, next
door, he had entertained with a raffle making people spend
"a great many guineas" for boxes and knives—"none of
which were worth half a crown apiece"—that belonged to
his servants.

Four days later she is suffering from gout; has not drunk
the waters; is "extremely weary" of Scarborough; and—having begun a book "by one Dr. Wittie written sixty-five
years ago"—tends to agree that "drinking nothing but good
water . . . is best for one's health. . . . I am convinced
that the less wine or malt drink young people take, it is

[8] On such reasoning the whole trip was unnecessary, for Scarborough
waters "well cemented down in the bottles" were all the time on sale in
London.

much the better. But for people of my age that have been used to drink wine"—naturally, circumstances alter cases. Some ten days later, though she had not "taken the waters this fortnight . . . I was well enough to play at quadrille yesterday and dined with company, but I believe I shall be sooner well if I don't hang down my legs and therefore I will keep my chamber today."

And so, what with her sending to York for coach horses, and desiring letters of Lady Di to be sent to "the post house at Nottingham," the correspondence tails off and the stay at Scarborough ends. On August 30, after six days on the road of a "tedious disagreeable journey"—three and a half miles an hour was the average speed in a coach—she is back at St. Albans: "I don't think myself better for the great trouble in going to Scarborough"; and so far as lameness is concerned, she is "worse." At journey's end, as at journey's outset, she speaks of the ailing Duke of Bedford. Lady Di has evidently been shocked on seeing him, and though he is "really a loss to nobody but the sharpers," Sarah confesses that "it is impossible to see anybody . . . in such a condition as he is said to be and not be touched by it." The Duke died, some two months later, while en route, without his Duchess, to Lisbon.

The Scarborough sessions of quadrille reflect Sarah's lifelong love of cards while caring very little for books. But one book that she read during her later years had her in raptures, even when she found out who had written it: *Gulliver's Travels*. No one had been more implacable toward John and her than Swift; and no one, we must add, had at times been more unfair. But now he conquered her: she was ready to forgive "all the slaps he has given me and the Duke of Marlborough," and could only wish he would join the present Opposition. In any case, "Dean Swift," she remarks, "gives the most exact account of kings, ministers, bishops and the courts of justice that is possible to be writ"; and "I really have not been pleased so much [for] a long time as with what he writes." One might think it required Swift's depths of savagery to earn Sarah's degree of praise, yet what very specially beguiled her were "those charming creatures . . . the Houyhnhnms, which I understand to be horses, so extremely polite." [9]

One other book she had returned to, again and again, over the years—her own Memoirs. The *Conduct*,[1] as the book was finally called, the *Vindication* as it was always thought of and meant to be, was completed in its first form hard on the heels of all it chronicled. This draft, composed in 1711, Sarah (as she later stated) planned "to publish immediately, but was dissuaded from it by a person of great eminence in this day whom I thought my friend"—Walpole. A "more connected and regular sketch" was written in 1713 and 1714 with the help of a secretary of John's, while the Marlboroughs were in exile. Early and late Sarah must have tinkered at this account of her persecutors and defense of herself. The work was certainly known to be writing; Voltaire indeed—when he visited Blenheim in 1727—begged Sarah for a glimpse of it. "Wait a little," she answered. "I am at present altering my account of Queen Anne's character. I have begun to love her again since the present lot have be-

[9] In the animal kingdom, Sarah had generally to go beyond human beings to find what was truly desirable. "I am very fond of my three dogs," she writes,

> they have all of them gratitude, wit and good sense—things very rare to be found in this country. They are fond of going out with me; but when I reason with them and tell them it is not proper, they submit, and watch for my coming home, and meet me with as much joy as if I had never given them good advice.

[1] *Account of the Conduct of the Dowager Duchess of Marlborough from Her First Coming to Court to the Year 1710.*

10*

come our Governors." And she herself, after waiting a little, is said to have asked Voltaire whether he would edit the MS. Tempted at the outset—so Oliver Goldsmith tells the story—Voltaire, after reading the Memoirs, remonstrated with Sarah over their bitterness of tone. Withdrawing the offer, Sarah said afterwards that she had supposed Voltaire a "man of sense, but I find him at bottom either a fool or a philosopher."

Finally, in her old age, she asked Pope to find her a collaborator who could knit her fragments into a whole; and Pope, after conferring with Chesterfield, suggested his friend, a barrister named Nathaniel Hooke. Chesterfield having brought Hooke and Sarah together, at once withdrew, not caring, as he said, "to meddle myself in an affair which I am sure will not turn out . . . to her satisfaction, though I hope . . . it will be to his advantage." The collaboration, which at any rate brought Hooke a handsome £5,000, consisted largely of Sarah lying in bed propped up by pillows dictating for hours on end. Tradition has it that Sarah would not permit her collaborator any access to her materials, and that Hooke in turn contended they were "sadly garbled." His activities were perhaps largely confined to details and, one might suppose, to abridgment. The book came out at last in 1742, and, though concerned with far-off things and battles long ago, it fomented—like almost everything connected with Sarah—an uproar. Her Queen-Anne enemies might by now be dead or senile, but she had antagonists enough in the present to raise the dust, and her need to show herself always in the right provoked jests as well as rejoinders. The *Conduct*, as far as it goes, is often amazingly truthful, and even oftener vivid, though from what Sarah left out or slurred over there might be compiled a no less truthful and vivid *Misconduct*.

One further piece of writing diverted Sarah, it may be, most of all: her will, but this, appearing posthumously, must not be examined out of order. And with those whose names it would naturally contain or more unnaturally omit—with the members of Sarah's family during the last years of her life—we have now to concern ourselves.

XV

About Sarah as she grew older there is the sense of a most numerous progeny: one is forever encountering a reference to one grandchild or an anecdote about another. And one's confusion mounts, what with three Marys in the family, three Annes, two Henriettas, and two Dukes of Bedford—and mounts the more because commentators understandably mistake them for one another or kill them off out of turn. In actual fact, however, it was not a specially populous breed, but only seems to be because of so many flavorsome references, because Sarah's relations with her grandchildren were so public or so punitive. Sarah had in all well over a dozen grandchildren who lived for any length of time; but of these, three died years before she did, and several hardly entered her life. To be sure, her grandchildren-by-marriage virtually doubled the chances of collision and uproar; nor did deaths necessarily end them. And there were also the two undutiful daughters from whom Sarah was estranged, and who did not have to meet their mother to meet with her abuse.

Sarah in old age might have grievances and to spare against her eldest daughter, but had she ever chosen to read over the letters Henrietta wrote to her as a child, she might have wondered how such affectionate prattle could pass into such stony silence:

> My sister and I took physic on Saturday, and are very well after it. Pray mama, present my humble duty to the Princess. My sister presents hers to you, I believe I have said enough to tire you, and so will end.

Sarah might actually have found Henrietta what she subscribes herself—"most dutiful":

> Pray, my dear Mama, send word when you send the fans, which is to be mine, for I had rather you should choose for me, than myself.

And Sarah might have found that she herself was proving a little difficult: "I will do another letter for you," wrote Henrietta on another occasion, "quickly and better than the other was, for I am afraid it did not please you."

Much else, in any case, did not please Henrietta's mother as time rolled on, with Henrietta herself showing less and less contrition, and at length showing none at all. The friction did not really have consequences, however, till a good while after Henrietta's marriage. As a young wife she could write to her mother: "Where you say your heart is so full of kindness for me has done me more good than I can express." Indeed, Henrietta can even show signs of jealousy: "I was mighty sorry not to have a letter last post, especially when my sister had one." Actually, the young Godolphins had moved in with the Marlboroughs, where Sarah and her daughter lived, as the mother put it, "like sisters." But later the young couple went to live with Lord Godolphin, in whose widower's house Henrietta was under no one's thumb and could assume a hostess's role. And beyond being seated, now, at the head of the table, Henrietta could have at her side, and down its length, such guests as she herself had a mind to, and it was just here, perhaps, that things began to go astray. For Henrietta, it appears, had ambitions—which Sarah disapproved of—to know and even be numbered among the wits. Sarah was possibly right to sniff at Henrietta's way of going about it, at her "giving 100 guineas to a very low poet that will tell her that she is what she knows she is not"—the poet presumably being John Gay. But, whatever her mother might think, Henrietta could boast that, at the opening of the playhouse in the Haymarket, in 1705, Congreve and Vanbrugh called her "the learned Minerva"; and indeed Sarah, coming to consult Henrietta "about Lady Harriot, whether she should have pinners with lappets, or without," found her daughter "at ombre with Mr. Congreve and a woman that I did not know. I thought he looked out of countenance but showed more willingness to talk to me than you did; I soon put you at ease by going away." Worse, when Sarah called the next day, she was informed that Henrietta was out—when all the time, as her mother discovered, she was writing in her dressing-room.

From thenceforth, relations between mother and daughter rapidly declined, one explanation being what Sarah scrawled on a letter of Henrietta's: "This . . . was from Lady Godolphin before she was ruined by the very bad company she kept." Elsewhere Sarah was perfectly explicit about the "very ill company"—"My Lady Oxford, and her daughter Mrs. Ramsey, and Mrs. Hamond . . . and at last . . . Mr. Congreve and several poets." Henrietta, without doubt, was pleasure-loving and vain: even her fond father-in-law admitted that she had had the colic "enough to hinder her from sleeping, but not from going to the play," and she herself, taxed with liking country dances, snapped back at her mother: "For saying I don't love country dances when I really do, I could not think of denying such an inclination as that."

But whatever the perils of country dances, or Sarah's insistence that "there was not upon Earth so vile a woman as my Lady Oxford," it was Mr. Congreve who would leave the greatest mark—and, as Sarah might think, stain—on Henrietta's reputation. For more and more, as the years passed, he was to be seen in Henrietta's company. Henrietta "mothered him," and truly enough, in early middle age, gout plagued him and cataract left him all but blind. The year after Henrietta became Duchess, she and Congreve both spent the whole season at Bath, and were always together. At Bath, noted a contemporary gossip, the "waters have a wonderful influence on barren ladies, who often prove with child, even in their husbands' absence." And in due time, some twenty years after she had left off child-bearing, Henrietta was "brought to bed," as her husband informed their married daughter, "of a little girl."

The husband was to become very fond and fatherly toward the little girl, but it was on every tongue that she was Congreve's daughter. Henrietta, wrote Lady Mary, "is as much embarrassed with the loss of her big belly as ever a dairymaid with the getting one." Sarah herself referred to her Duchess daughter as Congreve's moll. There were to be scurrilous poems and the like for years to come. Boswell—in his *London Journal*—says that

> Mrs. Douglas, who has a prodigious memory . . . told me that Congreve the poet lived in the family of old Lord Godolphin, who is yet alive, and that Lady Godolphin was notoriously fond of him. In so much

that her lord having gone abroad upon an embassy for
two years, on return she presented him with a fine
girl by the author of *Love For Love*, which he was
so indulgent to accept of. . . .

Indeed, Boswell adds,

the young lady was most tenderly educated, and . . .
was never suffered to see the moon for fear she would
cry for it.[1]

Certainly, in their way, Congreve and Henrietta went
far toward affirming the truth of his paternity—he by leaving Henrietta (what would otherwise surely be strange,
seeing how rich she was) almost his entire £7,000 estate,
and she by leaving Congreve's entire bequest to the child.
One feels considerable sympathy with Henrietta's husband, who not only had to put up with a virtual *ménage à
trois;* but who, while gossip was flying about concerning
the baby, received angry screeds from Sarah concerning
his wife. "The ill treatment," Sarah wrote, "which I have
had from the Duchess of Marlborough . . . I believe there
is no instance of to any mother since the world was made."
Henrietta's husband outlived them all, however, even the
late-born child he came to love; and, dying at eighty-seven,
asked to be buried "without pomp" at neither his wife's
side nor his father's.

[1] The child in time became Duchess of Leeds, and seems to have had
a gay, exuberant nature. She wrote letters in the vein of: "My sister
flatters me we shall have the pleasure of your company to eat eels . . .
but does not *promise* anything more. . . . I'm always happy in your
company; besides . . . I've been at the expense of a new mattress for
your bed." It would be pleasant to detect in her letters some inheritance
from Congreve; but she wrote precisely as scores of eighteenth-century
ladies of fashion were wont to do.

Henrietta died some thirty-three years earlier, in 1733, when she was fifty-one. To the very end she sought to make something of a figure in artistic circles, and to the very end she and Sarah remained alienated. When Handel and Buononcini split London into camps, Sarah was ranged with George II on the German's side, Henrietta with the Prince of Wales on the Italian's. Henrietta died of the dropsy—going hence, in her husband's words, in a "kind of dreaming rather than a downright delirium," and Sarah could only write from Windsor to Lady Di of her "several attempts to be reconciled to that unfortunate woman. . . . But nothing I said or did had the least good effect." As to the pain she felt at Henrietta's death, "I do acknowledge," Sarah continued,

> it would have been much greater had she . . . loved me as she once did. It is certain that her nature was tender and that she . . . was the modestest young creature that ever I saw, till she was flattered and practised upon by the most vile people upon earth.

Henrietta, though she died Duchess of Marlborough, chose not to be buried at Blenheim, but (by instructions in her will) near her father-in-law in Westminster Abbey—which would be near Congreve as well. She had not only given Congreve a magnificent funeral, but—to quote Boswell's received account of a famous and doubtless fictitious story—had "an image of him in wax daily set at table and nightly in her bedchamber, to which she spoke, believing it . . . to be Congreve himself." Far more certainly—and, if the wax-image tale is true, rather inconsistently—she put up a monument to Congreve in the Abbey, with an inscription recording what happiness and honor she had had in his company. "I know not what happiness she might have had in his company," Sarah muttered, "but I am sure it was no honor."

Of Sarah's children there remained now only the Duchess of Montagu, of whom Sarah was writing as of old: "As she has been an ill wife, a cruel daughter and mother, and a very harsh mistress, she must have a very bad heart." How outrageously her youngest daughter had behaved toward her Sarah explained on another occasion: "I married her to the chief match of England in all respects, and the settlements which I made for her were uncommon." As for the girl's ingratitude, "if it had not been for my favor she must have been married to some country gentleman with £1,500 or £2,000 a year.[2] Of the "chief match in England," all the same, and despite his being of her own choosing, Sarah could only say:

> All his talents lie in things only natural in boys of fifteen years old, and he is about two and fifty: to get people into his garden and wet them with squirts, and to invite people to his country houses, and put things in their beds to make them itch.[3]

How violent was Sarah's feeling about the Duchess of Montagu comes out in the fact that, where she had unsuccessfully made overtures of reconciliation with Henrietta, of the overtures that—in Sarah's extreme old age—the Duchess of Montagu made toward her she would have no part. And to a common friend who tried also to reconcile mother and daughter, Sarah wrote: "After all that has passed in so many years I will never have anything more

[2] There is a tradition—which may account for part of the ill feeling—that it was just such a man that the Duchess of Montagu had set her heart on.

[3] The Duke of Montagu also originated a famous hoax at the Haymarket Theatre, of a man squeezing himself into a quart bottle.

to do with her. . . . My life is very near run out, and I am sure she can never give me any more pain or pleasure, and therefore I desire that you would never name her more to your most faithful, humble servant, S. Marlborough." In this last reference to the last existing of her children, Sarah seems to write out of more than pique or ill temper: she is indomitable, not merely willful; granitic, and no longer just hard.

Sarah as a grandmother was, if at times implacable, generally far more indulgent; and manifesting devotion and even restraint. As a grandmother, too, she can be observed full-face, close up, and in revealing detail, for she was now much more of a private person than a public figure. She had grown old and crippled, and been widowed, and plainly craved notice and affection. Of some dozen grandchildren at the time of John's death, several entered very little into her existence, but collectively the grandchildren play a great role in her old age—if not in terms of personal feeling, then of family prestige, or of that quality she abounded in: moral indignation she would have called it, but moral irritation is a more accurate phrase. It is a common trait in humanity still, and consists in exalting personal grievances or annoyances into high-minded questions of ethics.

Even those of her grandchildren who interested Sarah very little as people, she was concerned about as *partis:* however extreme, the maneuvers involving Vanbrugh over marrying off Lady Harriet Godolphin are not untypical of her matchmaking. Thanks in part to Sarah's determination and tactics, five of her six granddaughters became duchesses. Sarah, again, was on at least a civil footing with two of her grandchildren because they, like her, were on bad terms with their mothers. Presumably young Isabel Montagu was treated coldly by her parents and pushed into a loveless early marriage with the Duke of Manchester. She had when young been often with Sarah, who "pitied her . . . and loved her as much as if she had been my own child." Grown into a "witty, extremely agreeable but sharp-tempered woman," she seems to have retained her grandmother's regard. "You're a good creature," Sarah told her once, "but you *have* a mother!" "And *she* had a mother," the granddaughter replied.

Sarah also—though here it was more difficult—maintained good relations with Henrietta's son. Lord Blandford, as he was known after Henrietta became Duchess, was always spoken of in the family as Willigo (except when he was referred to as Lord Worthless). Growing up to keep bad company and be constantly drunk, he got into his mother's ill graces. Sarah accordingly went out of her way to be kind to him and so arranged matters as to make him independent of his parents. Running wild on the Continent in his youth, he wrote suddenly to Sarah from Utrecht that he was engaged to a rich burgomaster's daughter; knowing his grandmother, he married the girl before Sarah's outraged letter forbidding the match could reach him. Sarah now wrote again, substituting for the "ingenious curses" of her first letter a grandmother's blessing. She urged Willigo to come back to England and seek his mother's forgiveness —which, Sarah wickedly pointed out, Henrietta would doubtless refuse, and after that, grandmama added, Willigo's father could have no valid complaint and would not stay on bad terms with his son simply "because he has . . . a mad woman for his wife." Blandford answers more wickedly still that he has no intention of seeing his mother— which, since that means flouting his father's commands, will save him the trouble "of seeing either of them."

When, at length, he arrived with his bride in England his charming manners helped reveal Sarah in an unexpected light. Blandford gave a dinner party at which his grandmother was one of the guests:

They were all there a little after three. Four o'clock came, and five, but no Ld. Blandford, and by that time my Lady thought fit to call for dinner, and when they had half dined he came in, so that the D[uches]s of M[arlborough] said, in all the good humor in the world, "Oh my Lord, I conclude you have been in the House of Commons." "Indeed, madam, but I have not." "Then," says she, "I wish I was nearer to you, that I might beat you." "Then I am very glad you are not. I did not think you would have come before five, nor did I not [sic] think you would have stayed for me," says my Ld.

Around six, Blandford went off to the play, leaving his guests behind to play quadrille. When he got home again— continues the Duchess of Newcastle—

he came into the room . . . for a minute, went away again before the D[uches]s of M[arlborough] went away, and Ld. Winchelsea put her into her chair. To complete my history, the occasion of his being so late was, that he went and dined at Lady Meadows', and so came to his company at his own house between five and six o'clock that he knew was waiting for him all that time. I fancy t'would be entertaining to hear the D[uches]s of M[arlborough] give an account of it. But Lady Evelyn says she kept her good humor all day, and was perfectly easy, and did not seem as if there was anything odd or wrong in him, any more than what she said to him, which was quite in good humor.

Not much more than a year later Willigo died of a drunken fit at Oxford. His mother could only say how glad she was that the title her father had borne would never, now, be sullied by her son. Sarah, sent for without being told that Willigo was dead, murmured on learning the truth: "I hope the Devil is picking the man's bones who taught him to drink." She stayed on at Oxford to discuss his case with the doctors and to comfort the young widow (whom she never saw again), then hurried back to Blenheim.

It so happens that the grandchildren who aroused really strong feelings in Sarah were all of them Spencers, children of the rasping Lord Sunderland and of Sarah's much loved and lamented daughter Anne. The four Spencers included the grandchild Sarah most loved, the one she most hated, the one she most indulged, and the one she most kept changing her mind about. Being themselves, moreover, a loyal and close-knit group, each is often involved, in Sarah's tribal dramas, with one or more of the others.

In that copious anthology of abuse which will someday, perhaps, be culled from Sarah's speech and writings, her granddaughter Lady Anne Spencer, who married William —afterwards Viscount—Bateman, must boast very nearly the foremost place, and by all odds the most famous example. For it was Lady Bateman's portrait that Sarah caused to be hung in her drawing-room with the face blackened over and an inscription reading: "She is much blacker within." Apparently Sarah had never liked the girl, and at the time of Lady Sunderland's death, when she took little Lady Di into her household, contrived not to take in Lady

Anne. For violently disliking Lady Anne after she grew up and married, Sarah had what for her were weighty reasons. It was Lady Bateman who introduced her brother Charles—the new Duke of Marlborough on Henrietta's death—to the girl he married; and as the girl's father had been a bitter enemy of John's, this was the basest treachery. As if that were not enough, Lady Bateman also introduced Charles to Henry Fox—and so into the hands of the Walpolites. Sarah came to see in Lady Bateman a determined enemy, someone who, wherever possible in family matters, sought to flout and discredit her. Even Lady Di, the one grandchild whom Sarah steadily adored, got into her grandmother's black books for remaining friendly with such a viper. "She is a disgrace," Sarah wrote, "to be anybody's sister" and decreed that Lady Di must choose between her sister and her grandmother:

> I desire, my dear, that you will consider very well before you take your resolution. . . . If you determine . . . not to take away those few comforts I have left . . . you must be very plain with Lady Bateman . . . in letting her know that you can have no commerce with her; that you are very sorry that she did not reflect upon . . . what she has done; that . . . there is no predecent of such a treatment [4] to a grandmother that for thirty years has been laboring to assist and serve the whole family, and has done it with great success.
>
> . . . I am the more persuaded my notions are right in this, because . . . those of the most cool temper can't help saying that nothing was ever so scandalous

---

[4] It may enliven some student's leisure to count up the number of insults, outrages, and misdeeds against Sarah for which she claims there is no equal or precedent in recorded history.

as all that Lady Bateman has done,[5] but . . . I wish to have you do as you judge best and right, and . . . whatever you do, I shall always be most affectionately yours, S. Marlborough.

Lady Di apparently ignored Sarah's ultimatum, while yet managing to pacify her, but neither was she infected with any of Lady Bateman's hostility toward their grandmother. Lady Bateman did, on the other hand, have a certain influence on her two brothers. Charles, whose marriage she had helped bring about, was in later years a sturdy soldier who actually died on active service, but in early life he was a good deal of a coxcomb and spendthrift, and a sort of foolish stubborn liar. "I remember," Sarah wrote,

> when he was a very great boy, he had burnt the hair of his head almost down to his forehead. I . . . asked him how it came in that condition, and who had cut it to hide its having been burnt, but he stiffly denied that it was either burnt or cut, saying for half an hour . . . that he knew nothing of it. . . .

Sarah, when he grew up, indulgently bailed him out of a number of tight squeezes over money—never knowing that she was also a source of supply to him through loans raised against her death. She had once given him a diamond sword that the Emperor had presented to John; learning that the moneylenders were about to pounce on anything available, she went to law to recover her gift and argued the case herself: "Shall I suffer the sword which my lord would have carried to the gates of Paris to be sent to the pawnbroker's and have the diamonds picked out one by

[5] And if the student has any leisure left, he might count up the number of times Sarah has consulted others and been assured she was in the right.

one?" Then came the far more heinous offense of his marrying a daughter of John's enemy Lord Trevor: Sarah did not attend the wedding (nor did Lady Di), and the soon-to-be Duke was in the deepest disfavor. His grandmother was now speaking of his "monstrous usage" of her and accusing his bride of having looted Windsor Lodge, where Charles had been staying before he fell into disgrace. Sarah, indeed, even rigged up a symbolic puppet show in which eight Miss Trevors, cousins of the bride, pulled up every shrub in the Windsor garden while the bride herself walked off with the chicken coop under her arm.

But when, in his own good time, her grandson came calling on Sarah, she quickly changed her tune. "I have a mind to tell you," she wrote to Lady Di,

> that the Duke of Marlborough has been with me this morning, though I endeavored in my letter to save him that trouble. It is not easy for me to describe without lessening it, the goodness of his behavior in every respect. All that he said was so extremely good natured, and with good sense. And I do really believe, he is very sincere. . . .
>
> Before he went away, he desired that his wife might come to me. . . . I told him . . . that I should be glad to see her, when I came to London. For I never had anything to say against her.

Of the wife, Sarah also confessed she had never "heard any one speak of her that did not give her an extreme good character." All the same, says Sarah, it was "not a natural match." Less than a week after the Duke's conciliatory visit, his grandmother announces that she loves him "much better than I ever did in my life, which is saying a great deal." The new love affair continues for a little; then tiny clouds appear. "I have not heard from your brother Marlborough," Sarah writes to Lady Di, and "cannot help apprehending that the lady [Bateman] who has formerly done so much mischief is contriving some new plot." More time passes, and though the young Duke still has "a great many very good qualities," he has also a decided number of bad ones, not least his extravagance. His grandmother concedes that he gave up "some very useless horses," but only, she contends, to be at "a much greater expense in building a ship." Yet more time passes, and though, Sarah complains, she is "laboring like a packhorse . . . to save him from the cheats," the ungrateful Charles barely bothers to answer her letters. A further interval, and he has left off answering at all, but that is not why Sarah is indignant; it is that "he never writes to me but as one would do to an enemy or at least to one that was mud."

Pretty plainly Sarah liked the young Duke, but, what is more to the point, nowhere better do we get a sense of her craving (despite all disclaimers) for attention, of her susceptibility (despite all denials) to flattery. When Charles failed of giving these, she fired up; and at length, for want of a better target, went back to railing at his marriage, notwithstanding its success.

Charles's younger brother Jack—whom Sarah always speaks of as Johnny—was a much steadier favorite, not for being any better behaved, but for being so naturally engaging. He had grown up the very model of a gay, wild, dashing, extravagant young man about town whose scrapes sometimes ended in the guardhouse. He never, it was said, "soiled his fingers" with anything so paltry as silver, and chair men virtually ran one another through competing for his custom. He lived off his charm and his talent for small attentions: Sarah, for example, would be sent grapes or game or honey. At times—as in being present at Charles's wedding—he displeased her, only to redeem himself by paying her the "high compliment," as she put it, of making a troublesome journey to see her in tacit apology. Or Sarah would order him out of the room and he would make her laugh by vaulting back next minute through the window. She got him a seat in Parliament; she virtually chose him his bride. He and Lord Carteret's daughter "were married between eight and nine o'clock at night. After they were married, they played a pool of commerce, supped at ten, went to bed between twelve and one and to Windsor Lodge next day."

Johnny could get back into Sarah's good graces by dint of dash and charm, but of all the brood only "poor dear little Di" never really forfeited Sarah's affections. Her grandmother, as we know, had brought her up and had seen her married at twenty-one, with a magnificent dowry, to the future young Duke of Bedford (the younger brother and successor of the Duke who died en route to Lisbon.) During the three years preceding Di's death at twenty-five, Sarah wrote constantly to her, seeing her as often as circumstances, and scolding her as seldom as temperament, permitted. Writing to Lady Di, her grandmother reveals what was best in her nature as well as most touching about her lonely old age. But if Lady Di is the truest source of happiness left in life to Sarah, she is equally the readiest outlet for Sarah's recriminations and complaints. No letters of Lady Di's survive, and, perhaps because she was sweet-tempered and tactful, virtually no anecdotes either, so that of all the grandchildren with any place in Sarah's life, this greatest recipient of her love and greatest repository of her annoyances remains in a sense the most shadowy. Yet, by way of Sarah's letters, she brought out what was both central and special in her grandmother.

She brought out, for example, the awful pertinacity and meddlesomeness: Sarah—to give just one instance—felt there should be better stairs in Lady Di's town house, and though naturally this is only a suggestion on her part, she goes on and on about it, in letter after letter, fanning out into suggestions for building, rebuilding, and altering generally. (In the matter of houses, to be sure, Sarah had become one of the most experienced people alive, and one of the most put upon. "I have always had the misfortune," she elsewhere tells Lady Di, "to suffer very great mischiefs from the assistance of architects.")

Again, Lady Di can bring out a comic jealousy in Sarah: "A great while after you had left me," her grandmother tells her, "I went out in my coach to take the air, and saw your coaches standing at her door, in a violent rain, though you were in so much haste to leave me."

For a long time, in high eighteenth-century style, Sarah always addresses her favorite grandchild as "my dear Lady Russell" and then "my dear Duchess of Bedford," and it is only at the granddaughter's solicitation that she at last calls her "my dear Di." Finally Sarah hit upon the idea of "my dear Cordelia." "That is the name," she adds, "I intend to call you, for the future, which I think is the name of King Lear's good child." One could hardly ask for a more deliciously misapprehended allusion, for clearly Sarah saw Lady Bateman as Goneril and Regan rolled into one without ever for a second thinking of herself as Lear during the earlier half of the play.

The later letters, in which the young Duchess, while supposedly going through a difficult pregnancy, was the victim of galloping consumption, are full of real anxiety on

Sarah's part. Actually, however, Sarah's letters cease before she had learned the truth, and nothing is told of the final weeks of Di's life. But eighteen months after Diana's death in September 1735, Sarah wrote Diana's husband one of the most extraordinary letters of her whole life. During her illness Diana had asked her grandmother for the tent that John had used on his campaigns. This tent the Duke of Bedford, who was now about to remarry, had never returned after Lady Di's death: "I might well have expected your Grace," Sarah tells him, "would have sent it home to me, for I never gave it to your Grace, tho' you say in your letter I did." There follows a long harangue about the tent, then: "You say . . . that, as I gave your Grace my picture standing in Bedford Hall you will never part with it. This requires some answer . . . for I never gave your Grace that picture." And there follows a long outburst concerning the picture. Later Sarah speaks of jewels she lent for Diana's marriage to the Duke, "to save your Grace's money," and of her receiving "a letter from your Grace, which I have by me, which plainly shows that you had a mind to keep them." And there follows a bitter disquisition concerning the jewels.

But the heart of the letter concerns a quarrel Sarah had had during Diana's lifetime with the Duke, and what she had then assumed to be a reconciliation. But at the time of Diana's death she learned otherwise. "I believe," Sarah writes,

> there is no instance of such a treatment as I went through . . . It would be too much to repeat the monstrous usage which I received. . . . I sat silently in outward rooms, bathed in tears; and I own I flattered you upon every occasion that offered; which was out of

fear that if I did not take that way, you would order the porter not to let me in.

It is not just an old wound that all this seems to open, but a cavern of human contention round a dying girl. And Sarah ends:

I come now to the conclusion of your letter . . . that you are with due respect, etc. But I am so sincere, that I will end with saying that I wish I could with truth profess I had any respect for you: which I do not think anybody that reads this account can really have, since there is not one tittle aggravated but a great many things omitted of the same nature to save tediousness, and, therefore, I am sure your Grace in your own mind, will excuse me for saying no more than that I am

Your Grace's
most humble servant,
S. Marlborough

Thus ends Sarah's connection with her favorite grandchild.

If, as age crept in, Sarah's perceptions were sometimes blunted, her eyesight was always sharp, her sense of the vivid small point fully alive. Now she will note a detail that seems far ahead of its day:

Instead of a partition or a wall [the room] is divided with glass the same as in windows from the ceiling to the floor, so that everybody that sits in the room sees those that go through the passage and they see those that sit in the room. And this I must acknowledge is extremely new.

Or she will recount anecdotes of the Queen:

Two or three days ago, Her sacred Majesty was in great danger of being ravished. She was walking from Kensington to London early in the morning and having a vast desire to appear more able in everything than other people, she walked so fast as to get . . . quite out of sight [of her companions.] . . . Lord Grantham meeting a country clown asked him if he had met any person. . . . To which he answered he had met a jolly crummy woman with whom he had been fighting some time to kiss her. . . . Lord Grantham was so frightened that he screamed out and said it was the Queen. Upon which the country fellow was out of his wits, fell upon his knees, cried and earnestly begged of my Lord Grantham to speak for him for he was sure he should be hanged for what he had done. But did not explain further what it was. And her Majesty does not own more than that he struggled with her, but that she got the better of him.

Or she will announce that

Vandyke has been dead I suppose three hundred years.

Or she reveals herself, during a very formal age, as a very modern kind of hostess:

I dare not fix a day for going to Windsor; but I really think it will be the end of the week. I have told my Lady Muskerry that I will carry her with me. And I have made a bargain with her this afternoon that she should not take it ill, if I never see her but once a day at dinner and she is to entertain herself as she pleases, as if it were her own house.

Or she gives us, quite as Horace Walpole might have done, one of those low-comedy scenes, so frequent in her century, involving the highborn:

I never in my life heard so strange a thing as happened at an opera not long before the King left England. Mr. Seymour, who is a member of Parliament for Marlborough, at a great distance from His Majesty was in some box over the stage, or somewhere high, and His Majesty observed that there was a man in a hat, at which he was very much offended; and after speaking of it with some warmth he sent my Lord C—— up to him, and he told Mr. Seymour as civilly as he could, that His Majesty would have him pull off his hat. Mr. Seymour answered that he was ill, and could not do it for fear of catching cold. Several very curious messages followed, but all in vain; for Mr. Seymour said that he had paid for his place and he would not prejudice his health. . . .

Another extraordinary thing happened of much the same nature. The famous dancing woman . . . in the opera, the audience were so excessive fond of her that they hollered out "encore" several times to have her dance over again, which she could not do, because as she was coming on again, the King made a motion with his hand that she should not. At last the dispute was so violent that to put an end to it, the curtain was let down, whereby the spectators lost all after the third act.

I forgot to give an account in this great struggle concerning the hat, His Majesty ordered the guard to go up and take it away; but his servants in the box prevailed with him not to do it, saying [Mr. Seymour] was an ill-bred country gentleman but was of a great family and had many friends and it would make a noise.

It is amid such scenes and by way of such intelligences that we watch Sarah grow old, and older, and at length very venerable indeed. The mental alertness is so striking, the human energy so continuous, that we have to remind ourselves of the bodily aches and pains, of the hobbling or the being carried about. Weariness of a sort did certainly come at last, but we do not quite believe such remarks of hers as "If I could have walked out of this world, I would have departed long ago if only to get rid of so many tiresome people." As a younger woman she had summed up her truer feelings very well:

> I have always thought that the greatest happiness of life was to love and value somebody extremely that returned it, and to see them often, and if one has an easy fortune that is what makes one's life pass away agreeably.

And we catch the true voice of the older woman when, lying ill at eighty, Sarah heard the doctor whisper: "She must be blistered or she will die" and bellowed forth: "I won't be blistered and I won't die!" There was too much that concerned, not just the present, but also the past and the future, to keep her occupied: the writing and reading about and rebutting of her *Conduct;* the buying and building and rebuilding of her houses; the berating those she hated and indulging those she loved; the tearing up old wills and making new ones, what with "the lawyers who lived at her bedside." At eighty she dictated from memory a vast inventory of Blenheim—sixty-seven dozen nap-

kins plus five; ninety-three tablecloths "of the best sort";
the gold plate and hangings she had got from the Electress
of Hanover in exchange for a portrait of Queen Anne.
Twice—in 1736 and again in 1743—she read through John's
love letters to her as a girl, writing the second time: "Read
over in 1743 desiring to burn them, but I could not do it."
At the very end of her life she engaged two men, David
Mallet and Richard Glover, to tell John's story; and she
set to work with Mallet, speaking to him of men who "came
to be Admirals without ever having seen water but in a
basin." Remembering, for the book, this detail or that from
the days of her ascendancy, she was living happily in the
past as she imperceptibly drifted out of life. "Old Marlborough is dying," Horace Walpole had announced, with
his too vivid instinct for news, long before it was true; and
it was quite without drama, and with no one who was consequential, or close to her, at her bedside, that suddenly
on the 19th of October 1744 Old Marlborough was dead.[6]
Four days later she was buried very simply in the private
chapel at Blenheim, where—by her wish—John's body had
been brought from the Abbey. "My funeral," she had directed, "must be only decent, and without plumes or
escutcheons."

She left a very great estate and, as might be suspected,
had found interesting ways of disposing of it. The will,
dated August 15, 1744, left the poor of Woodstock £300;
each of her servants "one year's wages";[7] and her "first
woman," a clergyman's daughter named Grace Ridley, the
really notable sum of £15,000 outright, besides £300 a
year for life and various mementos. The Duchess of Mon-

---

[6] Jack Spencer was sent for, but arrived after her death.
[7] For her day, she had been rather notably charitable while she lived,
giving away "during her widowhood alone" more than £300,000.

tagu received gold and jeweled objects containing pictures of her father and sisters. Henrietta's late-born daughter received diamonds; and her husband, the Duke of Leeds, £3,000 and some property. Various members of Sarah's acquaintance—the Duchess of Devonshire, the Countess of Burlington—received money or mementos or both. The younger children of Sarah's grandson, the then Duke of Marlborough, were suitably provided for; but the bulk of the estate went to Jack Spencer. In addition, there were two rather famous bequests and a curious injunction. Lord Chesterfield, who had sought to be her grandson, at the last was treated like one, receiving her "best and largest brilliant diamond ring," some land, and £20,000. William Pitt, for his "noble defense . . . of the laws of England"—i.e., his steadfast opposition to Walpole—received land and £10,000. And Glover and Mallet were given £500 each for writing the history of the Duke, but enjoined that "no part of the said history may be in verse." (Little if any of it was ever done in prose either.)

Sarah was not mourned, and has never been very much esteemed or honored. But she has always been most vividly remembered. She was not at all, by happy standards, a great woman, but by any standards she must rank with the very greatest personalities. She was, as C. V. Wedgwood has said, impossible but also incomparable. In one sense she was all the more a grande dame for being so thorough a barbarian, and all the more stridently impolitic for living in an age of canny whispers. But the truth is that, more than anything she achieved, or lost, or represents, more than she was the commandant of so tremendous a general or the coercer of so obstinate a queen, she was inextinguishably herself. She persists even now; almost every anecdote concerning her is an encounter.

BIBLIOGRAPHICAL NOTE

WITHOUT intruding upon the reader the great mass of material that necessarily goes into the writing of a biography, I might—for his possible pleasure—remind him of such enjoyably relevant classics as Pepys's and Evelyn's Diaries, Swift's *Journal to Stella*, Pope's *Imitations* and *Moral Essays*, Lady Mary's and Horace Walpole's *Letters*, Hervey's *Memoirs*, and Macaulay's *History*. The reader may also find of interest some recent biographies of personages in Sarah's life. There is notably Sir Winston Churchill's *Marlborough: His Life and Times* (6 vols., Scribner); also —for the family connection generally—*The Early Churchills*, by A. L. Rowse (Harper); *Godolphin: His Life and Times*, by Sir Tresham Lever (John Murray); *Mary II, Queen of England*, by Nellie M. Waterson (Duke University Press); *Sir John Vanbrugh: Architect and Dramatist*, by Laurence Whistler (Macmillan); *The Life of Lady Mary Wortley Montagu*, by Robert Halsband (Oxford); *Lord Chesterfield*, by Samuel Shellabarger (Macmillan); *Caroline of England: An Augustan Portrait*, by Peter Quennell (Viking); and the presumable first volume (which ends before Sarah's quarrel really begins) of J. H. Plumb's *Sir Robert Walpole* (Houghton Mifflin). Of Queen Anne, as of several other people, no good modern biography exists; but her *Letters* (Cassell) pair off very well with Sarah's *Memoirs* (Routledge), and the history of her whole reign is brilliantly set forth in George Macaulay Trevelyan's *England under Queen Anne* (3 vols., Longmans, Green).

INDEX